Mountains
of the
Mind

How we get depth from flatness

Trevor Rollings

Mountains of the Mind

Printed by Kindle Direct Publishing 2021

tjrollings@gmail.com

Also available by the same author
in the series
Empires of the Mind

We are More than our Brains
Putting our minds to neuroscience
No Man is an Island
How pain, suffering and hope bind us to each other
The Mosaic of the Mind
Where does our mind go in sleep, dreams, hypnosis and meditation?
In Our Right Mind
Sex, drugs, kicks and control
The Mirror of the Mind
Seeing personally, seeing really and seeing sanely

Contents

Mountains of the Mind

Introduction

In the mountains, there you feel free.
T S Eliot

In his short life as a Catholic priest in the nineteenth century, wrestling with the twin peaks of faith and doubt, the poet Gerard Manley Hopkins wrote: 'O the mind, mind has mountains'. He lived a century and a half before cognitive, evolutionary and social psychologists came up with a very different reading of the contours of our mental landscape: the mind is flat. According to the behavioural scientist Nick Chater, writing in 2018, 'There are no mental depths to plumb'.

Gerard Manley Hopkins
1844-89
As a Jesuit priest, Hopkins wrestled with his faith, but he also saw extraordinary beauty in ordinary things. His poetry is still widely read today.

Mountains of the Mind

This conflict of views from above and below, or clash of perspectives from inside and outside, possibly arises from the huge burden of expectation we place upon the word 'mind'. We use it to imply reason (of sound mind), intelligence (a sharp mind), opinion (to my mind), imagination (all in the mind), wisdom (a deep mind) and spiritual contentment (peace of mind).

This is too much for one word to bear without running into difficulties sooner or later, especially when we try to reduce the 'idea' it represents to its component parts, 'flatten' its operations, subject it to scientific investigation, or ply it with psychometric testing.

The chasm between the mountains and valleys in our mind is not a recent phenomenon. It is as old and wide as time itself, buried deep in our evolutionary story. We inherit two worlds, one of thoughts and subjective awareness, guided by the moral law of interpersonal relationships, the other of things and objective systems, overseen by the laws of physics which rule the cosmos.

Some believe it is only a matter of time before science brings all phenomena, including Hopkins and his 'inscape', into the purview of material explanation. But science is a very late arrival on the human scene, occupying only a tiny fraction of our lengthy gestation as hunter gatherers. It is also a product of the same mind that writes poetry, gives and does not count the cost, and asks ultimate questions about its own existence.

The African savannah is littered with the skulls of our ancestors, hinting at the size of brain they contained, and the kinds of tools they were capable of making. Our story did not become fully human however until we started to bury our dead with treasured objects, daub paint on cave walls, and generate myths about our origins. Through these cultural practices we became minded creatures, inhabiting an inner world nurtured in a network of other minds.

Science offers us our most up to date myth about who we are and how our mind works. It presents itself as our 'first order' way of knowing, able to quantify the fall of a leaf, track the orbit of a star, and follow the trail of a chemical messenger in our brain.

As a result, philosophy, the humanities, the arts and religion, engrossing pursuits as they are, have been relegated to 'second order' enquiries. It's not that they fail to give answers but, according to the strict standards of science, they don't frame their questions in ways that produce answers that can be checked empirically. They don't create knowledge that can send a probe to Mars, or cure a cancer.

The sciences, which are increasingly converging in their understanding of the universe, and our evolution in this small corner of it, reign supreme. Very soon we will know all there is to know about the cosmos, and we will understand enough about the human brain to create digital doppelgangers of ourselves.

If Hopkins were alive today, mindful that the burden of suffering in the world is just as great as in his day, he would smile wryly at this bullish view of progress. He would be intrigued by the explanation of his agonised soul-searching as the operation of fizzing neurons and Darwinian gremlins. He would point out that mind and culture, not easily measurable by scientific rigour, require a broader and deeper analysis of the human condition.

He would be amazed at the ways in which the sciences have helped to unlock the secrets of cognition, and to transform medical treatment for those with brain injuries. But he would also know that the existential challenges faced by his parishioners remain as pressing as ever: the need to belong, the search for a life purpose, the yearning for self understanding.

By training and conviction he belonged to a tradition which viewed cognitive flaws as character failings, which only God can redeem. But he would also have been aware of the warnings given by Buddhist and Stoic teachers, going back over two thousand years: we entertain false views about self and reality, we hide behind subterfuges, we never see things for what they are, we are vulnerable to unconscious cravings, and we do not know our own minds. This is flat mind theory in all but name.

He knew that self knowledge is a greater challenge than knowledge about the physical world. The great philosophical and spiritual traditions have long taught two truths: the journey inwards is much harder that the journey out, and the answers we seek are within us, not outside ourselves.

For all his high Victorianism, he would not necessarily have seen the divide between his concern for the salvation of his soul and the naturalistic explanations of science as unbridgeable. The gap between the 'two cultures' of science and the humanities was already beginning to narrow in his lifetime. Since then, physicists have come to realise that the brain is a dynamic system, and biologists are fully aware of the role of ideas and culture in the shaping of the mind.

Mountains of the Mind

There was a fashion for a while of seeing ourselves in the stark light of evolutionary necessity, but it was gradually abandoned, because it cut us off from the existential aspects of being a person in the world, and the things that concern us ultimately: the nature of consciousness, the self, free will, spirituality, forming a worldview, finding a meaning to our existence.

Unlike the facts and theories of science, these are not givens, but realities we have to construct as part of a well-lived life. We are more than the sum of our parts, and we are forced to be free. Science can deepen our understanding of what goes on in our brain when we make a choice, but it cannot make our decisions for us.

Hopkins would be perturbed by some of the stronger claims of 'The mind is flat' school of thought. It calls into question core 'myths' we have long cherished: our sovereignty, authenticity, capacity for reason, reliance on memory, freedom of will, certainty of knowing, justification of belief, innate goodness, independence of thought, and sense of progress. All of these assumptions, say the flat minders, are flawed and biased.

They have plenty of ammunition in their locker. Our mind is easily hijacked by demagogues and conspiracy theorists, we occasionally lapse into barbarism, we struggle to think straight, we entertain irrational beliefs, we delude ourselves that we know more than we do. These are cosy illusions, or fronts that we present to the world.

Hopkins managed to get depth from flatness, and there is no yardstick by which we can say he was deluded, or wrong, or unhappy. Like us, he was a compulsive maker of theories, eager to know which ones pass muster. Flat mind theory is just that, a theory. If however it helps us to know more about what goes on in the lumber room our brain, debug our mind, question our assumptions and improve our reasoning about reason itself, it demands a considered response from us.

It is time to set off into the mountains.

How has our mind been flattened?

Vitalism - loss of transcendence - the ghost in the machine - the death of old mind – the shortcomings of reason – giving the mind a makeover – the fake mind

- The mind is older than the brain, in the sense that it has a longer recorded history.
- Our ancestors became gradually more mindful, or self-aware, through rituals, paintings, dances and myths.
- These myths of human specialness and mental depth have been challenged by the theory of the flat mind.
- Self, consciousness and free will have been exposed as illusions, or tricks of the brain.
- Flat mind theory 'works' however only by subjecting all traditions, ways of knowing and areas of experience to a simplistic formula.
- Using the reasoning of science, flat mind theorists have reduced the mind to the 'ghost in the machine'.
- Reason is not however without its own blind spots, flaws and limitations, nor can everything in the mind be put to the scalpel of science.
- This does not mean that we should doubt our ability to reason well. By applying flat mind theory creatively, we can get to know our own minds better, and learn to apply reason more wisely.

Mountains of the Mind

The deep mind

In 1884 Edwin Abbott wrote a novel called 'Flatland', in which the characters are geometrical planes. The story is an allegory in which those who are two-dimensional, which is most of us, look down on one-dimensionals, or those we consider to be our inferiors. Two-dimensionals lack the insight to imagine what life might be like in three-dimensions, which for us means a realm beyond sensory perception. Abbott was trying to warn us of the perils of prejudice, and reminding us how poor we are at grasping higher realities.

Today, Abbott's strange musings sound not so far-fetched. Scientists now describe us as living in four-dimensional spacetime, and if we are to believe string theorists, there may be as many as twenty six dimensions, the vast majority of which our humble brain is unable to access or compute, making reality anything but flat. Films like 'The Matrix' (1999) have taken Abbott's thinking about our limited perception of reality into even weirder realms: everything we see is a giant computer simulation, not even the product of our own mind.

In desperation we might turn to physics to adjudicate between what is really real and what is a projection of our mind. There is little clarity here however. Classical physicists confirm that we live in a world of rocks and trees, made of real stuff that we can touch and hear. Quantum theorists challenge this naive view of the world, suggesting that we don't see the depth of what is really there, only a quantum reality of what our 'flat' senses give us, as interpreted by our brain.

Edwin Abbot
Abbot's 1884 novel 'Flatland', considered to be the first example of 'mathematical fiction', makes us wonder how our brain allows us to see in three dimensions, how our mind allows us to live in four dimensions, and why neither allows us to conceive what lies in the fifth dimension and beyond.

Mountains of the Mind

Common sense tells us that evolution has not tricked us: what we see is what we get. Without this pragmatic assumption, our concepts of self, consciousness, free will and responsibility fall to pieces. Common sense however is often misleading, and these 'essences' may be illusions of our over-inventive brain, merely words with no substance behind them.

The mind is a hallucination of the brain.

In recent years cognitive scientists have taken pains to introduce us to the phenomenon of the flat mind: our minds are not as deep as we think, and most of the time it plays tricks on us. In fact, the mind is a hallucination of the brain, so if we want to understand the mind, we must start with the brain.

This is counterintuitive, because the mind evolved to be our sole window onto reality. For reasons we shall never understand, and in ways we shall never know, something new in nature began to take shape in the brain of our hominin ancestors, potentially always there, but awaiting expression. We are made aware of this rich legacy through the wealth of words we use to describe the ways in which our mind goes beyond what it is given: we dream, speculate, imagine, theorise, idealise and create.

Culture and ritual leave few traces for historians to pore over, but we start to hear the musings of a fully human consciousness in the 'wisdom literature' of the ancient world, both East and West. We encounter for the first time the myth of a stairway to heaven, or an ascent of expanding insight. Like Jack, we become climbers of the beanstalk, looking for an alternative reality at the top, just beyond our earthly perception.

We see this myth at its simplest and most beautiful in Michelangelo's image of Adam reaching up to touch God's finger, and God reaching down. Renaissance painters like Michelangelo show an increased confidence in being and perception. Before then, human figures were seen against a flat background, drawing in the viewer as part of the scene, with no special point of view.

Gradually however the new trick of perspective created a sense of depth, and the illusion of the viewer outside the frame, as a separate self contemplating its subject from a distinct vantage point, giving us a sense of the mind contemplating itself. The mind became personalised, endowed with self, character and

11

individuality. In the literature of the period, we begin to hear voices and meet minds that we recognise as distinctly modern.

Enter the brain

In this sense, the mind preceded the brain in the human journey to self discovery. The brain, as in our awareness of it, did not make an appearance until about three thousand years ago. As a biological organ, it had always been there, but barely noticed. It gradually dawned on a few perspicacious physicians that the contents of the skull were more than a mush of jelly. Head injuries to soldiers on the battlefield suggested a strong link between brain injury and loss of faculties.

For all sorts of reasons, brain science and psychology did not advance very far in the ancient world, Aristotle remaining of the opinion that the brain's principal purpose was to cool the blood. For two millennia the mind was largely left to priests, philosophers, gurus and artists to play with. In the West it was seen as an image of God in the next world, in the East as an illusion of this world.

The brain is the apex of the nervous system.

About five hundred years ago a more inquisitive science, based on what can be seen and known by observation, readmitted the brain to the debate. Dissections and post mortems in the seventeenth century forced a rethink of centuries of superstition, and revealed that the brain is the apex of the nervous system. If the mind resides anywhere, it is here.

There was more to come. To the Renaissance vision of shared divinity, the thinkers of the Enlightenment added the secular god of Reason. Even without God, we are independent rational minds, capable of taming our base impulses through higher thinking, and realising the beautiful through refining our feelings.

By now, the uplifting 'deep mind' narrative that had sustained philosophical and religious thought for over two millennia was under siege. The twin pillars of transcendentalism and rationalism, which served so long as the cornerstones of humanist thought, no longer define what it means to have a mind. All the hot money is on brain research and cognitive psychology.

12

Mountains of the Mind

The mind is flat

Building on insights first mooted by Charles Darwin, that the shape of our mind is as much a product of natural selection as the curve of our lip, flat mind theory upends the dogmas of human specialness and rational invincibility. Deep mind is a fiction, albeit a powerful one. According to cognitive scientists, social psychologists and evolutionary biologists, it is little more than an elaborate myth, a self-deluding optimism that has been undone by the advances of our post-technological age.

We are as flat and two-dimensional as the screen that
frames our social media profile.

Postmodern theorists and cultural critics agree, but for very different reasons. We have lost touch with our spiritual and cultural roots, our ancient cosmogonies and epics becoming strangers to us. Depth of awareness, response and feeling have been flattened out to relevance, psychometrics and neural circuitry. We're all two-dimensional now, as square as the screen that frames our social media profile.

Our politics is dominated by 'what you see is what you get' populism, we are failing to find global solutions to our ecological crisis, and our public discourse is hijacked by the most strident voices. Our notions of traditional wisdom, sovereign individuality and self determination, for so long regarded in the West as the hallmark of a deep mind, are superstitions, largely put about by educated white males.

Depth is dispelled, and flatness is the new normal. When we put our behaviour under the microscope, we expose a catalogue of failings. We think with our gut, ignoring the good stuff. We notice only the bad stuff, or what bolsters what we already think. We jump to conclusions, rush to all-or-nothing judgment, over-generalise, catastrophise, fall victim to false memories, look out for our own, are deluded that we are always right, and know far less than we think.

There is no 'essential' mind. Instead, our fabled self image is the plaything of the new gods of our destiny. We are the sum total of our class, suburb, tribe, sexuality, education, genes, neurochemistry, work, leisure, personality type and social media profile.

13

Mountains of the Mind

Our much vaunted intellect is riddled with gremlins. When we set out to make a decision of any kind, large or small, our brain becomes a battleground of warring impulses and conflicting interests. In one corner is our ventromedial cortex, urging hot feeling on us, as 'system one' kneejerk responses. In the other is our prefrontal cortex, pushing us towards cool thinking, or 'system two' reflection. Gut feeling screams out for that ice cream, but reason says the long-term impact of the extra calories on our waistline isn't worth the temporary thrill. Guess who wins. The flat mind theorists have us worked out to a tee.

Why then did we ever think we had a deep mind, and how did we lose it? To answer this, we need to go back to the origins of Western thought. Over two thousand years ago, Plato encapsulated the essence of mind in the idea of the Logos, an eternal principle that underpins both cosmic and moral law. In the human mind, this quality is experienced through the power of contemplative reason.

By the time of Christianity, the idea of a rational mind had morphed into a soul that survives the body after death. Both Plato and the early Church Fathers reasoned that the mind and the soul must relate to something larger than our mortal selves, on the grounds that a cause cannot be less than its effect.

This doctrine of a mind free of its body was not however without problems. It made an enemy of the body, either as a drag on the ascent of the soul, or as the fiefdom of doctors who pronounce that it is blighted with cancer, coronary disease or dementia. But it did reserve a special 'out of body' place in humanist thought where conscience, sense of purpose and 'me-ness' can reside, a personal voice that we hear when we think to ourselves, or imagine ourselves into the minds of others.

Empirical research within the cognitive and social sciences in recent years shows however that dualism, or the idea of a mind mysteriously detached from its body, is unsustainable. Our musings are not profound insights in some free-floating realm, but superficial glosses and tricks of our brain. We derive meaning and achieve happiness by delusion at best, and self deception at worst.

The deeper we dig, the more we realise that the mind is flat. Consciousness, self and free will are clever illusions created by a default network we are never consciously aware of. We think we are running the show, but our behaviour is determined by cognitive machinations beyond our control, down in the lumber room of our unconscious.

Consciousness is a mask, a home-movie cobbled together from fleeting perceptions, a tapestry of fluctuating feelings, the effervescence of billions of neurons going about their business. The self is the shop window of a biological computing machine and an algorithmic data cruncher. 'I' is the metaphysical glue that binds together moments of mind-magic that would otherwise have no coherence. Free will is a thin cover for decisions that the brain has already made.

In other words, we are flawed creatures suffering from a user illusion that we are running the show. Our senses are not infallible guides to reality, we make ourselves up as we go along, we are much more impressionable than we realise, and the only depth we have is subconscious urges that do our thinking for us.

What appears to the mind
Plato is of little interest to flat-minders. He was too rationalist and idealist. The story must jump ahead to two English scientists working within the empirical tradition, using the power of observation to move from the particular to the general. Look first, and only then suggest a theory that gives overall meaning to the data. How does a better grasp of things-as-they-are enrich our understanding of things-as-they-appear to our senses?

Isaac Newton (d 1727) focussed on physics, the domain of inanimate things. His work on gravity and light showed that the universe is a giant clock working to unerring laws. He retained belief in a divine creator, and wrote a million words on religious matters, but the cosmos that he revealed requires no God to keep it going.

The mind is just data and DNA going about its business.

Charles Darwin (d 1882) chose biology, the domain of living creatures, and his grand but simple idea of natural selection with modification took him one step further than Newton: there is no need of any hypothesis of God, even for the phenomena we can't yet explain. His catch-all theory can account for the evolution of every species and the niche it occupies, including Homo sapiens.

Mountains of the Mind

Our science lessons at school are basically footnotes to Newton and Darwin's discoveries, right up to the digital revolution. Within this materialist frame, the mind is physics and biochemistry, information and instinct, data and DNA going about their business.

The problem with this theory, and all attempts to explain the mind empirically, is that it ignores the rest of the curriculum, or what we call the humanities, accounting not just for the other half of our intellectual activity, but also our feelings. To see ourselves whole, or understand our psychology in the round, we need also to study the ways we are shaped by culture and language. Neither Newton nor Darwin, brilliant minds as they were, factored the power of the personal and the social into their thinking. The lived or 'existential' reality of having a mind is conspicuous by its absence.

Insight into these other ways of knowing was developed by four thinkers from the German-speaking world, whose ideas have for cultural reasons been largely ignored if not dismissed by the English-speaking community. These continental thinkers did not underestimate the empirical observation of particulars as a starting point, but they were equally swayed by the power of reason to grasp a general truth and then work backwards to the particular. In other words, start with an idea, then look closely to see how well it fits the phenomena.

They were rationalists, whose guiding theory was that our mind, far from being the mere recipient of things-as-they are, is the principal architect of things-as-they-appear. The mind is far from flat. It has surprising depths, because it helps us to make our own reality. Ironically, this is exactly the conclusion reached by modern flat mind theorists, but they read very different things into their findings.

Deconstructing the mind

Immanuel Kant (d 1804) was no physicist or biologist, but he suggested that the mind is like a pair of goggles that colours everything we see. Our life's task is to work out what things look like when we remove the goggles. This is a difficult idea which suggests that what we see, whether by scientific observation or through moral conviction, is not always what is really there, but what our mind gives to us.

16

Mountains of the Mind

Georg Hegel (d 1831) added a further twist to this thinking. Not only does our mind act as a filter, it also makes the very reality is it is contemplating. This is never an absolute view, because our mind is at all times caught up in the contemporary unfolding of history and progress. The modern mind sees the world very differently from the ancient, the primitive from the civilised, the eastern from the western. Reality is never pure, but a shifting human construct, constantly in the making, shaping consciousness from the top down.

Karl Marx (d 1833) was impressed by Hegel, but thought he was working from the wrong end of the scale. Hegel was an idealist, who saw the mind as superior to matter, guided into the future by clever thinkers like himself. Marx was a materialist who saw consciousness as shaped not by airy thinking, but by hard-edged economic forces, creating a never-ending class struggle in which those at bottom of the heap never get a look-in.

In an attempt to explain how the exploited worker occupies a very different mind-world from the prosperous factory owner, he turned Hegel's thinking on its head. The superstructures of society pit the powerful against the weak: masters and slaves, bosses and workers, husbands and wives, luxury yacht owners and homeless rough-sleepers. If we want to bring about a change of consciousness, it can only be by bottom-up systemic change, brought about by violent revolution if necessary.

Western politicians were initially afraid of Marx, and then dismissive, but the impact of technology and the digital revolution on all aspects of our life, largely beyond our control, gives us cause us to think again. If we try living without our iphone or computer for a day or two, we are brought up hard against the power these superstructures have over us. We are not captains of our soul, lords of all we survey, or masters of our destiny. We are ciphers in a giant data storage facility in the Californian desert.

If the mind is a human construct, it can be deconstructed.

The final German-speaking dismantler of the mind as a transcendent essence was Sigmund Freud (d 1939). He turned his attention to the part of the mind that lies beneath the surface, the bit we never see: our unconscious. Mind is not the apogee of reason and rationality, but a cesspit of guilt and fear. We have been talking about our fantasies and neuroses ever since.

Freud had no access to modern scanners or genetic decoding, but his insights have nevertheless directed the course of modern debate about the mind/brain. By suggesting that the mind is a human construction, he opened the door to its deconstruction. By suggesting that the mind is a moveable feast, he provided food for thought for generations of cognitive scientists, psychology researchers, cultural critics and postmodern theorists.

Loss of vitality

Thinking about the mind was dominated for over two millennia by a belief in vitalism, acting as a kind of secular religion. According to this theory, there is an energy in living things, coming not from on high but from within, as a spirit or subtle agent that mysteriously enters each creature at birth and just as mysteriously disappears upon death.

> *Nature was seen as infused with mind all the way down,*
> *things below mirroring things above.*

The life-force of vitalism was accompanied by teleological or final-goal thinking, inherited from Aristotle. Everything, animate and inanimate, has a purpose or aspiration towards a natural end, working for the common good. Not only does the acorn 'want' to be an oak, fulfilling its final form as an organism, the stone also 'wants' to fall to earth when dropped, seeking its natural resting place. Mind, operating as a divine principle, was seen as running through all things, even grains of sand blown in the wind. In what is known as panpsychism, nature was seen as infused with mind all the way down, things below mirroring things above.

The idea of a vacuum, or a space where mind is absent, was anathema to early philosophers. Even outer space, which looks to all appearances to be empty, was presumed to be filled with a substance called the aether, without which light could not pass between the planets, or reach us on earth. It was not until the nineteenth century that experiments revealed that no such luminiferous substance exists.

Mountains of the Mind

Eastern philosophers were not generally given to scientific experiment, because they belonged to an even more ancient tradition of thought, telling a different kind of story. There is no duality of above and below, or separation of self and the world, but a unity of earth and heaven, each contained in the other, mirroring human affairs: if all is harmonious in the human heart, all is balanced in the cosmos. In Chinese thought, *qi* is the vital energy that runs through all things, from the coarse-grain of the simple bacterium to the fine-grain of subtle human consciousness.

In India, *prana* or breath was equated with the soul, hence the focus on breathing in yoga and meditation. *Prana* and breath were absorbed into Western thought as Greek *pneuma*, to do with air and lungs, and Latin *spiritus*, both the respiration of our body and the spirit that leaves it on death. This suggested an upward flight, the mind rising towards the top of a great chain of being, stretching like a ladder from the amoeba to the angel. On the top rung sits God.

In an early stab at evolutionary theory, which simply means an unfolding, the thirteenth-century theologian Thomas Aquinas saw each created thing, from the simple cell to the complex mind, as aspiring to be the best of its kind. God was not an add-on, stranded in some transcendent realm outside of his creation, but immanent, visible even in the image seen through an electron microscope. What Aquinas could not provide however was a mechanism by which such order emerges from chaos.

Leonardo da Vinci
1452-1519
As artist and inventor in equal measure, was Leonardo one of the last minds to see things whole, untroubled by the duality of body and soul?

Mountains of the Mind

Leonardo Da Vinci was a keen student of anatomy, intent on seeing how muscles ripple beneath the skin, but he did not regard the body as mere matter or machine. He believed it was the seat of the soul, the culmination of divine creation. But he was also aware of the 'new science' that was emerging from the European universities. Though his paintings are infused with a heavenly light, they also mark the beginning of a fascination with worldly empirical observation. We might say that Leonardo was one of the last minds to see things whole, untroubled by the duality of body and soul.

Since the Renaissance, the vertical aspirations of the soul and the mind have been decapitated: there is no divine provenance or heavenly elevation, only successive events on a horizontal plane. Four hundred years ago, under the scrutiny of materialist Western science, the motivating narratives of the upward ascent of matter and progress of history began to lose their powers of persuasion.

By the mid-twentieth century, vitalism, teleology, panpsychism, *qi* and *prana*, not to mention soul, mind, self, free will and idealism, had all been put to the sword of naturalism, materialism, reductionism, empiricism and a 'connectionist' view of the brain. There is no magic or mystery going on, just the robotic crunching of algorithms and the reliable networking of neurons.

A new genesis story

We now have a new version of Genesis. There *is* a system, but it is determined by chance and necessity, not guided by providence and purpose. There *is* an energy, but it is mechanical, not divine. There *is* a 'user', but s/he is created by computation, not communion. There *is* a goal to human endeavour, but it is the survival of the fittest, not heaven. There *is* an after life, but it is the infinity of the cosmos, not the eternity of the soul.

This new narrative also redefines the human mind. It is not part of a grand ascent, but part of nature. It is not a vital spirit breathed into the body, but an evolved organ, on a par with the kidney and liver. It is flat, subject to the same laws that make the leaves fall from the trees in the autumn. It is the projection of a brain that does not give us a finished version of reality, but an improvised consciousness that constantly disappears before us.

Mountains of the Mind

We hear this new teaching in the writings of Francis Bacon, who lived around the time of Shakespeare. He conducted few experiments, but in many ways he was the father of the modern scientific outlook, because he established the principle that experiment is the key to new understanding.

His first step was to sweep away superstition, bigotry, group-think and reliance on authority, which he called 'idols of the mind'. These are dirty mirrors which distort our understanding, but if we clean the glass, science can see through them to banish ignorance, destroy illusions and generate knowledge that is its own reward.

Bacon staked a claim to being the first flat mind theorist.

In line with this fresh approach based on observation, not hearsay, Bacon suggested that the mind itself ought to be an object of investigation. Previously our mental life had been beyond the purview of science, but he was not deterred. Staking a claim as the first flat mind theorist, he saw the mind as a cracked mirror, full of flaws and bad thinking habits. It is made of mortal stuff, just like the body that houses it, of a piece with nature, comprising the same molecules found in a potato, but differently arranged.

This was challenging stuff, causing Bacon's contemporary John Donne to remark that the 'new philosophy calls all in doubt'. Over the next four centuries, physics laid bare the mind as a machine, going through the gears of pneumatics, hydraulics, electricity and electrochemistry as explanatory drivers. The animal spirit of pneuma was converted to action potential and positively charged ions.

Two centuries after Francis Bacon, Darwinian evolutionary theory exposed *qi*, *prana* and *spiritus* as distinctly animal in origin, void of transcendence. The mind is material, mortal, no deeper than a pancake, its 'idols' traceable to glitches in our ancestral psychology. If Bacon were alive today, he might target our modern idols of the mind: continuing superstition, tribalism, populism, consumerism, obsession with technology and our ambivalent relationship with the truth.

There have been several rearguard actions to keep alive the idea of a mind 'higher' than its body, or of a vital force guiding evolution in a human-friendly direction. In the seventeenth century the mathematician René Descartes proposed a dualism of body and mind, setting the mind free of its physical shackles. In the twentieth century, the philosopher Henri Bergson suggested there is a creative impulse behind each organism, and the French priest Teilhard de Chardin believed that life on earth is moving towards an Omega Point, or ultimate union of mind and matter.

These ideas are too metaphysical for some but ironically, in an effort to replace all the 'dead' metaphysics that it has consigned to the cemetery of ideas, materialist scientists are slowly coming full circle. For all their knowledge, they are no closer to accounting for what the poet Dylan Thomas described in 1933 as 'the force that through the green fuse drives the flower'. In search of an answer, they are resurrecting the old idea of vitalism, but in a bold new way.

Physicists and biologists, traditionally separated by their disciplines, are forming a new alliance in realising that life forms, as well as exhibiting movement, food consumption, excretion, reproductive capacities and possibly consciousness, are not just arrangements of chemicals or assemblies of cells. They generate energy fields which are as yet barely understood, or explainable by conventional means.

How for instance does our body know, when it is wounded, where the hurt is, and how does a cell know how to fettle itself to repair the damage? This type of holistic thinking is even more essential if we are to appreciate how our mind works in all its complexity.

The disappearing ghost
It remains the case however that modern science has firmly ousted the notion of a mind distinct from matter, and spirited away the 'ghost in the machine'. We have been shown that our 'true nature' is the outcome of several billion years of evolution by natural selection and descent with modification from these raw materials on this remote planet.

Meanwhile, philosophy and psychology have unmasked a creature that is barely rational, seldom right, easily deceived, often mistaken and always riddled with faulty habits of thought. The brain that we glibly think we control is in fact in control of us, because it was never made perfect. For all our progress, it remains an improvised 'idiot' brain with many design faults, as we shall see.

Mountains of the Mind

Reason shares the same animal origins as our
primitive fears and sexual desires.

For a couple of centuries the 'ghost' that allegedly haunted our head at least had reason to fall back on, as a free-floating essence or mental faculty that not only distinguishes Homo sapiens from the rest of creation, but also underwrites the logic of progress. Since the Enlightenment, reason has been our secular religion and guiding light, dispelling the darkness of ignorance and superstition. We have dared to know, even though such knowledge has taken us close to the brink of mutual destruction.

But even the male preserve of Reason with a capital R has been dismantled and debunked, as a biased, lazy and manipulative evolutionary adaptation aimed at bolstering our pre-existent convictions. We are capable of applying reason, but only up to a point. It is a bounded rationality, constrained by our limited intellect, sensory myopia and tribal attachment. In the public arena, we use its sidekick logic as much to dupe others into thinking as we do, as to help us to think straight. Reason, sharing the same animal origins as our primitive fears and sexual desires, is not so elevated after all.

The ghost in the machine
If the mind is reducible to so many cogs and wheels, what ghost assembled it? If there is no ghost, what keeps it running?

Some believe that, as enlightened self-interest, Reason has brought us not a rational utopia, but a dystopia of planetary destruction and social collapse. It cannot alone create a perfectly just, happy or rational society, because we are not relentlessly logical thinking machines. Although mutual bonds of trust and obligation connect us to each other, they also cast long shadows of suspicion and manipulation.

Reason is at its most dangerous when it forgets its historical realities, social sympathies and moral responsibilities. It's not intelligence we need, but the wisdom to apply it humanely and astutely. It's not abstract reason we need, but practically grounded reasonableness. In an age of fake news, growing tribalism and weakening social connections, we need the solutions and insights of practical reason more than ever, aimed not just at the useful and pleasant, but also at what is good, as judged by outcomes that are in the interests of all.

Rebooting reason

Reason might need a reboot, but we are much better off with it than without it. All of our knowledge, not just our science but also our theology, is predicated on our belief that we live in an ordered world and an intelligible universe, with causes that are discoverable by an enquiring mind. Despite the late twentieth century drift towards relativism, we work on the assumption that truth, though never absolute, is at least ascertainable, and not just a matter of personal preference.

Reason in its present form however took a long time to appear in the human story. For countless millennia, the mental experience of our ancestors was largely grounded in sensation. As their heirs, we still need sensation to make sense of being conscious, and to keep us in touch with our body. It gives us the kind of joy and spontaneity we feel when we dance.

Reason is caught in its own explanatory loop.

We cannot however live by sensation alone, because we cannot use one feeling to justify another. We are caught in the loop of our emotions, and if we are to master ourselves, or make designs upon the world, we also need reason, which gains traction through language and logic. When we disagree with each other, we are more likely to resolve our differences if we talk them through, and parse them carefully. It can be no coincidence that when writing appeared on the human stage around five thousand years ago, thought became analysable. The subject could be objectified, and the steady march from prehistory to modernity could begin.

Since then society has become infinitely more complex, and rationality has become a condition of our existence. When we look around us, at both our arts and sciences, we soon realise that our life world has been created by those who have turned their emotions into reasons, and their feelings into thoughts, not merely given vent to their spleen or affections. Ideas and the intellect have been greater forces for change than the passions. We need to remember however that reason too is caught in an explanatory loop: to claim that reason is our backstop in all disputes is to rely on reason to supply its own reason.

To resolve this conundrum, we need two types of rationality, instrumental and value-based, which between them unite the affective and intellective operations of our brain. Instrumental rationality operates as a highly effective *means* to an end: if we want to build a pyramid, these are the steps we have to take. But there is another type of rationality, and it is value-based, more concerned with the *ends* of our actions: how does building a pyramid fit into an overall belief system that holds society together, creating a stability without which bread cannot be put on the table for the thousands of builders who toil daily on the megaproject?

Such a question shows that instrumental and value-based reason can never be neatly separated, because they always operate in tandem in particular social contexts. For some, they justify the status quo, bolstering centuries of tradition, for others they are tyrannies and superstitions to be overthrown. Either way, once the practical skills of constructing pyramids were lost, and the ideological reasons for erecting them in the first place disappeared, the foundations of Ancient Egyptian society crumbled, and the Pharaohs disappeared into the sand forever.

It would be folly to suppose that today, having dispelled old ghosts from our mind, we enjoy a superior rationality. We are faced by bewildering dilemmas in genetic engineering, cognitive enhancement and artificial intelligence, not to mention crises of rising sea levels, burning tundra and global pandemics. Like science and religion, reason evolves, and only engaged, wise and open minds can decide which way to steer it. We shouldn't therefore say farewell to the ghosts of our old mind just yet, because they might still have a few things to teach us.

Mountains of the Mind

Time for a mind makeover

Our new knowledge about the mind/brain gives us several suggestions for how we can give our mind a makeover. We can't change the hardware, but maybe we can reboot the software. This is hard, because we face an awkward paradox. One of the key lessons we have learned from cognitive scientists and evolutionary psychologists is that we have no privileged access to our brain. How then can we dispassionately interrogate ourselves, or be our own judge and jury?

'The mind is flat' message is that our mind is so full of prior expectations, shoddy thinking habits and cognitive fallacies that it does most of our 'reasoning' for us. It disguises its feelings and invents little stories to cover its tracks. It clings to what it knows, driven more by fear than curiosity, prejudice more than fairness and reflex more than reflection, which is why social change is so agonisingly slow.

We are rational choosers prone to making irrational choices.

When we're not downright biased, we are at best muddled in our thinking. Take for instance the conclusions of behavioural economists, who give us a confusing mixed message about ourselves. They suggest that our brain is in some ways good enough to 'know' more than 'we' do, in others bad enough to lead us in the wrong direction. This caricatures us as rational choosers prone to making irrational choices.

Our brain, so the theory goes, is shut inside the black box of our skull, receiving relatively limited information from the outside world, much of which is contradictory. It has to work hard therefore to build an inner model of what is 'out there'. It achieves this by operating as a predictive machine and belief engine, insistent on filling in gaps and justifying choices, which is why we occasionally hallucinate, perform actions we can't fully account for, or swear allegiance to a cause that is no 'truer' than the one clung to by our neighbours.

The problem is, although our brain is constantly 'on the go', even in sleep, it communicates only essential business to our conscious mind to protect us from overload. For every 'thought' that goes on up top, there are myriad slave systems propping it up down below.

26

Mountains of the Mind

This manifests itself as a body-awareness that operates below our mind's radar. If for instance we wish to make a left turn at speed while cycling, we must first make an imperceptible turn to the *right* to give a lean into the bend. Our conscious mind doesn't 'know' this, but our body does it automatically.

Poverty of information or automaticity of response in such circumstances means that our brain makes many of our decisions for us. There are sound reasons why evolution might have bequeathed us this facility. It can keep us safe, give us short cuts in our thinking, or fast-forward us to insight and creativity. The downside is that our waking mind is left in ignorance, playing catch-up, fabricating reasons for actions that we have not consciously chosen, or accounting for ideas that seem to come out of the blue.

The fake mind

This means there *is* a ghost in there, but it's not the self-directing mind beloved of ancient philosophers: it's the neurophilosopher's lackey of evolutionary imperatives, neural necessities and downright self-deceptions.

These are strong charges, but they are not new. Socrates was persuaded that our prime quest in life is to know ourselves, but Freud insisted that the self is not ultimately knowable. This means that the self that we present to the world is at best an act, at worst a deception. Shakespeare's character Edmund, an arch schemer, declares that we are all guilty of foppery: 'when we are sick in fortune....we make guilty of our disasters the sun, the moon, and the stars, as if we were villains by necessity'. We put on a show to the world, faking it until we make it, intent only on furthering our ambitions or covering up our failures.

> *Our mind is a 'kluge', a clumsy piece of engineering,*
> *badly designed for its purpose.*

We shall investigate whether these charges can be made to stick. If we are to lay claim to a mind of any substance, it should be tough enough to defend itself under empirical interrogation. If not, it is guilty as charged, ready to be 'sent down' as a 'kluge' or clumsy piece of engineering, badly designed for its purpose. It's just an assembly of nerve cells, collection of memes, lumbering robot, set of obedient algorithms, or chemical scum with barely any more meaning than the life of a slime mould.

These charges are real ones made by some of the authors listed in the bibliography at the end of this book. On one hand they do not rate our species too highly, on the other they do not appear to think so badly of themselves. If they're right, and the self is an illusion, full of deceptions and miscalculations, and human nature is ape behaviour in fancy dress, we can't defend ourselves, because we have no mind to rise above ourselves and judge the case impartially. There is no external court of appeal to tell us that all we are getting back is the verdict we want to hear.

Scientising the mind

According to flat-mind theorists, we are inheritors of a new kind of original sin, not moral but cognitive: we are deeply flawed, over-reliant on instinct, with a tendency to overrate ourselves and conflate our thinking into all-consuming ideologies. We are hopeless optimists, taking a far more positive view of our future prospects than the situation warrants. One explanation they give for these blind spots is that our ancestors might have evolved a capacity to 'big up' themselves, giving them a false confidence without which they would never have found the courage to leave their caves.

It does us no harm to puncture our complacency, confront our limitations or query what we assume to be 'natural' about our thinking. We also however need some grounds for our dignity, and a vision to aspire to. Science is only one perspective on the world, and we go astray when we look to it for a theory of everything, or of human nature. Scientists do well to avoid an air of omniscience, because science that goes beyond its brief becomes scientism, just another ideology that is no more true, reasonable, fair or informed than any of the other worldviews that it dismisses as superstitious or ill-informed.

Scientists like to say that their findings do not reduce us in stature, but offer a straighter path to self-knowledge than the tortuous route taken by philosophers and mystics. Rather than seek for imaginary treasures buried somewhere deep in our spiritual locker, it is better to know what is really in our cognitive cupboard. Only then can we give it a proper spring clean.

Mountains of the Mind

Scientists deploy modern methods, but they subscribe to an ancient myth: knowledge is not only desirable, it is inevitable, whatever the consequences. They do not believe therefore that their discoveries disenchant the world. On the contrary, they reveal its wonder. But so does the realm of culture, mind, art and spirit, albeit in qualitatively different ways.

We draw strange conclusions if we fail to see how the brain and mind, or material science and felt experience, are complementary aspects of being human. The cognitive scientist Steven Pinker describes music as 'auditory cheesecake'. We enjoy a more elevated experience than eating dessert however when we hear a slow ballad, a sacred mass, a rousing march, a holy requiem, a soulful serenade or a raunchy rock number. We sense we are doing more than sweetening our neural taste buds. We don't dismiss our auditory thrills on the grounds that they seem to be pointless, or serve no obvious purpose. We enjoy them because they are *there*.

Cognitive neuroscience has not been all about reducing our mental life to pleasure seeking or pain avoidance. It has also explored other contours of the mind. Research on creativity acknowledges our brain's expansiveness, imagination and ability to generate new ideas. But what happens when we finally discover the 'genes for' creativity, 'neurons for' insight or 'neural substrates of' spontaneity? We have scientised them, perhaps even 'explained' them, but without enchantment and wonder, their significance to us as lived experience is hollowed out.

'The mind is flat' mantra ultimately leaves us feeling parched, empty and politically vulnerable. We become the 'Unknown Citizen' of W H Auden's 1940 poem of that name. As malleable functionaries, our individual actions have meaning only within the larger system, which merely requires us to be 'normal in every way', and to 'hold the proper opinions for the time of year'. As creatures of 'flat affect', possessing no feelings we can genuinely call our own, even to rebel is to respond as 'they' wish us to do.

Flat mind theory therefore misses the point of having a mind in the first place, which is to impose ourselves upon the world, and to discriminate between artistry and dross. The evolutionary rationale of consciousness is that it makes sense of experience. It is always about something else, beyond raw inputs, and it always expresses something about 'us' in response to 'them'.

Mountains of the Mind

Flat mind theory is behaviourism in modern guise.

By missing this point, flat mind theory is behaviourism in modern guise. Behaviourists believed that the inner workings of the mind are impenetrable, behind lock and key. Flat-minders have found the key, and have even gone inside, but they still struggle to help us understand who is at home. The short-comings of their thinking are cruelly exposed in the fashionable attempt to rebrand ideas as 'memes', to which we now turn.

What is the new mind meme?

Meme theory – selfish genes – evolutionary psychology - the postmodern self – nature and nurture

- Meme theory is a biological model for explaining how non-genetic ideas parasitise our minds like viruses.
- It cannot however tell us how to judge good ideas from bad.
- Selfish gene theory, from which meme theory derives, is similarly limited, good at explaining our biology, less so at accounting for our sense of being a person in the world, what makes for a good life, or why we should be kind to one another.
- Selfish genes and memes became influential in the biological and cognitive sciences, but they have given way to a broader understanding of how genes and culture interact.
- Evolutionary psychology is good at speculating about what motivated our ancestors on the African savannah, less so about what drives our behaviour in the complex modern world.
- Our genes are prompters, not determiners. To be fully human, our nature must be nurtured, while not forgetting that our nurture is equally conditioned by nature.
- Around two hundred thousand years ago, the human mind developed a self-directing capacity, amplified by the passing on of extra-genetic culture.
- During this time of cognitive expansion, driven by a more complex social existence, we became conscious moral choosers, born of the need to balance self interest with the needs of the group, and to temper emotion with reason.
- Around the same time the idea of the soul emerged as part of a search for oneness and cohesion. Some see this as a vital spiritual legacy, others as a gremlin which we need to expel from our brain.

Mountains of the Mind

Meme theory

We do not need to engage in futile culture wars between 'scientific' and 'religious' mindsets, because our mind has evolved to cope quite comfortably with both. We can entertain different 'magisteria' or domains of knowledge, and accommodate complementary truths. Faith can be rational, and science regularly speculates about the deep nature of reality.

After four centuries of drifting apart, science and the humanities are increasingly finding common ground, accepting the overlaps between biology and culture, giving us our diverse worlds of mind. It is not an absurdity for a nuclear physicist to profess religious convictions.

Reconciling our different ways of knowing requires latitude and insight. Scientists come unstuck when they over-apply materialist reasoning to spiritual phenomena, just as poets lose their mojo when they seek to objectify their inspiration.

Sharing metaphors between domains of knowledge can stimulate new understanding, but not when one is privileged at the expense of the other. It is one thing to propose that genes control our genome, another to extend this logic to our mental life: memes direct our connectome. In this view, our mind is characterised as a meme machine, and our trains of thought, from daydreams to quantum theory, are memeplexes.

By what criteria do we rate one meme above another?

Giving something a different name, preferably with a technical twist, does not amount to an explanation, and a theory that sets out to explain everything ends up explaining nothing. What advance is 'meme' on 'idea', a much older word for a thought held in mind? How does 'memeplex' shed more light on the architecture of our thinking than worldview, theory, philosophy or ideology? Radical terrorism and scientific method are both memplexes and 'cultural attractors', engaged in a struggle for air time and dominance, but by what criteria do we rate one above the other?

Meme theory proposes that our thoughts are 'bits of information' that get passed between us, just as genes pass on our hair or eye colour. Straight away however we hit a problem with this biological analogy. Our bodies pass on genes, often with little say-so on our part, but our minds possess an element of choice in which memes we adopt.

Consider what happens if we catch a cold virus from someone else. We didn't intend to, and our body reacts accordingly, usually badly. But what if we are exposed to the 'virus' of joining a terrorist cell to bring about political or religious revolution? There has been contagion, and we have been infected with a dangerous idea, but we are at liberty to walk away, or campaign to eliminate this threat to our community.

If not, the meme has bypassed our moral resistance and entered our mind like a nasty germ. Instead of us thinking it, it now thinks us. Our sense of agency, imagination and creativity have been reduced to the burrowing of a clever parasite. 'A person is a hominid with an infected brain', writes the philosopher Daniel Dennett. But how did his mind become infected with the virus of this provocative idea? If the idea is his, and his alone, that makes him the possessor of the only hominid brain that is parasite-free.

Dennett takes his idea of the meme as a 'unit of culture' from Richard Dawkins, who popularised the idea of the selfish gene in the 1970's. As shapers of our body and determiners of why we look increasingly like our parents as we age, our genes form our genotype. Dawkins realised however that we are made not just by our biology, but also by our culture, which he called the phenotype. We are born into a social community of language, ideas, values, rituals, which fashion our mind as surely as our genes mould our body.

Once the trope of the 'selfish meme' had been set in motion, like any new or catchy idea (sorry, meme), it transmogrified into an epidemiological model of the spread of culture. Our mind was portrayed as vulnerable to infection, like an unvaccinated population in the midst of a cholera outbreak. Memes are powerful replicators, spreading like wildfire because they answer deep emotional and psychological needs, feeding on low-resistance default mechanisms and cognitive habits that are intrinsic to the evolution of our brain.

Those that spread fastest are the ones that parasitise our vulnerable wants, desires and fears, pressing the buttons of sex, pleasure and insecurity, which hark back to our fractious times on the savannah. Of course we want to be loved and famous, make a quick buck where we can, keep up with the Joneses, enjoy perpetual nirvana, and avoid being murdered in our bed. Memes are expert at targeting these rapid-response 'system one' instincts. They are not so good at accounting for how we arrive at our lengthily deliberated 'system two' moral choices and cultural values.

Brain worms

Memes are selfish brain worms, intent only on their own propagation, their 'fitness' judged by their ability to replicate, not by their impact on the well-being of their host, or fellow organisms. Instead of being helpful symbionts, they are potentially deadly toxins.

We don't choose memes, they choose us.

The rapid-spread ability of memes, which are invisible and subliminal, means they can multiply without any conscious input from their hosts. This means we might adopt them without understanding what they mean, who made them and where they come from. We don't choose them, they choose us.

This leaves us dangerously exposed, because the normal nexus of cause and effect is reversed, sometimes to preposterous effect. A mind is a meme's way of getting around, a dope addict is cocaine's way of getting sold on the street, a scholar is a library's way of getting its books read, a suicide bomber is a cult's way of getting itself noticed.

That said, memes often do wriggle past our defences, like that annoying ear worm of a tune that we can't get out of our head, or that seductive eye worm of a fashion accessory that persuades us we would look good in it. A meme might start as a fad, but when it reaches critical mass it becomes a fashion, creating its own magnetic field. Now it can begin to manage its popularity, and freely self-create.

Employing the biological model of a contagious virus does not however shed much light on how cultural ideas spread through a population, or down the generations. A successfully propagating meme does not tell us whether it is mad, bad or dangerous to know. So rather than judging its 'fitness' as a virus by the number of followers it infects, we need to consider the virtue of its argument, or its contribution to the greater good.

34

Mountains of the Mind

Richard Dawkins
Dawkins coined the term 'meme' in 1975, as a self-replicating mental phenomenon, to complement what the gene does for DNA. Since then his meme of the meme has had a good run, though it might also have run out of steam.

Otherwise we cannot make a judgment whether a meme is worthy or plain nasty. Memes are amoral, careless of whether they are right or wrong. Only minds are moral. This means we need to develop cognitive and collective immunity to bad memes, so that we can choose which ones to allow into our private brain and group mind. Do we pass on that racist joke doing the rounds, or spread that good news story about people from different communities getting on well in our neighbourhood?

For generations, good memes were naturally selected, with little conscious input from the minds that transferred them to the next generation: they were the ones that contributed to human flourishing, not private gain. As knowledge advanced, beneficial memes could be consciously selected and disseminated. It was a clear win for everyone three hundred years ago when doctors stopped bleeding their patients willy-nilly, and began to diagnose symptoms more precisely, so that they could be matched with appropriate cures.

Good memes favour the whole group. Where bad memes prosper, such as fake news, conspiracy theories, internet scams and extremist propaganda, they serve the interests of unscrupulous individuals or disaffected minorities, but only for a while, against the common good, and in defiance of the moral arc of progress. Such antisocial memes do indeed deserve to singled out as pathological mind-viruses.

Mountains of the Mind

Top of the memes

Aristotle proposed human flourishing as our most wholesome and healing 'top' meme, and it is clear that down the ages our best cultural memes have been those that maximise survival, freedom and dignity: the family, the social contract, altruism, the rule of law and education. Goodness, justice, truth and beauty are dismissed by some as mere abstractions, but as noble ideals they have played an important role in the human story.

More recently, free will, the self, consciousness and spirituality have been put under the spotlight of neuroscience, but they haven't been neurologically 'explained' in any meaningful sense, because such memes are 'high information'. A 'low information' meme like a pop song lasts only five minutes, but the essence of what makes a human mind is a bit more complex than humming a catchy tune. It has been part of who we are since we descended from the trees.

This does not mean that longevity of a meme is a guarantee of its worth. Pharaohs do not build pyramids any more, and the gods they worshipped, or declared themselves to be, have long disappeared. We have generally turned our backs on infanticide, slavery, capital punishment and fascism. The fact that these memes existed at all, or seemed to possess some staying power, does not prove that they are right, only that they served a purpose at the time, however dubious.

Like any infection, a bad meme can break out any time, or re-infect a population that has only just recovered from the previous bout of illness. Copy-cat suicides, religious cults and political purges always lurk in the wings. The idea that there is progress in human affairs is itself a contested meme, but it is difficult to maintain that memes like liberalism, reason and scientific method do not serve as a strong protection against slipping backwards into autocracy, ignorance and superstition.

Many good memes are so integrated into our lives that we are not aware of them, and take them for granted. If we're lucky to live in a good neighbourhood, we don't see a predominance of burglars, bullies, bums and beggars in the street. We see well-kept homes, orderly traffic, children going to school, delivery vans and public services. These are the mere tips of complex memes whose roots go far beneath the surface and into a sustainable future, not reducible to what is simple, catchy, predictable, temporary and accidental.

36

Mountains of the Mind

Memes are not therefore isolated bits of 'sticky' information that spread merely by contact. They are given meaning only in communities of like minds and engaged choosers who reject or approve of them. They gain effect and traction by their interconnections with countless other memes, and have to wait until their time has come, 'catching on' only when the political, moral and intellectual climate is right. It took centuries for instance for slavery to be abolished, and the struggle is still far from over.

The 'bad meme' of slavery is a constant reminder of our moral responsibility as human beings. We cannot un-invent it, pretend it is not there, or hide it under a new name such as indentured labour. 'Bad' memes have to be constantly called out, faced down, exposed for what they are. To do this, we have to be capable judges of what a good meme looks and feels like, and learn how to inoculate ourselves against bad ones.

There is no defence in claiming 'my memes made me do it'.

For many years it was assumed that our genes are fixed, passing on us a life or a death sentence. We now know that the life-style decisions we make feed back to our genes, and this is even truer of our memes. We both create and are created by them, underlining the importance of education, open-mindedness and the exercise of critical judgment. If our memes are as potent as meme-theorists claim, they must be constantly weighed in the balance. They have to be *our* ideas, because there is no defence in claiming 'my memes made me do it'.

Many memes have obvious cash value, such as learning our times tables, or waiting our turn in a queue. Just as many however develop more subtle symbolic power and psychological force, kept in circulation because they are cherished and passed on to the young. The same cannot be said for the cult of Kamikaze pilots, that eliminated many of Japan's brightest and best young males from the gene pool in World War Two. It is true that every now and again a powerful 'popular' meme operates like a superbug temporarily infecting the mind and body politic, but it withers away unless it is able to root itself deeply in a wider human story.

Mountains of the Mind

Mental parasites

When we are children, we have little choice which views our parents foist upon us. In preparing us for life's challenges, they regard it as their moral duty to fill our heads with their values and example. But at what point does this concern for what we think and how we conduct ourselves become indoctrination?

Some meme theorists are particularly critical of the contamination of young minds with religious or political propaganda. Aristotle remarked, 'Give me a child until he is seven, and I will show you the man', a sentiment which became a cornerstone of the spreading of the Catholic faith through education via the Jesuits.

Many of us grow up as mini-versions of our parents, though we would never admit this. We are just as likely however to rebel and go our own way. The key point is that we are allowed the freedom to do so. When we are older, we might choose a belief system, not because it was drummed into us as a child, but because we have thought deeply on an issue, or the claims of a particular faith. We might have a life-changing experience which radically reshapes our views.

This is the way with memes. They are brought to life in minds, not as dumb replicators or mindless algorithms. They are acquired, not inherited. We can't choose the length of our middle finger, but our big brain gives us the processing power to negotiate which complex memes we adopt through words and symbols.

Or does it? An effective meme is one that deceives us into passing it on, having first convinced us that it is our choice to do so. History shows only too graphically how vulnerable the human mind is to religious and political indoctrination. Romantic love might be our craftiest meme of all, a clever trick that keeps us alive just long enough to infect those around us, or make more of our own kind.

The larva of the lancet liver fluke or flatworm is even more calculating. It kick-starts its life cycle by worming its way into the body of an ant deep in the grass. When it gets into the brain of the insect, it turns it into a zombie, making it do its bidding by climbing to the top of a blade of grass. The ant is not doing this for exercise. Perched in mid-air, it is eaten by a cow, which simultaneously becomes host to the liver fluke, the eggs of which are eventually dumped in a juicy cow pat onto the grass, where they incubate and hatch as new larvae, which start the cycle all over again.

Mountains of the Mind

Liver fluke
It's not likely we have some of these wriggling around inside our brain, but might they symbolise certain unwanted ideas that we just can't get out of our head?

We might object to the claim that religion works to the same principle as the liver fluke, but a meme theorist would point out that both have been cunningly designed to hide this possibility from us. Why else do most religions insist that the good disciple is the one who proselytises, winning the most converts to the cause?

Some suggest that our brain has evolved software that makes it particularly vulnerable to indoctrination, propaganda, superstition and paranoia. No wonder the Book of Isaiah opines that 'All we like sheep have gone astray'. Rules of thumb such as 'follow the leader', 'look out for your own kind' and 'don't trust strangers' would have given any clan or tribe the edge over its neighbour in the precarious struggle for resources, territory and influence.

As the current surge in populism shows, these are powerful memes, never far from the surface, gaining traction because they go with the grain of our nature. They are not however what we teach our children. In the family and in school we offer them a 'hidden curriculum' of memes which include showing gratitude, working hard, helping others, aiming high and taking pleasure in sharing.

We also encourage children to think for themselves, or to use their imagination. Taken literally, imagination means the art of picture-making, but the pictures on the screen of our mind are not all dependent on what is received from outside. From a young age we are able to project our own pictures onto reality, largely through the power of symbolism, or the ability to draw together seemingly unrelated ideas in our mind in a novel way.

Meme theory accounts only for ideas that come to us externally. Only imagination is able to explain how one thought can spark another inside our head, or inspire us to conceive a new reality that transcends our senses. Without this alchemy of mind, which meme theorists are at a loss to understand, and neuroscientists to explain, we could not make sense of figurative language, such as Ted Hughes' simile of a black-backed gull in flight bending in a strong wind 'like an iron bar slowly'. In the same instant we feel the light strength of the bird in the heavy invisibility of the wind.

Imagination is not confined to poetry lessons. It infuses all of our thinking, and is therefore the fount of all our knowledge. Isaac Newton needed the power of metaphorical thinking to see the moon 'pulling' the oceans towards itself, creating the phenomenon of tides. Albert Einstein needed the ability to make a greater reality from two simpler ideas if he was to see time and space as 'curved'.

The most powerful memes need first to be conceived as ideas,
and for that we need imagination.

According to meme theory, memes propagate by being passed on from mind to mind, and by talking about them now, we are doing just that. Gravity and spacetime are now common knowledge, powerful memeplexes that are part of the culture and zeitgeist. They could not however have come to Newton and Einstein as ready-made memes. The most powerful memes need first to be conceived as ideas, and for that we need imagination.

Deadly memes
Terrorism through suicide-bombing or mowing down pedestrians with a vehicle might be seen as highly successful memes from the perspective of fanatical jihadists who want only for their ideas to poison liberal debate, or sow religious division. Some commentators believe these violent memes have now entered the mainstream, and will be social realities for decades to come. They are therefore 'strong' memes.

Strong memes are almost impossible to stamp out, because they reside not in individual brains, but in the culture that created them. They will persist as long as their ideological cause remains, such as spreading the faith or punishing the infidel, or the environmental catalyst persists, such as social exclusion or extreme poverty.

Persecution and martyrdom do not weaken a meme, but strengthen it. Crucifixion could not eradicate Christianity, and drones cannot kill jihadism. Martyrs may be killed, but their ideas live on, often invigorated. Scans of the brains of evangelicals and jihadists show similar areas of the brain lighting up, as if both see themselves as engaged in a holy war. We need more than meme theory to judge the truth or wholesomeness of such beliefs.

Another failing of meme theory is that it cannot explain how we come up with a new idea, or have an epiphany. Did Einstein come up with startlingly new insights, or was he replicating earlier memes? In a peculiar updating of Marx's claim that our consciousness is the product of our own creations, meme-theory has even been extended to 'temes' or technology-memes in the digital world: eventually our minds become the extensions of our electronic devices and their algorithms.

The problem with the germ or contagion model of the spread of memes is that it negates human agency, reducing us to puppets and mimics. Ideas are no longer actively chosen by minds, but passively 'caught' like microbes. Our ideas, say the meme-theorists, accumulate us as much as we accumulate them.

It's hard however to equate the copying of the local graffiti 'tribal' style with our arrival after long reflection at a life-changing decision. Also, our deliberate reasons for rejecting certain ideas matter as much as our unwitting compliance in accepting others.

Critical thinking, or thinking for ourselves, has the power
to undermine meme theory.

The most powerful meme of all, because it is a primary act of mind, is the skill of critical thinking, our chief defence against humbug, lies, irrationality, superstition, propaganda, conspiracy theories and mediocrity. Without it, our only protection against skulduggery is to hide ourselves away from new memes altogether, good or bad, like the Amish. Without it, we have no way of discriminating between the 'good vibrations' of the Beach Boys and a Bach cantata.

Mountains of the Mind

By encouraging us to think for ourselves, develop immunity to bad thinking habits, resist unthinkingly falling in line, and recognise ideologies that set out to control us, critical thinking has the power to undermine the simplistic claims of meme theory, which is the meme that failed. It is hoist by its own petard, because it has not proved strong enough to enter the mainstream. Like behaviourism before it, it hasn't caught on, because it can't account for the inner workings of the mind in its personal and cultural manifestations. When we reflect, we find that we can rise above mimicry and flatness.

Selfish genes

Evolutionary psychologists set out to explain how our mind has evolved to solve the problems faced by our evolutionary ancestors, taking up where Darwin left off. He proposed that evolution by natural selection has shaped our body, but he refrained from insisting that our mind too is a product of nature, if only because there was no ready evidence. He did point out however that he believed an attempt to understand the behaviour of a baboon would teach us more than a volume of metaphysical speculation about human nature.

The problem for evolutionary psychologists is that we are not baboons or any other kind of furless bipedal primate. Nor are we still hunter-gathers roaming on the savannah. We are inhabitants of modern cities and complex cultures. Many of our inherited cognitive programs which once served us so well, such as suspicion of strangers and sexual jealousy, are therefore no longer adaptive. Cooperation is more important than survival, and we are here today because of mutuality, not selfishness.

And yet, for biologist Richard Dawkins, coiner of the term 'meme', survival is the name of the game. Evolution works at the level of the gene, not the individual or group, and to ensure this, genes are selfish, looking out only for themselves, or the replication of their own kind. Sperm cells would kill their own grandmother if it meant getting first to the egg.

An organism is a confederacy of co-operators, not a riot of rivals.

Unfortunately the metaphor 'selfish' has generated more heat than light. It was chosen by Dawkins to describe a *biological* truth, that what makes a gene successful is its survival into the next generation. He published 'The Selfish Gene' in 1976, at the height of the Cold War, and biology has since moved on: we now know that genes are as likely to form collectives as to try to exterminate each other. An organism is a confederacy of cooperators, not a riot of rivals. Genes, like the members of society, need each other's help. There is as much 'snuggle' on display in nature as there is struggle: even crocodiles nurse their eggs.

In our case, as advanced primates, we are highly dependent on cooperation, both within our bodies and between generations. If this weren't the case, we would all die at birth, because our genes would be too busy assassinating each other inside us, and we would die of neglect in the crib.

Nevertheless, the meme and metaphor of the selfish gene has stuck, and by association has been applied to our mind, masquerading as a kind of *human* truth. We are merely the carriers of our genes, and if our mind has any substance at all, it is only as a vehicle to transport our genes from one generation to the next. Any sense of mental depth we have is illusory. Even our finest achievements of mind are merely the random results of time plus chance plus necessity.

Moral memes
Dawkins, one of biology's great meme-makers, is of course a more subtle thinker than his tabloid 'Selfish Gene' book title suggests. He points out that evolution is not the random fumblings of a blind watchmaker. We like to wear 'designer' watches, but evolution offers us a different model of design. The result however is the same: we end up with the best solution to a problem, because each evolutionary advance is stored as a 'good trick' or winning combination in an organism that is 'fit' to survive.

Out of selfishness can arise selflessness.

The best genetic forms are 'saved' and 'sent' to the next generation, not lost in the recycle bin. Only the winners get to reproduce, so chance is 'tamed' to create something immensely complex from simple ingredients, such as the human eye, without the need for a watchmaker, or Intelligent Designer outside of time and space.

43

Mountains of the Mind

So the process is not blind, but sighted in a special non-human way, which nevertheless gives rise to our human kind of consciousness and society. 'Selfish' genes are as capable of favouring altruism and sacrifice as they are ruthlessness and revenge, as we see in any beehive. Out of selfishness can arise selflessness.

In that sense evolution is cleverer than we are, and morality and religion are not illusions. They are sound long-term strategies for the survival of the species. We can dress them up as 'moral memes' or 'spiritual neurons' if we prefer, but 'the ties that bind' does the job just as well.

Neural complexity, serendipitously arrived at or otherwise, has given rise to mind and culture, and these give us vision, or the foresight to choose our next step, not to be swept along by forces beyond our control. Mind and culture are non-genetic and extra-biological, allowing us to make human choices beyond the inhuman exigencies of natural selection.

The concept of the person for instance is something new in nature. So is language, or our ability to express complex ideas in strings of words, or think them as ideas inside our heads. Attempts to teach language to chimpanzees show how clever they are at gesturing with signs, but more importantly underline how brilliant we are at *speaking* with sounds. Our symbol-soaked culture has replaced our genes as the driver of the evolution of the human body and brain. Why else would we bother to *talk* about abortion, gene editing or the curing of cancer?

A material explanation based on the patterning of amino-acids in the spiral helix of our genome does not therefore prove that mind is merely a biological accretion. Similarly an evolutionary history of mind does not show that it is little more than a sophisticated entertainment system or sugar-salt-fat search engine. To know ourselves for what we are, and to rid ourselves of debilitating ideologies, we have to aim higher: we are conscious symbolic meaning-makers, morally interconnected and responsible for our own future. Our brain might be made of physics, but our mind is fired by ideas.

For these reasons, and more besides, biology's post-Darwinian synthesis has moved beyond a rigidly genetic model for explaining the human condition. As our species became more conscious and interdependent, 'fitness' became as social and cultural as it was biological and genetic. Evolutionists now talk not just of natural selection shaping our bodies, but of multilevel selection shaping our minds. Non-genetic innovations such as group living, language, introspection, art and reason became our greatest ideas.

Dangerous ideas

A strong advocate of the 'flat mind' argument has been the philosopher of mind Daniel Dennett, who describes Darwinian evolution as a 'universal acid' eating away at the foundations of all we thought was somehow special about human minding.

This is a dangerous meme indeed. Dennett insists that mind isn't special: it's a product of biology, or millions of little robots mindlessly going about their business. We make decisions without knowing how or why we make them. We are unconscious schemers, deceived about our own motives and our ability to influence others. Up top 'we' may feel free and sovereign selves, but deep down, 'we' are only the shallows of information processing and statistical analysis.

Some point out that the true acid is not the application of Darwinian thinking to all things human, but overly-reductive thinking. Certain types of reduction are highly useful memes. If our car breaks down, we need to know exactly which component has failed, and how to fix it. This is reduct*ionism* at work, tracing backwards to a cause. If however we say that our mind is 'just a Darwinian meme-replicating machine', this is reduct*ivism*, or taking reduction too far.

The mind is a culturally 'thick' concept, not reducible to 'thin' neural wiring. As we trace back along the chain of causation (why do I feel so tired today?), we start with a complex self-directing organism, and end up with incomprehensible quantum effects at the sub-particle level. This is why most cognitive scientists and biologists now start at the bottom of the chain, working their way slowly up through particles, atoms, molecules, cells, individual organisms (that's you and me), and the large cultural groups we belong to.

If we want to understand consciousness, mind and culture, as well as reductionism, we also need constructionism. Changing the metaphor from chains to building blocks, we must look not at the lowest courses of brick, which we're never aware of anyway, but at the magnificent building that rises up as more than the sum of its parts. This is where we live our lives, as self-directing members of a wider community.

45

Mountains of the Mind

It makes little sense to go hunting for 'neurons for' being kind to each other, 'genes for' being reasonable, or 'algorithms for' enjoying music, because such qualities don't exist in the footings and foundations. They 'emerge' at a particular point in the building project, as the living quarters take shape, and complexity increases. Beyond this point, something else takes over, beyond determinism, a self-organising occupant of the house who adds something new to the evolutionary process.

We can debate exactly when in the evolutionary story this transformation takes place. What matters is that we realise its significance in our progress from synapses to Shakespeare. The point of 'emergence' might be life itself, and nature's discovery of the spontaneous generation of energy. Even the humblest bacterium is in a constant fight to defy entropy, and make more of its own kind.

It is more likely however that, the more biologically complex the creature, or the bigger its brain, the greater the step change towards self-determination and creativity. We find that the life of the organism transcends the life of its cells. Once mind enters the scene, it begins to create its own order and reality, which need more than biochemistry to explain them.

The feed-back mechanisms become just as important as the feed-forward, if not more so, in a kind of reversal of the arrow of time and chain of causation. Our genes may prompt or incline us in a particular direction, but we evolve the capacity to say no, or switch course. Our mind becomes its own end, not a means to lots of sub-goals, always an indivisible experience, never reducible to its parts.

This puts 'minding' our own business in the same category as 'looking' out for ourselves. We don't worry about the definition of look. We just look. Either we see or we don't. Even if we're blind or visually impaired, we can still 'see' each other's point of view, because we are endowed with inner ways of seeing.

Spirituality is also a state of mind, not a style of meme, because like mind, it belongs to the realm of being. Any attempt to trace spirituality, insight, and intuition back to genes, neural networks, a 'God spot' in the cerebrum, hearing voices, a bang on the head, a psychedelic drug, a comet flying overhead, a hallucination on the mountain caused by lack of oxygen to the brain, or the vividness of a dream, without probing the mind's openness to symbol, feeling and meaning in a cultural context, is bound to fall sadly short as an 'explanation'.

46

Mountains of the Mind

We have reached a point in our evolution where mind and culture are increasingly controlling the biotechnology of our body. The truly dangerous meme therefore is the belief that we can improve or alter the complex inheritance that nature has bequeathed us, perhaps enhancing our intelligence or gifting ourselves immortality, without trusting equally to tried and tested beliefs that are part of, but also stand outside of, our successful biology.

Daniel Dennett
b 1942
As a philosopher of mind, Dennett has consistently maintained that everything in the mind can be explained naturalistically, either by biochemistry or Darwinian evolution.

Dawkins and Dennett have dominated debate and captured the public imagination in their intelligent books popularising their scientific and philosophical ideas. This has goaded postmodern theorists working in the humanities, who have traditionally regarded themselves as both strangely detached from 'mere' science and the true custodians of the zeitgeist, to flatten the mind from the perspective of culture.

They agree that the mind is flat, but for very different reasons. Whereas evolutionists see the mind as written on by nature, explaining many of our inherited gremlins, they insist that the mind is a blank slate. As a result, we are merely the signs we give off, and our interpretations of them. All our disputations, even about science itself, are opinionated excursions and linguistic performances, more show than substance.

Mountains of the Mind

There is no depth, essence or meaning to anything, only the constructions and inventions we make in passing. We change our spots so often that some days we don't recognise ourselves, because 'we' are a confection of our consciousness, a story we make up as we go along, usually after the event.

The world is a revolving stage, and we are the actors that come and go.

Postmodern scepticism undermines itself: if everything is relative, so is postmodernism. It sounds a trendy meme, but it is not a new idea unique to Western thinking. It goes back to much older Eastern teaching, especially Hinduism, that the world is a revolving stage, and we are the actors that come and go. The postmodern twist is that, even in our short time on stage, we are 'sites of conflict', never one thing long enough to say 'this is me'.

Our claims to enlightenment, individuality, reason, culture, democracy and civilisation are therefore only skin-deep illusions. Our emotions are so powerful that they persuade our intellect that our convictions match how the world really is. The postmodernist hope is that we can at least become aware of our ignorance, which is the first step in bringing our default networks out in the open, where we can see them for what they are.

The impulsive self

Cognitive scientists, evolutionary psychologists and postmodern theorists have been painting their own pictures of the mind as a temporary delusion, and our sense of self as an emergent deception, but they arrive at their conclusions by very different routes.

Cognitive scientists believe our brain has evolved to make our biases *feel like* reasons. *Of course* we made the best choice when we changed our job or brought a child into the world. Our brain's trick is to take a thousand bewildering inputs and shred them down to one über-idea, oblivious to over-simplification. Without this ability, we would never be able to bring ourselves to mark a particular box with 'X' in the polling booth.

'Up top' we feel justified and rational, but 'down below' we are driven by prejudice, insecurity and a need to show we are 'right'. Whether we are liberal or reactionary, white or black, chauvinist or feminist, straight or gay, we put a

48

'reasonable' face on our unconscious biases. We rationalise our emotions into a credible narrative that holds together the faux-confident 'self' we present to the world. Our brains are so expert at this gap-filling confabulation that even our practised denials are part of the performance we put on.

Evolutionary psychologists look to the genes for more substantial 'causes' of our self-deceiving fickleness and irrationality. Can the drivers of human behaviour be traced back to our evolutionary past? Take for instance our craving for sugar, and the soaring rates of diabetes in the developed world. It's easy for us to scoff a sugar bun if it's on offer, but for our ancestors, sweetness was a rare, precious and nutritious treat, risking injury and pain to steal it from an angry hive.

Coming across a bee colony dripping in honey therefore prompted a reflex reaction from our forebears. It might be months before they come across another opportunity like this. They therefore want it *now*, and there's no question of waiting. There's barely a choice to be made, and no need for deliberation.

The difficulty with this 'gimme gimme' primary reflex choice-mechanism, useful during a precarious existence on the African savannah, is that in the modern world, where sugar is added to just about everything we eat, we need a secondary reflective choice-mechanism, the ability to 'just say no', buy sugar-free products, put off our treat until later or deny it altogether.

We are like a three year old in a sweet shop demanding the
chocolate placed temptingly at the checkout.

The problem is that our rational, deliberative and analytical capacity to act 'on second thoughts' evolved much later, and therefore ends up playing second fiddle to our desire for instant gratification. As a result, our modern psychology mirrors that of a three year old in a sweet shop demanding the chocolate placed temptingly at the checkout. Our parents say no, even though we throw a tantrum, because they realise that, if our desires go unchecked, we face an adult life of bad teeth, obesity, diabetes and insatiable craving for undeserved reward.

Similarly, we add salt to our food despite medical advice not to, even claiming that we deserve the treat. High blood pressure has become a modern problem because natural selection favoured an ancestral gene that promoted a craving to add salt to our diet. Our bodies need it, and on the African savannah it was in short supply. Our problem today is that salt is not a rare treat but freely available, added in large quantities to our processed foods to make us crave more of the same. Our taste buds just can't say no and we haven't evolved an 'off' switch, so hardened arteries are the price we pay.

Genes and nurture

Even if evodevo (evolutionary psychology in cahoots with sociobiology) is able to account in these ways for our modern high rates of obesity and heart disease, they don't easily map onto our wider worlds of morality and culture. Genes are not tyrants and determiners but enablers and incliners, and even then, are not always expressed. We're not 'naturally' aggressive or compassionate, adulterous or faithful, neurotic or psychotic, fat-gorging or ascetic, except in response to particular situations. Most importantly, our culture steps in to influence what response might be acceptable.

The binary nature/nurture debate does little to settle this argument, as nurture happens as much inside the body as outside. We are not just what happens to us externally, but also the product of an internal milieu of self-induced chemical and psychological states, based on what we consume and how we think. We are not the creatures of nature *or* nurture, but nature *and* nurture, operating on us at all times from every direction. Why else did nurture evolve in the first place, unless to transform nature?

Nevertheless, some hard-line geneticists insist on framing nurture as an extension of nature: it's all in the genes. Nursing mothers will stumble out of bed in the wee small hours to feed the baby while the father snores on obliviously: that's just the way things are.

This is partly a reaction against ideologically-driven 'blank slate' environmentalist thinking of the 1960's and 70's, based on the belief that cultural influences can outweigh the effects of the genes. Some 'social engineering' theorists were convinced that they could eradicate gender attitudes by giving dolls to boys and spanners to girls.

Not so, say the geneticists. Boys will be boys, if only because they carry the Y chromosome. If they don't, they will behave like girls. Boys, who eventually grow into men, behave in masculine ways not because they are taught to, but because they create environments that match and amplify their maleness: fast-action computer games, watching football, taking machines apart, shoving each other. Their bedrooms reek of testosterone. Whether their parents paint their bedroom blue or pink is neither here nor there.

Our genetic predisposition, according to the gene-genies, is a blueprint, or list of settings, not a recipe we pick and choose from. We have no trouble understanding this when it comes to our eye colour or height, though a nourishing diet might help us put on an inch or two. It's more controversial when we say that our genes also trump the nurture we receive and the life chances that befall us. Early conditioning and the input of our parents do little to change the genetic path we are on.

It's nice when our parents, partners or friends show us some love, but they don't and won't make a difference to the person we have it within us to become. Hundreds of studies with identical twins separated at birth and adopted children show that the genes 'come true' regardless of upbringing, not just in terms of appearance but also in personality, right down to uncannily similar choices of job, clothing and partner.

Whatever life throws at us, we will bounce back in line with our genes.

In other words, barring tragic accidents, if we're born a winner, or with a genetic advantage, we're set to do well regardless. Whatever life throws at us, we will bounce back in line with our genes. That's the science. What the implications are for social policy would require a whole book to itself, though preferably not written by a geneticist.

There is a silver lining to this tough argument that we cannot be made into something we do not have it within us to be. Our parents might insist on giving us expensive piano lessons, but when they realise we are not cut out to be a classical pianist, they can let us quit with a clear conscience.

Their money and effort to find out if we are 'musical' has not however been wasted. At least we can now appreciate just what it takes to become a skilled pianist, and there is ample research to show that learning a musical instrument when we are young helps to boost our overall intelligence in the long term. So nurture *does* make a difference, and it *does* improve on nature.

51

Mountains of the Mind

Nurturing our genes

The environment we are raised in does therefore influence our development, but not always in ways we expect. Each of us encapsulates the phylogeny or the genetic history of our species that goes back two million years, with a brain story that stretches three *billion* years before that.

We are shaped by the genetic 'memories' passed down to us.

Just as important however is our ontogeny, or the decisions our mother makes while we are in her womb, and the life choices we make after that. Her decision to smoke while she was pregnant, and even her own mother's decision a generation before her, can influence our propensity for smoking in adulthood. Our father's decision to smoke as a young man can raise our risk of cancer a generation later. The human condition is shaped therefore not just by the decisions of our own growing body and mind, but also by the genetic 'memories' passed down to us.

Explaining things backwards is problematic however, a bit like claiming that our nose and ears evolved to support our spectacles. We run into great difficulties if we try to judge our modern mind by what our neurons and DNA were getting up to in the Stone Age, or inside our mother's womb. Unlike the brain, the mind leaves no fossils, except in discarded tools, ruined settlements, cave paintings and what little archaic ritual survives.

It's pure speculation therefore to try to account for things we find hard in the modern age, such as resisting sweet food, accepting 'outsiders' or maintaining sexual fidelity within marriage, on the grounds that our brains were not originally 'wired' to cope with these challenges. Nor were they originally programmed to help us write our name or do sums.

And yet we learn these skills by exploiting ancient neural software to create something culturally new, shaped not just by genetics but also epigenetics, or the influence of upbringing and custom on the growing mind. Our genes can learn too, by adapting to feedback from our environment, giving nurture as strong a hand as nature. As well as neuroplasticity, we also possess genoplasticity, which is why doctors tell us it is never too late to adopt a healthier lifestyle.

There is now clear evidence that genes can be switched on or off by the life choices we make, the company we keep, and how we were raised. While it is true that the blacksmith's children won't be born with brawny biceps, their lives will be shaped by his kindness, attitudes, the example he sets, and the legacy of his father's father. Genes work vertically across generations, influenced not just by our parents, as previously thought, but also by our grandparents. Our genome carries the memory of their nutrition, drug habits and stress levels. They also work horizontally. By making life better for those around us, we give each other's genes a boost.

It's not therefore a simple case of nature, DNA, genes and instinct holding us on a shorter leash than nurture, our unconscious, culture or acquired habits. We don't have to choose between genetic determinism *or* cultural plasticity, because causes and motivations in human behaviour are not as simple as switching our central heating system on or off. Nature and nurture work as a complementary pair.

The self-directing mind
We have to understand that, as our brain complexity increased, our mind began to trace its own evolutionary path. Gradually, as our ancestors built up resources and established stable communities, survival became less a matter of ruthless chance, and culture started to domesticate and moralise us.

We can build whatever picture we like from the scanty fossil evidence of our ancestral past. Some anthropologists maintain that warfare is endemic in hunter-gatherer society. In one site in Kenya, twenty seven massacred bodies have been found, preserved in a lagoon, dating from ten thousand years ago, of men, women and children, their heads smashed in.

Others regard this as an exception, insisting that there is scant evidence of organised violence until the Stone Age, when social patterns changed. If there was aggression, violence and murder in Eden, there must also have been nurture, protection and stability, otherwise we would not be here to tell the story.

Somehow, despite our Jekyll and Hyde back story, greater mental processing power allowed us to reflect on our options, delay gratification, temper lust, interpret our emotions and control aggression. We find that we can walk away from that fight, or those buns in the bakery window. We can learn to live cheek by jowl with strangers. The aftermath of terrorist attacks does not have to be raw revenge but a quiet determination to show there is more that unites us than divides us.

53

Mountains of the Mind

Our life-journey engages us in a process of autopoiesis or self-making, shaped by the values, traditions and symbol systems of our culture. We need a sense of self to act as an autonomous agent, capable of reason and imagination. Only an individual mind is able to invest the world with meaning. In this sense, the shifting architecture of brain programs and the unfolding of mind are mirror images of each other, not opposites but as singular as a pair of socks.

And yet the socks do sometimes seem to make an odd pair, because mind and brain have grown at different speeds, not fully matched for style in the modern psyche. There is a fundamental and dangerous split between thought and feeling. Take the case of North Korea. This is a nation with the technical capability to launch intercontinental ballistic missiles, tipped with nuclear warheads, but with a political system possessing the mental age and emotional maturity of a petulant teenager.

It's as if evolution equipped us to survive, even to be technically clever, but not to solve complex moral puzzles or cope with high-level abstractions. So though we are smart enough to build a new car from scratch, our mind/brain comes as given, riddled with design faults that we can't reverse engineer or send back to the workshop for a refit. This makes us potentially very stupid, and possibly very dangerous.

Despite the best attempts of biologists, psychologists and cultural theorists, it's almost impossible to disentangle the growth of mind and brain in its long evolution on the savannah. Whatever intrinsic biological factors were at work, operating to the same algorithms throughout the living world, there was soon extrinsic moulding by the local influences of family and culture.

Anthropologists agree that culture offers each human group not a single model of reality, but a customised way of being and thinking. It also depends on mutuality, and this is rare in nature. Biologists calculate that insect species such as bees, termites and ants made the transition from solitariness to sociality about twenty times, whereas Homo sapiens needed to do so only once.

Once established, useful behaviours and ideas could replicate at a much faster rate than the slow evolution of genes. Our mind was no longer isolated and naked, but clothed by cooperation and custom. Each culture could not only develop its own wisdom, but also pass it on to the next generation or neighbouring tribe.

Mountains of the Mind

We spent as much time shaping our beliefs as sharpening our axes.

As a result of our sociality, genetic adaptation and cultural moulding could co-evolve. For instance, at about the same time that we started our technological journey of fashioning tools, we were also embarking on a spiritual adventure, believing in gods and making sacrifices, so our progress as a species was as much an affair of the heart as an exercise in logic. We spent as much time shaping our beliefs as sharpening our axes.

Balancing reason and emotion
There may have been a point in our ancestral past when reason and emotion complemented each other. That was our time of innocence, when we lived in small groups. But as 'civilisation' flourished, so did mistrust, power struggles and the vast armies dispatched to enslave the out-group. The wars and genocides of history suggest that technology and tribalism are a dangerous combination when not tempered by human sympathy of the in-group, and reason alone cannot teach us why we should accept each other's differences. As many myths attest, we became creatures of guilt with blood on our hands.

Charles Darwin
1809-1882
Darwin's theory of evolution by natural selection was an idea whose time had come, and it continues to account for how most biological phenomena came to be the way they are. Can it also account for mind?

So the dual realities of reason and feeling, science and spirit, tools and transcendence, emerged in tandem, simultaneously making sense of the physical world while suggesting that something lies beyond the senses. Even to fashion a flint, the idea of what it can be used for has to be in the mind before the brain guides the hand in performing the task. This need to visualise the unseen and second-guess the future was a great prompt in our cognitive development, but it also threw us into issues of purpose and meaning: *why* should we care for each other, or want to beautify our surroundings?

> *We are neither wholly good nor wholly evil, but*
> *agile opportunists and clever adapters.*

Something other than the instinct to survive was motivating our ancestors to develop moral sentiments and paint animals on rock faces. As far as we know, we are the only species capable of both laying down its life for a friend and wiping out a rival tribe. As well as reflecting on our own reflections, or expressing ourselves through art, we can build prisons or weapons of mass destruction. In other words, we are neither wholly good nor wholly evil, but agile opportunists and clever adapters.

Maybe we were once more 'together' and comfortable with ourselves, and the clash of hope and fear came much later, as human numbers increased, and a warrior class emerged to protect boundaries. Right at the start of the human journey, there were shades of Eden. The Blombos Caves in South Africa contain beautiful images and objects dating from seventy thousand years ago. One stone reveals a hatched pattern which qualifies as the first known attempt to store a message outside of the human brain. At about this time we also see the first signs of leaving gifts in the graves of our loved ones to take into the after-life.

To understand this step-change in human minding, we have to consider the role of *feeling*. It is a mistake to see our brain evolution purely in terms of a rational or 'winner takes all' ascent: we have also evolved the capacity for cultural 'non-zero-sum' cooperation. As our emotions became more refined, especially the more sophisticated social emotions of love, guilt, disgust, shame, embarrassment and pride, we needed a means of processing them, and a conscious self to own them.

Animals are conscious, but they do not wrestle with moral dilemmas. If a dog sees a bone, and he's strong enough to defend it, it's his. We however live in complex social networks with strict codes of behaviour and mutuality, adding memories, hopes and goals to what it means to be self-aware.

We had to evolve an additional brain layer to cope with this, the neocortex, which sends up to fifty pulses a second through the whole brain, creating a global perspective of other minds, triggering our moral sentiments, both to keep us this side of the law and to direct our compassion. What if somebody else has a prior claim to that bone, or there is a starving family next door?

The social mind
We cannot therefore overlook the social dimension of brain evolution as the catalyst for consciousness and morality. Navigating the perilous shoals of life is far from simple: whose food are we stealing, is it safe to eat, how do we fend off rivals, how do we share resources with an eye on future reciprocity?

> *The humanising presence of mind gives us*
> *the contours of a universal moral law.*

The start of the twenty-first century has been marred by upsurges in nationalism, populism, terrorism and isolationism, but this is not the only narrative we are capable of writing for ourselves. What about trust, empathy, generosity and the celebration of difference? When times are tough, we focus on physical survival, but in times of plenty, there is no need to unleash our atavistic fears. A full grasp of our evolutionary potential calls for the humanising presence of mind, which gives us the contours of a universal moral law. Whichever perspective we look from, the mind is not flat, and nor has it evolved to be so.

At this precarious point in our evolution, with the ability to destroy ourselves a hundred times over by a dozen different means, we need the concept of the social mind more than ever. Our big brain evolved to process all the challenges of group politics. From this shotgun marriage of sharp intelligence and cunning social skills emerged the frail offspring of our modern consciousness, not just as a bulwark for our sense of self, but also as an acknowledgement of the debt we owe each other.

The depth and range of human minding start here. Once freed from the dictates of raw sense experience, we could venture beyond stimulus and response into longer chains of thought, which have the added advantage of being reversible, allowing reasoning of effects back to causes. Only then could we become creatures of culture, generating the necessary symbols to communicate our ideas to each other and exploring alternatives. We could embrace a moral vision that takes us beyond our own immediate needs.

So in the beginning (perhaps) we were embodied brains at one with nature, participants and not spectators, our inner and outer worlds integrated and indistinguishable: the tool grew from our hand and the stars were in our eyes. Slowly however our newly-human rational left brain overtook our previously-primate empathic right brain, a cognitive transformation we experience as toddlers when we 'discover' speech and reason at around the age of two: we are no longer *infans*, or speechless.

Similarly in our hunter-gatherer ancestry we gradually realised we had a mind: we could make symbols which took on a life of their own, as ideas expressed in cave paintings and tribal chants, sculpting the brain that had brought them to life.

Finally we believed we had a soul: we began to leave offerings to nature spirits to persuade them to favour us, and to venerate fertility, the root of religion. The living world, including ourselves, was full of animal spirits, both present and absent. Through his magic and ritual, the shaman could bridge the gap between the human and animal worlds.

Even today, much of our modern science is a kind of magic, mixing a world of appearances with unseen forces. Modern physics has taught us that nothing is what it seems, solid matter is full of empty spaces, what appears as stasis is actually constant movement. No wonder then that we once viewed ourselves as psychic wholes, ensouled brains and minded bodies in a material world, unified in body, mind and spirit, our minding not split between our immersive right and our isolating left brain hemispheres.

Ghosts and gremlins

We need a new concept of mind if we are to replace the superstitions of ghosts and gremlins with an informed understanding of the relation of mind to body. Without it, we cannot counter the arguments of materialist science and evolutionary psychology. Our existential dilemmas come with our genome, their roots deep in our piecemeal evolution and opportunistic design.

Mountains of the Mind

There is always plenty of room for error and misjudgement.

Over fifty years before the evodevo theorists got onto the case, Freud was advising that we barely know our hidden nature. Evodevo translates this as follows: our brain is full of gremlins and self-deceptions, clumsy and inefficient. It is over-engineered in some respects and under-developed in others, too complicated for its own good. This means there is always plenty of room for error and misjudgement. We don't for instance always read our own sense impressions accurately: a cold coin feels heavier to us than a warm one.

The new explanatory myth of the mind/brain is flatness: most of our choices are made for us. Our brain is full of ghosts from an ancestral past, and gremlins from a shoddy construction process. It is like the QWERTY keyboard, initially designed to cope with the inefficient levers of early typewriters, but now an awkward limitation on modern keyboards.

It worked well then, but if we were designing it from scratch for a new generation of computers, we would start all over again, because its ancient design does not match the potential of the latest technology. But we can't, and we're stuck with it. We just have to learn to live with its gremlins.

Why is our mind so full of gremlins?

Ancestral glitches – bootstrap model – kluge theory – modular mind - tribalism – failures of rationality – uses of reason

- Our mind/brain evolved not as a flawless design but as a hotchpotch of tools untidily assembled to perform different functions, some of which occasionally conflict with each other.
- This means that our modern cognitive sophistication is a thin veneer over operations, responses and smart tricks that evolved for more primitive purposes.
- Thought experiments are useful in exposing some of the clashes and fault lines in our thinking, but they throw little light on how we make difficult decisions in real life.
- Rationality and logic are forms of thinking, but they are not alone able to teach us how to live together. For that we need practical reason, which is the foundation of our morality.
- The atrocity at Oradour in 1944 tempts us to believe that evil can be blamed on bad people who are nothing like us.
- The truth is otherwise. Our conflicted evolutionary inheritance makes us all capable of doing bad things in pursuit of what we are convinced is good.
- Being moral takes us beyond good and evil. It is about developing the character to do the right thing, even when it is the harder thing.
- This means that morality resides not in art, books or codes of conduct, but in cultivating the virtues of treating each other with justice and respect.

The tinker's brain

Our brain has not been specially designed for our personal use, but is the end result of the glacially slow twists and turns of evolution, which is not a clairvoyant process. Evolution is a tinker, driven not by what it 'intends' in the future, but by what was made available in the past.

Those who believe that things were created just as they are, or that evolution has a guiding force, often quote the case of the human eye: it is too complex to evolve by the chanciness of random mutation. What use is half an eye? Better than no eye at all, replies the partially sighted person. Evolution has 'invented' mechanisms capable of seeing, or deriving information from light, whether dimly or intensely perceived, several times in its long advance.

Genes that couldn't 'see' ended up as a hyena's lunch, but those that could, or that 'learned' how to cooperate with those that could, were able to pass on the trick to the next generation. By this means, chance and randomness were invested with what *seems like* design, meaning and purpose, even though there was no original designer, meaner or purposer.

We judge cultural and moral progress by their ability to improve the lot of mankind, moving ever closer towards a vision of what we could or should be. Evolutionary progress as judged by our biology is quite different, accounting for how things are, not what they should be.

There was no preordained goal when the first life appeared three and a half billion years ago, of creatures like us having thoughts like these, only the mechanism of natural selection gradually capitalising on successful adaptations to give the *appearance* of design without a designer, and intentional movement without a Prime Mover. This 'blind' process has proved itself to be astonishingly 'sighted', capable of creating from simple ingredients eyes and brains of great complexity, capable of 'seeing' into their own future.

We do not need to invoke supernatural explanations.

The human eye was not therefore specifically 'designed' to do its job, but just got better and better at seeing. It is an 'emergence', and by the same reasoning so are our mind and consciousness. Believers in creationism or intelligent design find this hard to accept, no matter how free and creative evolution might be, but we do not need to invoke supernatural explanations.

When we ponder the course of evolution, we realise that it is not just a game of roulette where all is thrown to chance and then lost every time. It is more like a

61

game of chess, where winning strategies are stored for the next game, banked in the genes that have already made the successful adaptation. There are rules, within which lies great scope for creativity, allowing the next game to be played more cleverly than the previous one.

This is not to deny that evolution is wasteful, or riddled with error, a truth we know if we have suffered from a burst appendix, erupted wisdom teeth or cancer. Many more species have gone extinct than survive today. Like any child, evolution goes down many blind alleys before it finds one that leads somewhere.

The dog asleep on our mat didn't suddenly appear in that form. It was domesticated from wolves about fifteen thousand years ago, to form a unique partnership: the dog gets food, while we get help hunting, protection and companionship. Dingoes, Great Danes, Chihuahuas and a thousand intermediate forms all descend from a common canine ancestor, which itself was an offshoot of a branch of tiny mammals that got their chance to flourish after the dinosaurs were wiped out sixty five million years ago.

We must not allow the phrase 'natural selection' to fool us into thinking there was a minded selector behind evolution. The only positive 'selector' at work was the ability of an organism to survive and reproduce, creating a self-replicating mini-cosmos of organisation while all around was threatening chaos and entropy. Negative selection, or what is weeded out in the struggle for existence, played an equal role. The feature common to all our ancestors is that they produced offspring, and didn't end up in the stomach of a predator.

Neither perfect nor special

This doesn't mean that all of those who survived were perfect, only that they were good enough to stay alive, explaining why a few design faults have managed to come down to us. Males do not need nipples, but it was 'cheaper' for evolution to keep them, and there was no way of going back to the drawing board to get rid of them. Males and females come from the same pod, the only genetic difference between us being a change of coding on the twenty third chromosome.

The stark truth that there is no final goal of evolution is the hardest lesson of Darwinian theory. We are neither special nor inevitable. Even if we establish causes, they are not guarantors of purposes. There is no Master Evolutioner at the birth of the cosmos laying out the future course of humanity, only millions of winning brain programs getting stacked on top of each other, each 'selected' because it solved a distinct survival problem *at the time of choosing*. The original reason for selecting a particular trait is lost in the past. We still feel our hair 'stand on end', but we long ago lost any fur to bristle.

The more we probe our cognitive back-story, the more we realise that our brain is not perfect, but a haphazard accumulation of strategies to answer the competing needs of a big-brained organism leading a challenging social life, with many conflicts of interest. Simplicity has been piled on simplicity to create a serendipitous complexity full of glitches and design faults that baffle its owner.

There is no final goal of evolution.

Anxiety for instance might be an inevitable consequence of a brain that is oriented exclusively to second-guessing the future, sensitive to threat even in the modern age where many dangers have been reduced or even eliminated. Our high stress levels fall into place if we remember that we are at the end of an ancient path, oblivious to the many pitfalls and broken slabs we have walked over to get where we are.

Anxiety was vital when the sabre-toothed tiger was on the prowl, but in the home or office it raises stress levels unbearably. Suspicion of the 'out group' was useful when we could not be sure whether there were barbarians or allies at the gate, but today it results in prejudice and xenophobia. Exclusive 'clean or unclean' logic mattered when food supplies were easily contaminated, but now they foster paranoia and homophobia. Curiosity was essential when it was important to know the local gossip, but not when our brain is flooded with emails and social media.

No wonder gremlins abound, emanating from both how the machine got put together, and what it is made of. This is why some cognitive scientists regard our brain as a kluge, not a purpose-built design, but the serendipitous outcome of eight million years of ad hoc primate evolution. It is the creation of a tinker, clumsily cobbling together whatever parts were lying around in the workshop, recycling odd bits of scrap, looking for anything that gets the job done.

Neurons are powerful things, but in their billions they leak vital energy, or don't always fire faultlessly. In our evolutionary journey, as more got crowded together, they swamped each other's signalling capacity, which led to a need for

Mountains of the Mind

even more neurons to compensate. Such overcrowding meant that simple tasks started to be performed in increasingly complex ways, some features became redundant, and key brain areas became isolated from each other. This made us vulnerable to duality, irrationality and mental illness.

The brain as a kluge
The cartoonist William Heath Robinson (1872 -1944) designed over-engineered contraptions to perform simple tasks. Might the brain have evolved to be similarly 'klugey', or over-complicated?

And yet from this very inefficiency (so the 'kluge theory' goes) came the benefits of choice and plasticity. Our brain had to develop multiple pathways for getting messages through if one line of communication was blocked or failed. The trouble is, our trillions of synapses transmit so many pulses that the outcomes are probabilistic, not always what we intended. They might go one way or the other.

Seen positively, this indeterminacy might be our doorway to free will, art, creativity and imagination. As a downside, it might account for our anxiety, tribalism, addictive tendencies, vulnerability to ambiguity, suggestibility and capacity for delusion. It might explain why we feel hungry or keep eating even when we've had more than enough.

No wonder our modern mind feels as if it lives on an evolutionary fault-line: it lives inside a tinker's brain. The old tools that were once so useful still lie at the bottom of our work-box. They are there if we need them, but they are ill-suited to a modern lifestyle.

Running on old software

This 'bootstrap' model of evolution, or pulling ourselves up by our own improvisations, suggests that no matter how smart we look on top, our boot-laces down below are still badly knotted, in tangles of racism, xenophobia, superstition and chauvinism. And yet it is the same brain that enables us to read, write and study interstellar physics. It seems extraordinary that NASA scientists are using the same neural software to send space missions to Jupiter as our ancestors relied on to track an antelope, or plot a raid against a rival tribe.

There is no evidence however that the structure of the brain has been remodelled by modern life, only our deployment of the programming. There is no part of our brain that evolved specifically for playing computer games, performing astrophysics or conducting international diplomacy, because these practices are very recent arrivals on the cultural scene. Texting, reading, calculating and negotiating are mental activities that feel civilised and modern, but they are merely primitive brain programs adapted to sophisticated new uses.

Recognising the symbols of a mathematical formula is an enhanced version of making out a predator through the dense leaves of the forest canopy, and predicting its next move, albeit carried to much higher levels of abstraction. This explains why we must go to school to be tutored in literacy and numeracy: they do not come to us as automatically as walking and talking.

We are saddled with ingrained 'bad thinking' habits.

The fault-line is not therefore cleverness versus stupidity, but the crevasse between our cognition and our feelings, two systems that evolved together but for very different purposes. As a result, we often feel pulled in different directions, saddled with ingrained 'bad thinking' habits. We jump to conclusions, seeing certainty where there is none. We misattribute causes and cling to irrational taboos, such as not eating pork, regarding cows as sacred or fearing the number thirteen. We fall for conspiracy theories that massage our prejudices, but don't exercise our reason.

65

Mountains of the Mind

This is because the sophisticated modern 'rational' brain is running on old 'gut instinct' emotional software. When threatened, we might be more tempted to buy a gun than to calculate that by doing so our chances of being shot are multiplied a hundred fold. When we dream, we believe our own publicity, so we set ourselves impossible targets. When we throw away plastic waste, we have no concept of how it might end up in a giant whirlpool in the Pacific Ocean.

When we contemplate a big decision with life-changing consequences, we find it hard to separate emotion from logic. We decide to get married today based on a present warm glow, not on how we might feel about each other after ten years have gone by, because we have no way of knowing what sort of person each of us will be by then. Nor do we run through the cold logic of how we'll be able to pay the mortgage or afford the college fees of the children we've brought into the world by then.

We are still tribal: we stereotype 'them' as an alien group who threaten our livelihood, but when we get to know two or three of 'them', we find out they are just like us after all. Despite reports to the contrary, we are not natural killers: we leave that to our machines. We can't bear to pull a trigger as we stare into the eyes of our enemy (an emotional taboo), but we can flip a switch that launches a missile into a populated area with a view to 'eliminating' a threat (a permitted rational calculation).

The trolley problem

Cognitive psychologists love to set up unsettling thought experiments which force decisions on us that we are unlikely to encounter in real life. Without inflicting real harm on anyone, they can probe how we make hard choices, expose clashes in our moral algorithms, and confront us with disturbing truths about ourselves.

In the 'trolley problem', we're placed on a virtual railway bridge where we can see a runaway train wagon coming down the line. We can also see five engineers working on the main track, and one person working in a siding. Are we prepared to pull a lever to divert the wagon into the siding, saving five lives by sacrificing one?

With time to think, and acting purely hypothetically, most of us elect to kill the one person. It's only a game, after all. This is a rational 'system two' calculation, firing the brain's 'reason centre': five lives for the price of one is a 'utility maximising' bargain. But then the psychologist adds a cruel twist: what if the one person, up to now a mere counter in a game, is our own child? Suddenly our 'feeling centre' kicks in, and with only a few seconds remaining, our decision becomes infinitely more complex.

We are caught between rival 'goods'.

Those who show lesions in their prefrontal cortex, where hard decisions like this are computed, exhibit a more utilitarian response: *of course* five lives are more valuable than one, regardless of whether the life of our own child is at stake. The rest of us with 'normal' brains don't get off the hook so easily. We recognise that we are caught between rival 'goods'. We are forced to commit, and cope with the guilt later.

Fortunately this thought experiment is precisely that, an exercise in rationality, which is not how we make most of our decisions. We go with gut feeling, because we cannot override our natural feelings, or predict the consequence of an action, no matter how strongly the numbers add up in retrospect.

Given the opportunity in 1933, it would have made rational sense in hindsight to assassinate Adolf Hitler before he could go on to start a war that would kill sixty million people (there was a botched attempt in 1944, which was too late to make a difference). But when placed in that situation, and faced with the urgent need to act, few of us would go through with it. We might set out with good intentions, but we would be plagued by the law of 'double effect' what worse terrors might we unleash?

Utilitarian thinking, or judging by the best outcome, serves us well when we have time at our disposal, and we are merely poring over which type of dishwasher to buy. It's the wrong calculus however when, whatever we choose, someone is going to get hurt, or we personally have to do the hurting.

When we get up close and personal, dealing with matters dear to our heart, our sense of justice is powered by our emotions, not our ability to calculate consequences mathematically. We rely on fast system-one gut feeling and intuition, not slow system-two cool logic and reflection.

Consider for instance the second version of the trolley problem, in which we are asked if we would be prepared to push a heavily overweight man standing next to us on the bridge down on to the track below to bring the wagon to a halt, saving everyone further down the line.

Ignoring the daft physics of trying to stop a runaway wagon with anything smaller than a megalosaurus, this scenario highlights a key difference between rational calculation and emotional processing. In terms of lives saved, pushing Mr Obese is a winner, because it saves five lives, not four. The problem is, to shove him we must put our hands on a *real person* and send him crashing down. This human contact elicits very different emotions from flicking a switch. While we hesitate, unsure what to do, the five workers below are crushed by the wagon.

Our inaction is understandable, because we find ourselves caught between two sets of moral algebra which evolved for different purposes. Moral *intuition* comes from our limbic region, deriving from what we *feel* is right, seeing people as ends in themselves. Moral *reasoning* is cortical, hinging on what we *calculate* is right, seeing people as means to an end. How can we reconcile these two systems, or determine what is good or right in any situation?

This dilemma is not hypothetical. It is an existential choice faced by the designers of self-driving cars. Should the car be programmed to swerve to avoid a child who suddenly runs into the road, even if it risks the life of all passengers on board? We would not knowingly buy a car that was programmed to sacrifice one passenger's life to save two pedestrians. Can we rely on the 'utility maximising' algorithms of an AI software program to resolve this crisis of conscience?

Such a machine would have to make a lightning choice between altruism and egotism, but it is incapable of 'thinking' in these terms. All it can do is follow the algorithms it has been programmed with. It cannot 'decide' to kill or not to kill, only to select an option that entails less harm. This is exactly what we would hope to pull off in the heat of the moment, except that we would probably freeze in a paroxysm of emotional overload.

Changing the algorithm
When a malfunctioning algorithm sends a plane crashing to earth despite the pilot's attempt to correct it manually, the human designer is clearly to blame. As self-driving cars become a reality, it will remain the case that no 'rational choice' algorithm can ever be a substitute for human agency, and no machine we program can ever absolve us from personal responsibility.

Mountains of the Mind

Remember that the trolley problem is a thought experiment, an extrapolation of an idea to its extreme, just to see how far we can take it before it breaks down. This means it is not something that any driving test could ever prepare us for. We often make a quick calculation on the back of an envelope to choose the lesser of two evils, but life hasn't prepared us for 'Sophie's choice' in William Styron's 1979 novel of that name. She is forced by the Nazis to sacrifice one of her children so that the other might live, a quandary for which there is no moral calculus, and for which evolution has not prepared the human heart.

Real life problems such as swerving to avoid a child, not to mention abortion and euthanasia, are 'hard cases'. Fast or slow, they are choices we make in a crowded emotional context, not in the rational isolation of a laboratory. Our moral choices are complex mixes of reflexes, motives, reasons and justifications, subconscious integrations of raw feeling and cool reason, rapid computations of our instinct for self protection, what we feel is our duty to others, and what we calculate to be the likely consequences of our actions.

When it comes to the small stuff, our algorithms often let us down.

In the busy thoroughfare of life we don't have time to stand and stare, or ponder statistical probabilities: we just act. We respond emotionally and intuitively. In the big decisions, when it matters, the algorithms in our brain help us to get it right, though occasionally wrong. That's what makes us human. The irony is, when it comes to the small stuff, our algorithms often let us down.

We think one more burger won't harm us (an ancient instinct to store fat for the winter) but we ignore the statistics on diabetes (they don't relate to us). We fall for the advertisement that appeals to our present desire, but fail to take out the pension that provides for our remote future. We get angry about a small annual tax to save the planet, but gladly spend more on a daily cup of coffee. The philosopher Peter Singer argues that the *rational* thing to do is to use the cost of that cappuccino to buy enough food for a child in Africa for a whole day.

The difficulty we face is that, though our brain evolved as an anticipating machine, it never sees the big picture. It did not evolve to simulate a future that includes starving children on another continent, who are neither kith nor kin.

Instead it focuses on immediate threat, short-term need and our nearest and dearest, not a future that hasn't happened yet miles away to people we don't know.

We find it hard to appreciate that actions we fail to take now can have disastrous consequences for our grandchildren. We can't see that the world can be changed only one mind at a time, or how our tiny decisions to conserve resources make a huge difference when everyone else joins us. Instead, in what is known as the 'tragedy of the commons', we take what we personally need, leaving it to others to look out for themselves. The result is over-grazed grassland, ravaged forests and polluted oceans.

We have to educate ourselves that our evolution is now conscious, that our cognitive choices can override the dictates of our genes, that we can replace fast reflex with slow deliberation about the direction in which our resourceful brains are taking us. If we are to solve our deep environmental problems or stay in control of our rapid biotechnical advances, we have to learn to think globally. We have to rewrite our default algorithms. The problem is, this is a new demand in our evolution which our tinker's brain has not prepared us for.

Choosing the right tool
Given the piecemeal design of our brains, and the presence of so many gremlins, thinking rationally beyond our own needs is not easy. Over evolutionary time and untold generations, our brain toolbox became so large that we needed lots of compartments, especially for the small fiddly tools in the top drawers. To fit all these in, our pre-frontal cortex trebled in size, and our brain surface became deeply folded to fit everything in.

What we loosely call intelligence, if it means anything at all, is the ability to use these tools in the right combinations, and knowing how to apply them to new situations. Our ancestors were those who were most successful in getting these things right. Evolution couldn't see what was coming next, only design tools for specific jobs as they arose.

There was not therefore a generalised drift towards bigger and better brains, but a steady accumulation of more sophisticated tools jumbled up in the tool box. The modular theory of mind likens the brain to a Swiss Army knife with different blades for different assignments. Analysing probabilities, generating theories,

70

judging distance, detecting cheats, sorting priorities, managing memories, all call for specifically tooled bits of kit.

This model sounds neat, but it is too neat. For a start, it overlooks the role of the person in the evolution story. Natural selection might have equipped with several smart abilities on the savannah, but it was people who integrated these into meaningful experience. Regardless of what particular genes or neurons won the battle for selection, it was the social interactions of our ancestors that defined a uniquely human identity.

The old script always remains visible underneath.

Our brain is not therefore a fine piece of precision engineering or a streamlined super-tool fit for the twenty-first century. It is more like a Heath-Robinson contraption of awkwardly assembled spanners, wrenches and pulleys. Changing the metaphor, it is like a parchment or animal skin, written on and then scraped clean for the next use. This explains why attempts to change human nature by revolutionary or bureaucratic means always fail. We cannot start again with a new sheet of paper, because the old script always remains visible underneath.

It's too late therefore for a complete brain makeover: it comes as found, complete with old messages and built-in faults such as anxiety, duality, boredom, addiction, aggression and constant craving. These are not the hallmarks of smart design but opportunistic construction, and yet they are the very qualities that make us human.

All our ancestral brain needed to do was to get us through another day with minimum fuss, not fathom the meaning of life, which explains why nirvana is so hard to find. It evolved as a what/where/when calculator, not to make us rational or happy, and if we achieve either, it is more by luck than design. If our brain is 'designed' in any sense at all, it is to keep our body intact, analyse threat and calculate probabilities: we just want to know what happens if we put our weight on this plank, or what is behind this closed door.

Looking for the meaning of life is a modern obsession, the province of mind, a luxury when all that our ancestors needed to do was to cling to life on the savannah for one more day. Nevertheless, purpose and goal-seeking are necessary and valuable traits if we are to progress to insight and learning. For this, we need to cultivate a product of the evolved mind/brain that is unique to our species: reason.

The rational animal

The Greeks who lived in the ancient city of Miletus on the coast of modern Turkey were the first to adopt what we would understand today as a scientific approach to the world, believing it could be comprehended by reason and analysis, not by myth and superstition. Divine revelation and priestly authority take us only so far. If we can discover by the power of unaided reason why there is a cosmos and not a chaos, we have proved that the universe is not absurd.

Two centuries later, the Athenian philosopher Plato elevated reason above feeling and desire. In the polity of our body, there is a clear hierarchy: reason is the guardian of the citadel, emotions are its bodyguards, and our sensual appetites are the slaves that service the system. In a well-run city, the passions must submit to the intellect, because justice and morality depend on rationality. In many ways, his tripartite structure of the soul foreshadowed Freud's superego, ego and id by over two millennia.

We have regarded reason as the gold standard
that saves us from error.

Aristotle, Plato's pupil, supported his master's adulation of reason. He called us the rational animal, as a way of distinguishing us from the rest of nature. We belong to a species called Homo sapiens, the wise one, and contemplation is our highest and finest activity. Reason is the gold standard that saves us from error, foolishness and insanity.

Over two thousand years down the track however, we are a bit wiser about the nature of reason. It is not an instinct, nor does it come naturally to us. It is a hard-won intellectual achievement and social practice, which means it can frequently falter. Some go so far as to question our right to claim the mantle *sapiens*. In many tests of reasoning, we perform little better than chimpanzees. Also it seems that we are not the rational animal, but the *rationalising* one, which is very different. We use our cleverness to justify the views we already hold, not to break through to new ones.

72

Mountains of the Mind

Aristotle
A polymath who wrote on many subjects, Aristotle (384-322 BCE) placed reason above all else. Every society since has had a different idea of what it means to act rationally, or be reasonable, which are not necessarily the same thing.

From an evolutionary perspective, reason is a cultural invention or social construct, not a 'drive' like hunger or sex inscribed in our genes. Our brain evolved to get us through the day, not to explain the universe to us, solve crosswords, score highly in computer games or understand quantum theory. It is a late cortical arrival, as improvised as the design of the brain that uses it.

Many cultures have no word for reason, expressing their rationality through practical action, not abstract musing. It is only in the literate West that Reason with a capital R has been enshrined as a stand-alone court of final appeal to settle our disputes, or to serve as the mark of a civilised mind.

On a daily basis most of us rely on reason as a guide to what is sensible, fair or workable, but even practical reason cannot alone make us moral. In fact reason, parading as enlightened thinking, can be used to justify grossly unjust practices. In the eighteenth century, certain wealthy or aristocratic white male slave traders and owners, presenting themselves to the world as civilised, rational and educated European gentlemen, invented the term drapetomania to describe the 'madness' that causes a slave to run away from his 'natural' state as a barbarian, which is

73

bondage. Their human reason did not stretch to questioning the inhumanity of the institution of slavery.

Some can't 'see reason' even when it stares them in the face. In 1847 the Hungarian physician Ignaz Semmelweis demonstrated beyond doubt that when surgeons washed their hands between operations, the mortality rate fell dramatically. The response of his colleagues and superiors was neither reasonable nor rational. Blinded by their prejudices, they expelled him from the hospital, and he was later committed to an asylum, where he died.

Being logical
At least we have logic to fall back on, as a sub-branch of reason. Our ability to juxtapose ideas is the foundation of our science and technology: if this, then that, if not that, then this, with nothing in between. But in the cultural realm, consequences are not always so predictable, or what we intend. It seems logical for instance to support the idea that the problem of starvation in India could be solved if the millions of cows that roam the streets freely are slaughtered for meat, not worshipped as avatars of the gods.

In this case however, logic can be culturally blind, and dangerously wrong. The cows provide milk for nutrition and dung for cooking, they cost next to nothing to feed, they pull the ploughs that till the fields, and their worship as 'sacred cows' is part of a belief system that holds society together. Killing the cows would make starvation worse, not better.

About a hundred years ago, logical positivism was all the rage. 'Coal is black' causes us no cognitive dissonance, even when white light is shone upon it. The poet W H Auden's plea 'We must love one another or die' is by contrast a meaningless pronouncement because it takes words beyond what they can logically signify, or posit. By the time we've deconstructed what we mean by each word, especially 'love', the last train has left the station. Some logicians even dispute the meaning of the word 'the'.

Perhaps then we can look to mathematics, where we can write 'QED' at the end of our calculations, 'that which was to be proved', proud that our systematic reasoning has led to an incontrovertible conclusion. There is a glitch however. Some mathematical problems defy proof, except by mathematical reasoning, which is a circular argument, relying on the system to prove itself with no external

74

court of appeal, or application in the real world. Mathematical calculations suggest that there is such a thing as string theory, but no scientist has yet 'found' a string, let alone one with a theory attached to it.

Also, mathematical logic can lead us into profound paradoxes. Take the case of the frog on the edge of the pond, proposed by Zeno of Elea. It wants to leap to the lily pad at its centre. The problem is that each jump it makes is half of the previous jump. Logic dictates therefore that the frog can never reach its destination, no matter how many times it jumps.

This brainteaser teaches us to be wary, because there are different types of logic, with their own applications. No matter how many times we chop up a piece of string, even to infinity, the pieces will always add up to their original finite length. In real life therefore, even if not in the realm of abstract logic, the frog will get there eventually.

Zeno, a child of the West, knew he was teasing, and he might even have been trying to teach us a lesson beloved of the Zen masters of the East: don't over-analyse, because rationality seduces our mind away from experience. Try instead to see the frog, the jump and the pond as one, and then we will experience the unity of the knower and the known. This after all is the only 'logic' that makes sense of our everyday life in the world.

The logic we are most familiar with is the polarity of either/or: a lion cannot be an antelope. Such a distinction was a life or death question for our ancestors on the savannah. Such binary thinking is not however always helpful or even relevant in resolving human dilemmas, or when we are faced by conflicting goods. When for instance is it 'logical', as in 'right', to turn off someone's life support machine?

We can be so smart at finding reasons that
we end up eclipsing reason itself.

We tend to see reason as an 'essence' or universal moral law that deserves a capital R. It all depends how we use it. At its simplest, reason is the giving of reasons, something we are all good at, especially politicians in full debating mode. It doesn't matter whether our reasons are good or bad, right or wrong, considered or opinionated, so long as we win our argument.

In such instances, reason is 'motivated', applied where it suits us, doing what we ask of it, whether helping us to make sense of the world or propping up our bigotry. We might be convinced that we can 'prove' that homosexuality is an abomination by quoting the Old Testament. We can be so smart at finding reasons that we end up eclipsing reason itself. We fall into dysrationalia, failing to match our smartness to the use we are putting it to.

Blowing hot and cold

It's better to live with reason than without it, but it is not divine, supra-rational or universal. It is not a birth-right but a man-made habit which, like all our tools, is forged in a particular culture, with many design faults and blind spots. This is because reason, that we use to detach ourselves from the complexities of personal entanglements, is always intertwined with feelings, which evolved to bond us ever more closely.

For many centuries, courtesy of Plato, reason was pitted against emotion, but modern research suggests this is a false dichotomy and dangerous polarity. On the savannah we needed reason to solve pressing problems of survival, but we also had to navigate a complex social existence. This is where our emotions come into play. We are not just clever thinkers but also deeply social animals, and our feelings, which are how we *interpret* our emotions, are our body's way of making sense of our cognition, and keeping us in touch with each other.

Aristotle compounded Plato's distrust of emotions by calling us rational creatures. It is our emotions however that shape our instincts and intuitions. They are threaded right through our body, far more deeply intertwined than any ideas or abstractions we entertain. When we communicate electronically, emojis try to shred our feelings into two-dimensional smileys or scowls, but all they do is remind us how complex and physical our emotions really are, often hidden even from ourselves.

We need our emotions to make sense of our reasons, and vice versa.

Patients with lesions in their prefrontal cortex can still make decisions, but because their feeling-centres are damaged, and their emotional circuits bypassed, they don't care one way or the other, and are indifferent to good and bad. This suggests strongly that we need our emotions to make sense of our reasons, and vice versa. Reason without the leavening of emotions becomes cold rationality, and emotions without the tempering of reasoning verge on sloppy sentimentality.

In other words, we are whole-body thinkers, not cold rational processors who can lay our hot emotional responses to one side for a brief while, and then go back to them as if nothing has happened. Our mind, or the thinking part of our brain, does not float free of the body that feeds it and motivates it. Our prefrontal cortex might be clever enough to pass a challenging mathematics paper, but our ventro-medial frontal cortex has to be switched on too: why do we want to put ourselves through this stress, or why should we care whether we fail?

We see this conflict between reason and emotion in our morality. Seen from a utilitarian perspective, arrived at through cool calculation, it makes sense to give any excess money we have to those who have far less than we do. This is what many religious teachers urge us to do, and so-called 'progressive' taxation schemes ask of us. As an example, we are pointed to the selflessness of St Francis of Assisi, who gave away all his family wealth and devoted himself to a life of poverty.

Sadly, the altruistic and saintly Francis is a rare exception. He is venerated because he challenges and defies the strong evolutionary impulses within our DNA: blood is thicker than water, making it our 'gut instinct' to give our worldly possessions to our nearest and dearest, not to random strangers. This is why charities have to launch emotional appeals when there is a humanitarian disaster far beyond our visible neighbourhood. The good news is that many of us do give, often generously, prepared to share our wealth and good fortune with people we have never met, beyond 'our' tribe.

The tension between calculation and compassion is displayed in the famous 'wisdom' of King Solomon. When two women appeared before him, both claiming to be the mother of a child, he proposed a simple 'cold' rational solution: cut the child in half, so that it could be shared. Solomon knew that this would force 'hot' emotional evolutionary logic to kick in. One of the women instantly but reluctantly offered the child to the other, and he knew immediately who the real mother was.

Wisdom aside, Solomon's life teaches us something equally important about reason: the bias blind spot. Famous as he was for recognising the fault in others, he was far less successful at seeing his own faults, struggling to manage his tricky relationships with his thousand concubines.

77

Mountains of the Mind

Crooked timber

It is tempting to equate reason with civilisation. One might encourage the other, but they are by no means interchangeable. The Ancient Greeks, often held up as paragons of reason, also endorsed slavery, euthanasia and the suppression of women. In the modern world, democracy is lauded in the West, but this is a cultural bias that does not necessarily 'fit' all jurisdictions, especially when it is forced on countries that have evolved different political traditions and institutions.

In the French Revolution, the 'will of the people' reigned supreme in the name of Reason. She was enthroned as a Goddess, one moment advocating the creation of a 'rational' ten day week, the next providing justification for the atrocities of the guillotine.

The French revolutionaries made two errors. They overrated reason and let passions run riot. People are emotionally attached to the names of the week, and even more passionately want to stay connected to their heads. As a result, the eighteenth century Enlightenment engendered a powerful counter-movement driven more by feeling than intellect. Traditional religion, superstition and magic had been forced to retreat, but the 1775 Lisbon earthquake, in which the beautiful city was destroyed and up to a hundred thousand lives lost, left a huge void which the cold comforts of reason, science and logic could not fill.

The nineteenth century saw an outburst of Romantic poetry, nationalist fervour, religious revivalism and expressive music, and as the century progressed, bold new thinkers began to shake some of the foundations on which reason was built: words are imprecise, civilisation is a veneer, savagery is noble, truth is elusive, humans are animals, the mind is unfathomable, time is relative, matter is unstable. The goddess Reason was herself sullied, embroiled in the hunt for proofs and reasons why the white race was biologically superior to the 'primitives' she vanquished.

In the twentieth century, she could not hold back the 'blood-tide' of nationalism and anti-Semitism which swept through fascist Europe. Democracy, liberalism and globalism won the day and cooled passions, but the populism that powered the Brexit vote and the election of Trump three generations later reminded politicians of the power of gut feeling, the pull of identity, and the politics of belonging.

78

Mountains of the Mind

Some, mainly of a religious persuasion, take Reason to task for demystifying the world, or debasing the sacramental quality of life. Others dismiss this as mystical carping, but the outcomes of three centuries of Enlightenment Reason and Progress have not all been sweetness and light. We have seen increased libertinism in our personal affairs, sentimentality in our judgments, and a decline in our sense of community.

The gains of greater freedom of thought and material progress have not been without cost: strains on our personal happiness, social harmony and planetary well-being. We are becoming more divided, childhood depression rates are on the rise, the political bonds that unite us are being stretched to breaking point, drugs are becoming mainstream, natural systems are breaking down, and machines that can emulate human minds are waiting in the wings.

Technophiles and rationalists insist that, if we are not already living in the best of all possible worlds, we soon will be. Ironically, technophobes and humanists agree, but for totally different reasons: this is as good as it gets, and it's downhill from here.

So what does the data say? We can read it any way we wish, but on balance, things are definitely improving, if by that we mean that more people have wider access to capabilities that enhance the quality of life. Across the world, fewer live in poverty, disease is being brought under control, wars are occurring less often, genocide is declining, and life spans are increasing. 'Enlightenment', as in the slow steady victory of reason over ignorance, is slowly happening.

The opposite of Enlightenment is living in the dark.

The Enlightenment thinkers never promised us perfection, only perfectibility. We are made of crooked timber, but we have the power through reason to make things a bit straighter, not suddenly, but one small step at a time. Despite occasional setbacks, we are rational creatures who can deploy reason to offset our failures of reasoning. The alternative is bleak: the opposite of Enlightenment is living in the dark, or being swept along in a tide of irrationality.

Whatever its virtues or failings, Reason has some difficult battles ahead, which cannot be solved by Reason alone. Some for instance believe it entirely reasonable to view human life as sacred, and insist that personhood is inviolable, setting their minds firmly against abortion, euthanasia, gene editing, and any form of transhumanism that alters the essence of what it means to be human.

Others, floating on a rising tide of technology, believe that the body is just as perfectible as the mind, if not more so. Biotechnology, integrated circuitry and augmented reality will give us eternal life, extrasensory perception and cleverness beyond our dreams. How do we square the tremendous power of our technical wizardry with our need to remember that we are mortal and fallible?

Practical reason
When we look at the state of the world, it appears that in many key regards we're neither rational nor wise, driven more by our faults than logic. Nor can we assume that a good education shields us from folly or guarantees reasonableness. For all our twenty-first century knowledge, we are hardly any more reasonable, and many of us choose to have no truck with Reason in the abstract unless we absolutely have to.

Some go so far as to suggest that not all people are capable of *exercising* Reason, an elitist assumption which can have very unreasonable consequences, and doesn't address the fact that, whatever our station in life, we are all reason-*seeking* animals.

Aristotle understood this dilemma, which is why he distinguished between different types of reason. He accepted that pure reason and logic are useful in the realms of abstract mathematical proofs, giving us a kind of universality. But he also knew that logic and reason alone cannot save us, or guarantee moral progress. He was wary of putting logic and reason on a pedestal, as Plato had. They are static nouns. What he sought instead was a verb, a form of reason*ing*, or way of acting in the world that integrates body and mind, and is in tune with our moral instincts.

He suggested that reasoning comes in different flavours. He admired reflective reason for giving us the power of metacognition, or the capacity to use our own thought to take our thought to pieces. He valued instrumental reason for its ability to generate a series of steady steps to solve particular real-world problems.

Reasons are not alone sufficient to serve as an ethical guide to life.

When we employ these forms of reasoning however, we always run the risk of over-thinking a problem to the point that we lose touch with reality. They are useful *means* for exercising our grey matter, but they don't give us the *ends* of our actions, or reasons why we should undertake them in the first place. They are not alone sufficient to serve as an ethical guide to life.

Aristotle therefore proposed that we also need practical reason, which he called *phronesis*. This is our best tactic for solving everyday human dilemmas, or acting ethically. It is the kind of evidence-based wisdom that we read in agony aunt columns. Does the advice they give map onto our daily interactions with other people? Does it contribute to the leading of a good life for all? In other words, does it strike us as.......well, reasonable?

Being reasonable

Being reasonable belongs to the whole person, and is not to be confused with rationality, which is disembodied reason. For thinkers of the eighteenth century Enlightenment, reason was the gateway to humanism, offering a break from authority, magic and ignorance through science, open enquiry and a bold vision of the future.

The promotion of reason over superstitious thinking didn't come out of the blue: there were many forerunners in the ancient world. Nor was it a sudden or clean revolution: there were many thinkers working on many fronts, and it took many years with several false starts.

What they held in common was their conviction that reason was then and remains now our principal means of ridding ourselves of bad thinking. It can achieve great things by thought alone, sitting down and pondering the world. In the scientific realm, this claim has much truth. Einstein's great theories arose largely from thought experiments, which were only later put empirically to the test.

In the social realm however, living inside our head can cut us off from our feelings, which have evolved to situate us in the lives of other people. If we're not careful, reason can be little more than a thin veneer masking the prejudices of our historical situation.

My survival is dependent upon your survival.

1

In many ways Aristotle's distinctions between types of reasoning foreshadowed what was eventually to emerge as sound evolutionary theory. Practical reason, like our morality, is grounded in strategies that proved to be win-win, or non-zero-sum on the African savannah. We instinctively recognise and reach out to each other as rational, sentient creatures. My interests are your interests, and my survival is dependent upon your survival.

Self-interest, rape, pillage and murder cannot therefore be seen as winning strategies. They are not universalisable, because if they were to become the norm, we would all perish. One person might get away with rape, but no human society could be founded upon it. Without the family as a unit of transmission, culture would collapse. Mutuality, respect, cooperation and trust by contrast are universalisable, which is why we cling to them. Practical reason therefore chimes with our morality, based not on divine command, but on shared sympathy, constantly put to the test of reasoned argument.

Unsurprisingly, we see practical reason shining through the political constitutions, legal systems and rights declarations of most countries. If one thrives, we all thrive. When we unite, we stand a better chance of allowing everyone to flourish equally, and of guarding against tyranny.

It is worth reminding ourselves however that the authors of the American Declaration of Independence who declared boldly that all men are created equal, with inalienable rights to life and liberty, were in reality land-owning white males who omitted to include women, displaced Native Americans and slaves stolen from Africa. Nevertheless, at the time they saw themselves as paragons of Reason and Virtue, upholding everyone's right to pursue Happiness.

Bureaucratic rationality

We might accuse the Founding Fathers of self-interested reasoning, only one step away from rationalisation. This kind of after-the-event reasoning sets out to justify what we already believe. It's what we do when we've persuaded ourselves that we are free to optimise our preferences and self-realise. This is the danger of rationality: it can make us peculiarly disembodied and strangely detached, alienating us from the deeper feelings that unite us as a species.

At the end of the nineteenth for instance, leading thinkers in several countries became concerned that the 'benighted' lower classes were out-breeding the 'enlightened' upper classes, leading to declines in average IQ levels, and creating a threat to social stability.

In what has come to be known as 'science's greatest mistake', sterilisations and incarcerations took place of people selected on the slenderest evidence as being idiots, morons and imbeciles, as measured by 'objective' tests. Many were abused, homeless or what we would now call 'special needs'. 'At risk' children were taken away from their parents and rehomed with more 'respectable' families. 'Rational' science promoted by 'elite' thinkers became embroiled in top-down eugenic schemes to 'improve' the stock of the race.

We now know that eugenic 'enhancement' and racial 'cleansing' are based on flawed genetics and sinister social theory, leading eventually to the 'Final Solution' in the gas chambers of Auschwitz. The moral outrage after the Holocaust killed all talk of eugenics for over half a century, but it has reappeared in a new form, of bio-engineering, prenatal screening and genetic repair. The ancient dream of helping the blind to see again and the lame to walk once more is almost here. It will require more than reason and rationality however to decide whether we wish to dabble in neural upgrades, bionic implants, and life spans of a hundred and fifty years for those who can afford it.

On a less emotive level, we are all victims of bureaucratic rationality in one way or another, aided and abetted by modern communications technology.

Obsessed with its own efficiency, it places us at one remove from each other, as isolated statistics or ciphers in the system. When we try to phone up a company and speak with a person, we encounter a machine that takes us through ten automated options, none of which is right for us.

From the company's point of view, this is an efficient, logical and rational system: it cuts down on the number of staff they have to employ, it makes us feel 'valued' as a customer, but it also makes us hang up, which is good, because then they don't have to waste costly staff time by dealing with our enquiry.

Rationality and logic do not therefore fit our social situation very well, or address our moral dilemmas as a society capable of changing the direction of our evolution. They are usually used as ends in themselves, which is to serve their own limited purposes, not the needs of others. They focus on form, not content, giving 'rationales' for past or future actions. We use rationality retrospectively to cover our backs or boost our reputation, not always as a vehicle for arriving at the 'truth', or what works in everyone's best interests.

Practical reason remembers that we are persons, not farragos
of reasons or configurations of genes.

Reason with a small 'r' differs from rationality in that it takes us out of our head and into the world. It does not emphasise intellect at the expense of emotion, but reminds us we are embodied creatures in specific social situations. Practical or applied reason gives us our moral knowledge, by turning our focus outside of ourselves, onto the relations between things, people and meanings, which form the foundation of our science, art and religion. It remembers that we are persons, not farragos of reasons or configurations of genes.

Sceptics or debunkers of reason ironically rely on reasoned argument to convince us of their case. Their time would be better spent examining their own cognitive biases or blind spots. The good news is that practical reason gives us a set of tools for doing precisely this.

It allows us the self-reflection to realise that we cannot solve our problems by the power of thought alone. It does not get bogged down in detached analysis, but remains alert to feedback. It gives us the power of self-correction, helping us to understand that we may be victims of uncritical group-think, dupes of a conspiracy theory, or plain mistaken. It reminds us we are rooted in the soil of thought, feeling and action, all of which are equal expressions of the Darwinian thinking machine we call our mind/brain, with no part privileged above the other.

The dangers of unreason

To show its best side, reason must work to a generous end outside of itself, taking in the whole of the human condition. A clue lies in our choice of words. 'Reason' sounds homely and user-friendly, while 'rationality' sounds Latinate and cerebral, at one remove from real life. This might explain why we are emotionally troubled by unreason, but we tend to laugh at irrationality.

Acting reasonably is not the same as thinking rationally.

Reason is not intellectual but intersubjective, found not in the ether above us but created between us when we listen to each other. It stays in touch with tradition, not as dead thought, but as a valuable record of what 'works'. Its readiness to see both sides opens up possibilities for compromise and mutuality. This is why acting reasonably is not the same as thinking rationally. In fact, on occasions the two may conflict.

Now that the genome has been decoded, we might for instance consider it rational to have our DNA tested, giving insight into our personality and intelligence, as well as our propensity for mental illness or physical disease. If the results give us cause for concern, a rational response might be to change our job, alter our life style to head off illness, or decide not to have children so that we do not pass on any bad genes we carry.

If we are prospective parents, and a genetic defect is identified early in the womb, we might decide that abortion is the best option. If we already have children, we might discover that they have potential to become a fine athlete, musician or mathematician, and would benefit from some form of neural enhancement, or attending a specialist school.

For many however, issues that affect human freedom and dignity cannot be judged on genetic profiling or neural potential alone. Down's syndrome can be detected in the womb, and it can be eliminated from the next generation of children, but many parents who elect to go to full term and raise a Down's syndrome child testify to discovering a new kind of love. In these cases, practical reason trumps rationality, but the age of biotechnology will increasingly confront us with rival notions of what is good or right.

The thinkers of the Enlightenment showed they understood the tension between reason and rationality by promoting the education of the sentiments alongside the schooling of the intellect. Reason acknowledges that we have to *care* about what we do, and for that we need our feelings and our thoughts to complement each other.

This explains the philosopher David Hume's remark that reason is 'the slave of the passions'. Without the force of feeling, he says, 'it is not contrary to reason to prefer the destruction of the whole world to the scratching of my finger'. It is the force of feeling that kicks in, or should do, when we are confronted with a hard choice.

This is why emotions evolved, to give direction to our reason. They make reason practical, by grounding it in the needs and interests of others. Only practical reason teaches us that killing all the citizens in a small French village as an act of revenge is an atrocity, while scratching our finger is at best a momentary diversion.

Oradour

In early June 1944, the German army was sending units forward to fight the Allied D-Day landings in Normandy. As speed was of the essence, the German High Command issued a 'rational' order to their units to eliminate any activity by the French Resistance that hampered the operation.

Some armed attacks on advancing German units were encountered near the French village of Oradour in central France. To the 'logical' end of discouraging further guerrilla attacks, and on the pretext that one of their men was being held hostage there, a Nazi Waffen-SS regiment entered the village on the tenth of June and as an 'example' murdered 642 men, women and children, or nearly all of its residents, including visitors who were just passing through, then set fire to the buildings, some with people still hiding in them. Those who tried to escape through windows were machine-gunned. Only six managed to get away. The village is now a memorial, untouched since that dreadful day.

Mountains of the Mind

Many of the SS unit were killed in action in the days following the massacre, and of those who survived the war, very few faced any charges. A large number hailed from the region of Alsace, making them half German and half French, so charging them with war crimes against their own people was politically sensitive. Some of the Alsatians claimed they had been forced into the SS, and committed no atrocities on the day, so they were never brought to trial.

Oradour-sur-Glane
The ruined buildings and rusting vehicles of the village have been left as a memorial since the fateful day in June 1944.

Also, after the war the Allies believed that de-Nazifying the German population was a better way of rebuilding a shattered country than executing thousands of camp-followers as an example. At the Nuremberg War Trials in 1946 however, thirty seven Nazi officials were sentenced to death, though not necessarily for crimes committed against Jews.

The responsibility for the Holocaust came to in a head in 1961, in the televised trial of Adolf Eichmann, one of the principal architects of the extermination of six million Jews. It lasted several months and heard the testimony of over a hundred Holocaust survivors. Throughout, the cameras scanned Eichmann's face for a flicker of humanity, perhaps a grimace or a tear from the man who had exacted such a grim toll of human suffering. This would at least suggest that there was a person behind the mask, not a monster. But there was nothing, just dull insistence that he had only been obeying orders.

It is tempting to rationalise what happened at Oradour with some simplistic explanations, but they would all be wrong. It is the expression of a uniquely German authoritarian personality. It is what happens when soldiers are deindividuated and ideologically brainwashed. It is what follows when unquestioning obedience to a rational 'system' backed by a semblance of legitimate command is allowed to obliterate feeling and reason. It is an egregious example of unadulterated evil committed by men who were out of their minds.

The truth is more sinister. It is not that there are some people in the world who are intrinsically evil, or born thugs. It is that anyone put in evil circumstances is capable of acts of barbarism. Beneath our veneer of reason, we are deeply tribal, and however good we consider ourselves to be, if we are so convinced of our cause to the exclusion of all else, we might find ourselves doing bad things.

Three thousand years ago, the Persian prophet Zoroaster established the dualistic myth that the world is engaged in a titanic struggle between light and dark, kindness and cruelty, forgiveness and retribution. The journalist Hannah Arendt, who witnessed Eichmann's trial, shocked the Jewish community by reporting that good and evil clash not on some cosmic stage, but in a much more banal place: the human heart.

Many wanted to demonise Eichmann, but Arendt insisted that he deserved a fair trial and due process of law, otherwise there could be no true justice for those he sent to the gas chambers. To condemn him as a monster would not only deny his humanity, it would excuse his barbarism as an aberration. It wasn't. It was all too human. He was a grubby murderer, with feet of clay.

She remarked that, in the face of Adolf Eichmann, despite his heinous crimes, she saw not the embodiment of evil, but ordinary unthinking obedience, void of personal responsibility. He was a common bully, a mere lackey of the Nazi party. The one concession she made to those who craved vengeance was that he had committed a new type of crime. By trying to wipe out a whole people and culture, he was guilty of a crime against humanity. He had gone against the very grain of what it means to be human.

Our angels and demons are interchangeable.

Arendt concluded that one of the most terrifying things about evil is how matter of fact it can look. It is not a rare and repellent moral darkness found in only a few, but a common potential in everyone. Our moral plasticity makes us capable of great acts of selflessness, but also of turning against our own kind. We all have it within us to be saints or sinners. Unless we learn how to recognise both, and perfect tactics of resistance, which can be taught and learned, our angels and demons are interchangeable.

The world is not neatly divisible into good and evil people. If it were, we could take all the nasty ones to one side and dispose of them. In doing so however, we might find ourselves wiping out not only most of the human race, but also something vital in our nature, or what makes us human. We admire saints not because they are sinless, but because they teach us how to struggle with our demons. By the reverse token, we are loath to condemn sinners because, like us, part of them strives to let their better nature flourish.

In other words, we are all like the curate's egg, good in parts, never perfectly good or totally evil, but a complex mix, depending on our intentions, decisions, and who we keep company with. Goodness is fragile, and we may even find ourselves doing evil in the name of good, or being duped by evil masquerading as good.

Good in parts

How can this be? There is no moral calculus that can justify the massacre of a whole village, but the stark reality is that, in our history as a species, war, atrocity and barbarism have come as easily to us as civilisation. If we must find a root cause, it is a shocking one. Empathy, the very urge which ensures that we care for our loved ones, even sacrifice our lives for them, has a dangerous flip side.

Empathy motivates us to rush to the aid of someone in distress, or to wince when someone else is in pain. It even turns soldiers into good fighters. They fight not because they hate their enemy, but because they are a 'band of brothers', 'Alte Kamaraden' sworn to death or glory out of loyalty for each other. Since ancient times, the toughest armies to beat have been those who fight back to back, watching out for each other, prepared to lay down their life for a friend.

But if empathy underpins our belief in the sanctity of life, how can it also justify killing? When our mind is young and impressionable, we can be conditioned to respond in different ways. If certain other humans are consistently dehumanised and demonised as vermin, we can end up having more empathy for our dog than for a perceived enemy of the Reich dying in the street. Our face is now set cruelly against outsiders.

Sigmund Freud accounted for this dark side of our nature by recasting evil as the 'id' of our unconscious. He believed that our polite manners are merely the thin veneer of our conscious ego, barely masking the primal urges of our unconscious id. We are all sick animals, never fully civilised, because we can never tame the promptings of the blood and the tantrums of the will, which plague us nightly in our dreams.

Freud died in 1939, having fled the Nazi regime, but he would have seen Nazism for what it was. It had dragged the Shadow of our unconscious self into the daylight, exposing its victims to our most vicious urges. By rationalising death, justifying evil and normalising psychopathy, it infected the whole psyche.

The problem with Freud's id is that it remains largely beyond our conscious reach. More potent is Carl Jung's portrayal of evil as our dark doppelganger that we can learn to confront and face down. If we don't, it will not only push back fiercely when we suppress it, but also project our unresolved inner conflicts onto those we single out as our enemies, not because they are evil in ways that we aren't, but because we punish in them the very failings we hate in ourselves.

Evil runs like a thread through all our actions.

These Freudian and Jungian ideas about evil suggest that when theologians pit God against Lucifer, Kali over Shiva, or Good versus Evil, they are merely externalising the enemy within. Evil runs like a thread through all our actions, as responsible for our best qualities as our worst.

Lady Macbeth for instance wasn't a 'natural born killer', evil through and through. In order to murder her king in cold blood, she had to appeal to the 'spirits that tend on mortal thoughts' to crush everything within her that cried out against the deed, such as her love for the baby she had suckled.

We tend to assume that people who do bad or mad things are bad or mad in themselves, but we are all capable of conforming, even when we know it to be wrong. This tendency was put to the test by various 'obedience' experiments staged on quiet American university campuses in the late 1960's.

90

Mountains of the Mind

Stanley Milgram and Phillip Zimbardo showed in different ways how upstanding citizens lack the moral resources to resist the authority of men in white coats or uniforms. Critics point out however that, not only do such studies breach ethical guidelines, their results have never been replicated, and later investigations reveal that the 'findings' were twisted to suit the agenda of the researchers.

On a closer look, these 'experiments' reveal that we are not all potential Nazis waiting for the right moment to exercise our sadistic urges. William Golding's 1954 novel 'Lord of the Flies', in which quiet English choirboys stranded on an island without adults quickly turn into whooping savages, is precisely that, a work of fiction. For obvious reasons, there are few if any real-life cases of children being left to their own devices for long periods, but when they are, they are more likely to invent games and look out for each other than revert to barbarism.

Just obeying orders
So what was going on in the minds of these young German storm troopers at Oradour? They had not been brainwashed, though their heads had been routinely filled with propaganda that they were elite warriors, the keepers of the flame of Aryan civilisation. They had their own morality, based on their own notions of goodness and strength. They became convinced they were right, and that the means of murdering civilians was justified by the end of a triumphant Reich. They confused being 'good' soldiers and servants of the Führer with being part of a collective that has the potential to 'do good' in the world.

This ethic was not however an inclusive, other-regarding or life-affirming one. It was based on the superiority of their in-group and the inferiority of their enemies, not a sense of universal brotherhood. This led to the paradox that they could be loving fathers back home, but executioners of those who belonged to the out-group. In their eyes, those they killed were culturally less evolved, and therefore less than human. Jewish and French people were not people.

Nor were these young soldiers of low intelligence, ignorant or naive. They were educated young men. Even a university degree cannot however immunise the intellect against the perverse charms of fascism. In our own time we see how a western education cannot insulate modern terrorists from radicalisation. Some young suicide bombers who intend the downfall of the system that nourished them are better 'educated' than the people they kill and maim. In such cases, über-rationality estranges thought from feeling, deadening the cries of women and children, blanking the right to live of the unarmed and innocent.

Nuremberg War Trials
Herman Goering, Hitler's second in command, on trial at Nuremberg in 1946. It's comforting to put evil in the dock, because this makes it someone else's responsibility. It saves us the worry of journeying into our own Heart of Darkness.

Nor were the soldiers the victims of child abuse, so they did not have the excuse of W H Auden's sagacious judgment, 'Those to whom evil is done, do evil in return'. They weren't psychopaths void of emotions, as this condition affects only one per cent of the population. They were potentially good people, with the same ethical constitution as the rest of us, but their minds had been steadily inured to violence and cruelty against those cast as parasites polluting the body politic.

Agency and responsibility ran all the way
down the chain of command.

So does it suffice to say they were just 'following orders'? This was the defence used by many of the leading Nazis at the Nuremberg War Trials. Orders presumably come from the very top, but ironically, although Hitler often incited violence and inflamed passions in his writings and speeches, he never gave specific orders about the Holocaust, or how it should be effected. Agency and responsibility therefore ran all the way down the chain of command.

Mountains of the Mind

Born to be bad

Moral realists believe that there is an essence called 'evil', but this is too facile an explanation for what happened at Oradour. These young German soldiers were not 'born evil', with intrinsically bad genes. They entered the world with the same moral intuitions and capacity for compassion as the rest of us, about sharing and caring, not maiming and killing.

We utter that verbal slur, spit in that face
and kick that body on the floor.

Normally our parents amplify these prosocial gut feelings by their approval of what is virtuous and their condemnation of what is vicious, until we have learned the perspective of the group and the benefits of reciprocity. This cannot happen if we are being slowly drip-fed insidious, racist and dehumanising thoughts about imagined enemies, until the balance of our hatred reaches a tipping point. Then our sins of omission, or simply failing to stand up for the underdog, become sins of commission: we utter that verbal slur, spit in that face and kick that body on the floor.

By the time they arrived at Oradour, these young men had slid remorselessly into evil habits, one cruel act at a time. They were brutalised by war, exhausted, staring down the barrel of defeat, some of them angry for being forced to fight, and looking for scapegoats. If they felt any empathy, it was not for these randomly chosen civilians, and without empathy, there was no scope for compassion, or urge to pull a screaming child from the flames.

We might blame the perniciousness of National Socialism, which urged them to project all their anger, frustration and hatred onto a single victim group. This does not explain however where such animosity came from, why these particular innocents were targeted, why so many Germans allowed themselves to be swept along by brute nationalism, or why so few resisted it.

Nazism duped them into believing absurdities as a preparation for committing atrocities. It operated as a cult, with its insignia, marching songs, rallies and idolisation of the Führer. It made them believe they were serving a greater cause. The collective will of the Reich of a Thousand Tears gave them a false myth of the Volk, or People, bound together by blood and soil, not reason.

Mountains of the Mind

This absolved them of personal responsibility and freed them of any cognitive dissonance: they were not murdering innocent civilians, but obeying orders, abandoning their private conscience for a cause greater than themselves, serving the call of the Fatherland.

They were victims of a strange 'flat mind' phenomenon: in the toxic cocktail of being caught up in a group convinced of its intellectual and moral superiority, human beings can be very cruel, ceasing to see their enemies as fellow human beings.

This phenomenon is not unique to what happened at Oradour. Ironically much of German military strategy had been learned from British tactics in controlling its vast empire. Local resistance against a thinly-spread occupying force was often dealt with by brutal 'pacification' policies in far-flung colonies or 'protectorates' such as India, Kenya and Malaya, that literally took no prisoners. In those days there were no prying cameras or news reporters to unsettle consciences back home, and poorly educated soldiers, sucked into a macho military culture and separated from the civilising influence of their women folk, generally did what they were ordered to do.

The 1981 American novel 'The Wave' shows how, even in peace time, compliance, mass mentality and thuggishness can increase when identity and responsibility are diffused. Subjected to sustained propaganda and sinister pressure, high school students brought up on cheesecake and baseball find themselves becoming mindless functionaries of a bullying cult.

Barbarism can therefore afflict anyone who puts on a uniform, signs up to an ideology or joins a mob. In the days of lynch mobs, the larger the group, the more brutal the lynching, because emotions usually kept under control were unleashed like a pack of dogs on the rampage.

Group violence affects both sexes. Since ancient times, women have urged their sons to return home a hero or on their shield, so the T shirt slogan 'Women make love, not war' is not strictly true. Some of the cruellest camp guards at Auschwitz were women. Research shows that, while women are better at resisting 'mass thinking' at first, once they have committed themselves, they can be more willing recruits than men.

Group violence also affects all cultures. The Greek historian Thucydides noted over two and a half thousand years ago that atrocities are committed by both sides

Mountains of the Mind

in a war. Genocidal rampages have been seen in Nanking, Rwanda, the Balkans and Myanmar, performed by the Japanese, Hutus, Serbs and Burmese, nearly always against unarmed civilians.

In 1968, American soldiers had their own Oradour moment in the Vietnamese village of My Lai, killing five hundred unarmed villagers over a four hour period. If there is any comfort to be taken from this incident, and it is only a crumb, American soldiers arriving later in the day from another unit could see that an atrocity was being committed, and risked their lives to stop it.

The physicist Freeman Dyson, who had used his considerable intellect and mathematical skills to assist the Allies during World War Two in designing ever more efficient means of killing the enemy, including the development of nuclear weapons, sagely wondered at the end of his life whether he was as guilty as some of the Nazi officers on trial at Nuremberg. He realised that it was his good fortune to be on the winning side.

Moral reasons

Oradour is a lesson to us all: this is what happens when we lose the ability to feel in our bones that we are committing a grievous wrong. We have to find *moral reasons* for choosing between burning children, biting our thumbs and acting humanely. This is not a question of reasons or rationalisations, but human decency and good character. If we can't manage this, we put ourselves on the side of evil, thwarting our full potential as human beings, becoming strangers to the good.

Good and evil are not the inventions of moral philosophers or prissy puritans. Like self and consciousness, our sense of what is good and right is intrinsic, an irreducible feature of what it means to be human. Some say the good is merely what aids survival or suits our private agenda, while bad is merely our disapproval of things and people we don't like. Infanticide and child sacrifice for instance have been practised at different times as the 'right' thing, and in some cultures female genital mutilation still is. Capital punishment was abolished in the United Kingdom in 1969, but in the nineteenth century it drew huge crowds of spectators at Tyburn gibbet.

Ancient burial sites going back forty thousand years don't settle the argument one way or the other. In one there is evidence of mass murder, the victims probably from a rival tribe, with skulls smashed and limbs severed. In another we

95

find the body of a disabled or injured person who had lived for at least another ten years, proving that the family were caring for close kin.

Experiments with the moral sensibilities of very young children give encouraging results. They show that caring for each other is not simply motivated by self-interest, but evident from the outset, part of our genome. They prefer toys that are seen to help others, not harm them. Even rats choose to press a lever to release a fellow rat over one which delivers a slab of chocolate, and adolescent chimp orphans have been seen caring for their motherless siblings.

> *Common humanity is our sense of what*
> *we owe each other as human beings.*

'Do the right thing' is therefore the default expectation, not an optional extra. If we do not feel in the pit of our stomach that it is wrong to deny a child a life-saving operation, refuse a sick person medicine or inflict pain knowingly, we lack common humanity, or a sense of what we owe each other as human beings.

We are constantly called upon to make judgments, between what is cruel or kind, wrong or right, shallow or deep, disgraceful or praiseworthy, unjust or fair. We cannot rationalise how we know which is which, or which faith system teaches it best, because it pre-dates religion. It comes from deep down, in our moral ancestry.

We know that if we knock over a homeless person while driving down a dark street, we are duty bound to stop. It doesn't matter that there are no witnesses, or that this person will not be missed by anyone. We don't behave ourselves just because we think are being watched, or because we have sublimated all those childhood tellings-off in what we call our conscience.

We are instinctively and intuitively appalled when we hear cases of children committing acts of cruelty, torture or murder, usually against children younger than themselves. We sense a breach in the natural order of things, but when we dig deeper, we discover that something has gone horribly wrong in their care and upbringing.

We accept unquestioningly that there are certain moral 'red lines' we must not cross, such as genocide or the slaughtering of innocents in reprisal, because we cannot imagine a human world in which such violations could be the norm, or be conceived as justified under any circumstances.

This does not mean that morality is obvious, or easy, or a matter of convenience. It may not be written in stone, like laws coming down from on high, but neither do we make it up as we go along. Where then does our morality come from, and how do we learn it?

Seen from an academic viewpoint, the young German soldiers had a choice of three 'models' of morality to guide them in their conduct at Oradour. They might have listened to the voice of their own countryman, Immanuel Kant, who presented a duty-based model: we do what we must, obeying a universal principle and overwhelming imperative that we should not do to others what we would not want done to ourselves. We should treat others with dignity, always as ends in themselves, never as means.

Kant's high-minded reframing of the 'Golden Rule', long established in the world's great religions, clearly did not fit in with National Socialism, so how about the more down-to-earth utilitarianism of the Englishman Jeremy Bentham: the end justifies the means, or the best course of action is that which benefits the greatest number? If the massacre at Oradour led to the French resistance being crushed, deterred subsequent attacks, or favoured the interests of the German people in the long run, it was justified. But none was the case. Even as retaliation the attack was a failure, because there probably wasn't a single resistance fighter among the victims.

Virtue ethics
What these young soldiers needed long before they arrived at Oradour was to be schooled in a much older morality, known as virtue ethics. Kant and Bentham's theories openly conflicted with each other in many areas, and were riddled with exceptions. Is it ever right to tell a lie, kill someone to save ten other lives, or set fire to civilians?

Virtue ethics, harking back to Aristotle, locates morality in the person, not in principle or rational calculation. Even in the heat of battle, common humanity should lead us to respect the rights of non-combatants or prisoners of war, which is the basis of the Geneva Convention. From a young age these young Germans should have been moulded by small acts of kindness and gratitude, not just towards blond Aryans but also to Jews, gypsies, the disabled, those who were different in any way.

When they fell short of this, they should have been corrected, and shown how to overcome their prejudice, however hard, improving with practice. They should have drunk in common kindness as naturally as their mothers' milk, and then painstakingly learned its ways, until it became second nature. These are the ways in which decency and kindness become not add-ons, but essential ingredients of our character.

Goodness must become our habit.

This is the only way we reach a point where we don't wilfully harm others, not because there is a moralising God tallying our sins, or a police force monitoring our every deed, but because our fellow feeling has become part of who we are, cultivated but spontaneous. We are no longer someone working hard to perform virtuous acts, or laboriously aping virtuous behaviour, but a virtuous person behaving humanely as a matter of course. Goodness has become our habit.

This was not the case with the men whose armoured vehicles arrived at Oradour. Their mission was clear, but their internal moral compass was broken long before they set about their atrocities. They had learned no kindness in the nursery, no shared humanity, no ingrained aversion to barbarousness, no whispering of conscience.

Far removed from the heat of the moment, we have time to intuit without much thought that what happened at Oradour was deeply wrong, and why. Steeped in the traditional classic virtues of temperance, prudence, courage and justice, to which Christianity added faith, hope and love, we are physically, emotionally and morally incapable of picking up a gun and shooting another human being in cold blood.

Everything in us screams against the deed. We declare, 'I cannot do this thing, because that is not who I am. Here I stand'. Doing the right thing has become intrinsic to who we are, even though it may be the harder thing, because to do the wrong thing offends something deep inside us.

Or does it? Oradour is not a thought experiment: it really happened. We will never know how we would have behaved, dressed in this uniform, surrounded by these fanatics, receiving these orders, inflamed by the euphoria of bloodletting. We can only hope that we would have resisted, or found a way of not being there in the first place. We breathe a sigh of relief that, being born at a different time, we escaped being tested.

We are the lucky ones, the generations raised in peace. As small children we were allowed to hear the still small voice of conscience, long before the big noisy concepts of right and wrong were drummed into us. What turns conscience into something of moral substance is when our parents start small, training us like naughty puppies not to snatch things from others, and to share what we have. Out of these tiny behaviour adjustments grow the good manners that make society polite, civil and a pleasure to live in.

Character formation cannot happen if there is no determination to become a better person, so perfecting the virtues has to begin in the nursery. At first we find this hard, but once we have learned to ride the bicycle, we can remove the stabilisers. We can stop chanting the Ten Commandments because they are no longer external to us, but inside us. When we choose to be celibate we show that we do not need to be the slaves of our desires: they can be sublimated to alternative or higher ends.

This personal investment in what is good, right, true and just, even beautiful, cannot be left to a vague notion of culture or custom. It needs to be drummed into us at the outset as the defining feature of what it means to be part of the human family, not just locally, but absolutely. The normally courteous Japanese behaved appallingly in the Rape of Nanjing, the usually harmonious Chinese turned children into their parents' executioners in the Cultural Revolution, and the traditionally urbane Germans brought up on Beethoven watched on dispassionately as they saw their Jewish neighbours being dragged from their homes.

Slave and master

In this regard, the young soldiers at Oradour were totally unprepared for the choice they had to make. Their parents, teachers, and the Kultur of the Third Reich had left them morally naked. Their judgment of right and wrong might have been based on a misunderstanding of the teaching of two earlier German philosophers.

Georg Hegel drew attention to the differing psychologies of the master and the slave. One of the driving forces of history is that the slave strives constantly to supplant the master. He did not however advocate the idea of a Master Race of

Mountains of the Mind

Übermensch subjugating a host of *Untermensch* through brute force, abrogating any claim to moral leadership in the process. In that sense, the true slaves at Oradour were not the defenceless French villagers, but their brutal oppressors, in the grip of a cruel and false ideology.

A later thinker, Friedrich Nietzsche, lauded the will to power, suggesting that the true hero is the one who forces others to comply with a superior vision. He admired the Ancient Greeks, but for their cruelty, not their reason: they faced life full on in all its suffering and brutality. By the same reasoning, he dismissed the traditional Christian teaching of turning the other cheek as 'herd morality', or the mark of weakness. Wimps are losers, and vice versa. It's highly unlikely that Donald Trump read Nietzsche, but he is one of his spiritual successors.

War, violence, division and destruction are seen by some as creating a terrible beauty, purifying the soul and essential for progress, but only at an appalling human cost. Death disinfects the body politic, disruption makes way for innovation, evil is more attractive than good. Without makers, breakers and shakers, intent on upending things and wreaking havoc, sometimes just for the hell of it, life would be dull indeed.

We want to live in a world where good is routinely done to us.

Our attitude to evil is ambivalent. Satan can be a more appealing character than God. In crime dramas, we find baddies more intriguing than goodies, even though we know they deserve their come-uppance. We are also deeply aware that, after the credits have rolled, and before our next excursion into imagined horrors, we want to live in a world where good is routinely done to us, and evildoers are brought to book.

History passes its own verdict on thugs and bullies. There is no memorial at Oradour to those who were responsible for the massacre, only the victims, though the monument was defaced by Neo-Nazi graffiti in 2020, showing that the fight against evil is never done.

Even if the German soldiers had disobeyed orders on the day of the Oradour massacre, it would have been too little, too late. They would have faced the firing squad, sacrificed to the Aryan myth of the fulfilment of history. Instead their future was much more prosaic. The few who survived the Allied onslaught had to return to a ruined Fatherland, their dream of a thousand-year Reich in tatters.

Friedrich Nietszche
1844-1900
Nietszche was a troubled genius who promoted the self as a heroic superman or *Übermensch* rising above mediocrity by force of will. He was not himself antisemitic, but his ideas were twisted by his sister after his death to endorse Nazi ideology.

Perhaps a few looked at themselves in the mirror, and found a way of becoming husbands and fathers in a new Germany. Their children and grandchildren might have made the pilgrimage to Oradour in later years, not to atone for the sins of their fathers, but to try to understand the dark forces that led to such an outrage, hoping to avoid repeating the tragedies of the past.

In the ruins of 1945, both Germany and Japan were forced to confront their demons, and find new moral resources to build a modern liberal society. The British and French had different ghosts to exorcise: the guilty debts of their colonial past. The Americans still struggle to find ways of atoning for the evils of slavery, while the Australians, New Zealanders and Canadians are charged with establishing just settlements and equitable relations with the indigenous peoples they often brutally supplanted.

Learning to be more civil
Morality's roots like deep in our ancestral past, and our slow acquisition of it is grounded in our evolution as a species. It is not so much an instinct, more a long, hard road of building up our shared moral capital, carefully passed down the

generations, and crossing individual cognitive thresholds as we learn how to balance the interests of self and others.

This means that our moral sense, or learning to be good, like our body, changes and grows. Only two centuries ago, many in the West saw nothing morally wrong in slavery, and it is still practised in some parts of the world. We can't lay any claim to becoming more just, progressive, enlightened or civilised unless we can agree that the rights to freedom from vassalage, relief from pain and protection from abuse are non-negotiable.

How then could a regressive ideology such as Nazism have marred the 'enlightened' twentieth century? The answer depends on our view of human progress. For centuries time had been seen as a cyclical eternal return, but the Judaeo-Christian faiths introduced into Western thought the idea of history as a linear ascent with an end goal.

The thinkers of the Enlightenment secularised this divine plan as Progress with a capital P, directed not by God but by secular humanism. Reason, science and intellect were seen as capable of furthering civilisation and generating ethical values not by divine fiat but by what works for human flourishing, based on experience.

There have been real enhancements in the quality of life.

If we judge flourishing by access to essential capabilities such as clean water, electricity, education, medicines and telecommunications, as well as entitlement to basic rights such as freedom from injustice, slavery, famine, civil war and persecution, we can justifiably claim that progress has been made, not just for the privileged few, but for the many. Across the developing world, millions have been lifted out of poverty, fewer mothers die in childbirth, fewer children die early, life spans have increased significantly, and barbaric practices such as female genital mutilation are on the retreat. There have been real enhancements in the quality of life.

Progress is seen by some as under-written by free trade and globalism, governments playing their part by regulating standards, upholding international law, spreading education, defending democratic freedoms and tackling outrages such as people trafficking. Some governments also concern themselves with raising happiness levels for their population, as measured by rising living standards, shorter working weeks, protected leisure time, improved health care and general sense of well-being.

Others dismiss such faith in progress as naive, as there is no guarantee that internationalism, reason, science and technology can alone lead us on to the bright sunlit uplands of material progress and utopian bliss. As Oradour shows, perfectibilism is a beguiling dream that just as easily ends up in the nightmare of the killing fields. Our moral progress seems to lag well behind our good intentions.

The young German soldiers who followed orders at Oradour were intelligent and educated young men, but they had forgotten Kant's warning that they were also made of crooked timber, from which nothing straight can be made. They may well have been brought up on Bach and Brahms, but high culture and grand reason could not alone civilise and humanise them. They also needed to learn humility and compassion.

Civilisation, as in behaving civilly towards each other, resides not in libraries or opera houses, but in the thousands of little habits and small acts of kindness that we afford each other every day, such as saying 'please' and 'thank you'. When city officials want to transform a run-down area, they start with the small stuff like litter-picking, jay-walking, parking offences, broken windows, hustling, petty theft and graffiti.

It is the small civilities like these that are the bedrock of decency, without which grander notions of justice, dignity and respect have no solid foundation. They are signals that people care about where they live. They take generations to build up as sociocultural practices and conventional acts of politeness, but they can be erased in an afternoon, as happened at Oradour.

Every so often, if put under intense strain, the thin crust of civility cracks, and the nasty stuff just beneath the surface oozes out, perhaps in a street fight, riot or orgy of bloodletting. This pus doesn't suddenly appear from nowhere. It is always there, and it is only by persistent effort, regularly cultivating the other-orientated side of our nature, that we keep it under control.

Our better angels

Progress is best seen therefore as constant vigilance against the worse angels of our nature. Our better angels are kept alive by the open exchange of ideas, not retreat into the enclaves of nationalism, populism, bigotry and superstition. A data-based approach shows that war, famine, murder, genocide and poverty are on the retreat across the world, but we also know that trolling, trafficking, depression, fundamentalism and white supremacy are poisons that lurk in the mud, always waiting their moment to hatch out.

Part of the problem is the way our perception is manipulated by knee-jerk social media, angry tweets, tribal silos, deep fakes and sensationalist news stories. We don't get to hear of the people saved from Ebola, only those that die. We aren't told about the girls who are the first in their village to be educated, only those who are kidnapped by Boko Haram.

What thought thinks needs to be balanced by what feelings feel.

The Enlightenment's gifts of reason and humanism, now over two centuries old, are not therefore open passports to a brighter future, unless we temper them with our deeper emotional needs. Rationality based on what works, or what thought thinks, needs to be balanced by our moral duty to each other, or what feelings feel.

Rationality alone cannot civilise us, motivate us to act well or teach us to choose wisely. Without values grounded in mutuality, rationality can in fact be used to achieve inhuman ends, such as the method used to solve the 'Jewish Problem' in 1941. Standing by the ruined church at Oradour, it is hard to imagine what kind of slide rule helped a German SS officer to make a rational calculation that the life of one of his soldiers was worth the lives of ten, a hundred or a thousand French civilians.

If we want to understand how our brain is capable of both genocide and genetic research, we need to work out how it came to be the way it is,. What are the gremlins that flatten our mind? Only then can we claim the title *sapiens*, and be sure we are progressing as a species, not because we are rational, but because we are capable of acting reasonably, guided by fellow feeling, and trained in practising the virtues.

Practical reason that balances the honing of our critical faculties with the cultivation of good character is our only defence against the unexamined and unrefined irrationalities of tribalism, prejudice, blood and soil. It alone can get us closer to resolving our interminable squabbles, making good our foolish errors, respecting each other as persons, helping us save our planet, and satisfying our craving for stimulus. But as we shall see, it remains a great struggle for us to know the *lived* difference between rationality and reasonableness.

Why aren't we more rational?

*Poor self knowledge – the progress trap –religion – spirituality -
atheism – belief – deceptive sense of self – duplicity*

- Though we seldom admit it, we are poor self-knowers, driven to act by our 'bottom up' unconscious default networks.
- A conscious 'top down' agent is however existentially necessary if we are to operate as self-directing persons, and establish a social identity.
- The question mark over our ability to know ourselves also hangs over our claims to making progress as a species. At best, progress is fragile.
- Religion is dismissed by many as a brake on our progress, something we need to grow out of.
- The religious impulse is however intrinsic to human experience, and not all religions subscribe to the supernatural.
- We can be 'spiritual' without believing in the transcendent.
- Spirituality predates religion and science, and remains common to both as a sense of wonder and a search for order.
- If we see religion and science as answering different questions, they form a continuum of enquiry, not a clash of ideologies.
- Atheism, materialism, reductionism and rationalism do not offer 'superior' ways of explaining the world to us.
- If we are to write an overarching narrative, and learn to live with difference, we need a synthesis of the sciences and the humanities.
- Belief comes naturally to the human mind, but there are many false gods, just as there are bad sciences. It matters that we reflect carefully on the causes we freely choose to believe in.

Mountains of the Mind

Poor self-knowers

Flat-mind theorists have got us bang to rights in many ways. They know that, suspended as we are between thought and feeling, we find it difficult to be consistently rational, because our body does not consistently perform. We make our best decisions in the morning, after our body temperature has risen. We experience an energy dip in the afternoon, and get a second boost in the evening.

This strongly suggests that our 'self' is the lackey of our body. Simply holding a warm drink in our hand can make us more responsive to the person we are talking to. If our bladder is full, we're more likely to refuse a request than grant it. If someone touches our arm while talking to us, we're more likely to trust what we are hearing.

These aren't such terrible failings, but there are more serious charges against us. Why do we continue to smoke despite the pictures of blackened lungs on the packet? Why do we go on an all-night bender when we know we have a big day tomorrow? Why do we fall for the myth that beer before spirits wards off a hangover, when it makes it worse?

It seems we hardly know ourselves, or at least not well enough to get a grip on our passions. In the heat of desire we forget that we haven't taken any contraceptive precautions. If meat balls make us sick once, we develop a phobia of all meat balls. Even sitting next to someone eating them makes us feel nauseous. When we fail at something, we catastrophise: we're useless at everything, and everybody hates us. We underestimate the effect of peer pressure on our choices. If our 'friends' on social media jump on a bandwagon, we jump on too so that we're not left out.

Not me, you might think, but social psychologists come up with the same findings, over and over. We're not very good at reading or predicting our emotions. We think that winning the lottery will transform our happiness levels, but the power of foresight eludes us, because we make the mistake of judging future happiness based on our present emotions. After six months, we revert to our default happiness setting, no higher or lower than someone who has adjusted to a life-changing illness or accident.

This undermines the idea that we can make an 'informed' decision about anything, because we have no way of second-guessing how we'll feel about things several years down the track. Logic can boast consistency, but our emotions are notoriously fickle.

Our auto-alarm systems stay on even though the threat has passed, making us unnecessarily anxious. We struggle to reach a decision, because impulse and reason often conflict. We want to trust our hunches, but we also crave more information. When we get it, we freeze, like a doctor surrounded by too many test results, unable to choose. If we don't get it, we invent the data we need, then press on regardless.

These half-grasped inconsistencies and laughable follies provide endless plotlines for the human comedy. We struggle to make the big calls in life: who to marry, whether to have children, which career to choose, whether to go vegan, which political party to support, where to live.

We can't really claim to know ourselves.

We can't live in a state of perpetual angst, so we have invented some excellent ruses for rationalising our thinking, or persuading ourselves that we've made the right choice anyway. Of course we don't regret buying that second car that's let us down twice already, despite our friend warning us off it. It's such *fun* to drive. Such levels of self-deception suggest that we can't really claim to know ourselves, or even recognise the reflection others give back to us.

Good self-promoters

Most of us over-estimate our abilities. In a survey of motorists, over fifty per cent claimed to have better than average driving skills. The irony is that the survey was conducted in a hospital ward with people who were recovering from being involved in a car accident.

Our technical abilities fare no better. We're surrounded by gadgets, but most of us can't explain how something as simple as a mousetrap works. This is because its mechanism isn't simple at all: we just cash in on generations of other people's ingenuity, allowing us to paper over our ignorance.

We convince ourselves that we are well-liked, unlucky not to get that job offer, deserving to be on television. We're insufferably right about everything, allowing us to occupy the moral high ground, bolstered by the gift of hindsight: I *told* you this would end in tears. We kid ourselves that we know far more than we do. Watching the film 'Gandhi' convinces us we know all we need to know about the subcontinent of India.

The Mousetrap
We've seen one, and we know it traps mice, but in what is known as the fallacy of assumed knowledge, if asked to make one from scratch, we wouldn't know where to start.

These blind spots and self deceptions are partly a consequence of how our brain works. To avoid overload, it operates as a reducing agent, grasping only the surface features of things and filling the gaps in our ignorance with supposition, giving us only the veneer of confidence.

Without a healthy smattering of ego bias,
we are more prone to depression.

We have evolved these positive illusions about our abilities because they are adaptive. They bolster our fragile ego, regardless of our true capacities. Self esteem based on a healthy and reasonable assessment of our potential is vital for mental health and social flourishing. Research shows that without a healthy smattering of ego bias, we are more prone to depression.

It's gratifying to feel that everyone loves us, that we are omniscient, and that we make the right calls every time, which serves us much better than being too negative about ourselves. In the cut and thrust of life, confident self-promoters get further than wilting self-doubters. If we are to get noticed, or achieve anything, we need to show our best face to the world. On the other hand, over-confidence that is reactive-defensive, based on little more than bluster, can do a lot of harm, and will one day come unstuck.

The flat self

Western religions have long taught that we are incarnated souls inhabiting dull flesh, shards of spirit trapped in dull matter. Secular philosophers have bigged us up as authentic, self-determining personalities, our relatively stable continuum of experience allowing us to recognise 'me' in the mirror.

This is a very Western view of the self, dating back over two millennia to Aristotle. He believed that we are rational beings, endowed with the thinking capacity to build an autonomous self, which is our natural 'end', the fulfilment of who we have it within us to be. We cannot achieve this in a state of nature, only in human society, through which we establish a personal identity, and without which we are little more than beasts.

Augustine's 'Confessions', written in the fifth century, took up the baton of the autobiographical self. By interrogating his memories and spiritual development, he explored the idea of life as a text, with salvation as its final chapter. He was the forerunner of all the characters in novels and films, who reflect our selves back to us as confused seekers after meaning.

Some say this privileging of the self has reached its zenith, or perhaps its nadir, in a culture of narcissism, with children as young as five or six parading in beauty pageants and having photo shoots. 'Look at me' celeb culture is not a good model for social cohesion, which requires a sense of contributing to the good of the whole, not individualism or egotism.

We have the power to change ourselves if we wish.

The Eastern model of the self is more circumspect. If the 'self' exists in any meaningful sense, it is in our ability to achieve harmony amidst a bundle of conflicting yin and yang energies, blowing hot one moment, cold the next. This insight chimes with the findings of modern social psychology: we are not stable or single selves, but a battlefield of unthinking habits, passing fancies, temporary upsets and mood swings. The good news, confirmed by the teachings of Buddhism, is that once we've experienced the light bulb moment of seeing ourselves for the conflicted and inconstant creatures that we are, we have the power to change ourselves if we wish.

Consumer culture by and large avoids such introspection, instead bolstering our idea of the self as a series of wants to be satisfied and amusements to be enjoyed. This 'surface' model of the self is so pervasive that we barely pause to think about it. Even when we're not shopping, practicality alone demands an 'agent' to unify our knowledge, control our urges and repel the slings and arrows of outrageous fortune.

Merely managing our social media profile calls for a strong sense of personal identity, someone to star in our own reality show, and the boss of everything we call our own. On a deeper level, our liberal politics and democratic traditions require a sovereign essence that we call 'the voter', on whom we base our notions of rights, obligations and freedoms.

To be or not to be
In recent years however, on the back of brain scans and social psychology experiments, cognitive scientists have suggested that the idea of a fixed self is little more than a consoling myth. There is no 'little person' somewhere in our brain flicking through television channels to decide which 'reality' to watch. When we talk of 'self-actualising', we are worshipping our own imagination, not dealing with a discrete neural entity. The self and the person are yarns that we spin from the random flow of experience, with ourselves as the lead character.

In other words, we are the victims of our own ego trick. We think we possess a sovereign self, unique, special and capable of achieving great things if only someone would notice us, but in reality we are just so many mini-robots and sub-personal routines going about their work. When we concentrate on something, our 'self' becomes for that moment whatever we hold in the spotlight of our attention, and the rest of our concerns vanish. Consciousness is not a single mind state, but a menu of modules that are activated for particular purposes.

We cannot say therefore that our self is stable, substantial or singular, nor is it always foolproof or truthful. It is a PR agent intent on getting us through the day and shielding us from criticism, not making us sit down to explain our actions, good or bad, sensible or silly.

Mountains of the Mind

William Shakespeare
1564-1616
Although Shakespeare wrote his plays four hundred years ago, his characters seem to speak directly to us, because they express a sense of self that chimes with our modern consciousness.

In 'Hamlet', Polonius advises his son Laertes, 'To thine own self be true', but without a core self, this is an impossible loop. If there is no quintessential self to be true to, or free agent capable of finding it, Laertes becomes just like all the other characters in the play, merely playing a part, struggling to establish who he really is, manoeuvring to gain some control over his destiny. In the cast of 'Hamlet', Shakespeare seems to be showing us a series of selves in search of an owner.

There is a self to be expressed, but it is uncertain,
making itself up as it goes.

Shakespeare was steeped in Renaissance humanism, which though no longer seeing human beings as god-like, did recognise them as earthly creatures of dignity and reason. As Hamlet addresses us in his soliloquys, especially 'To be or not to be', we gain a sense of a self unfolding before us, a consciousness listening in on itself, surprised to hear thoughts that he did not know lay unspoken within him. His modern self-doubt connects us to a lost classical ideal: there is a self to be expressed, but it is uncertain, making itself up as it goes.

We might contrast Hamlet's tentative self-searching with the fragile identity of someone in a movie scene standing on a ledge, being pleaded with or talked down by a friend or police officer. Which part of the prospective suicide's mind has decided to end it all? Which part is listening to the sensible advice to climb down? Which part decides to jump or not to jump? What if the jumper had decided earlier to go and join friends in the pub instead? Such vagaries hardly suggest a self deep enough to withstand the random blast of our volatile moods.

If the self is difficult to locate in the mind, it is even harder to find in the body. In the 'Monty Python' sketch of a sword-fight between King Arthur and the Black Knight, the latter gradually loses his arms, and then his legs, until he is just a torso with a talking head. But he remains defiant, his essential 'self' undefeated. His pluck poses a question which the best philosophers cannot answer: how far can we go in lopping off body parts before 'we' disappear? If our torso is hacked off, then our brain scooped from its skull, reducing us to a disembodied neural net, where does our self go? If we are religious, what happens to our soul?

The intention in this scene is comic, but for quadriplegics who live rich and fulfilling lives, it is a serious reality. What if, instead of shedding our limbs, we strip away our senses one at a time? At what moment does our core self disappear? If we go into a coma, with our self-awareness put on hold, perhaps even obliterated, we remain in the eyes of the law a person with inviolable rights to life and care, at the very time that we cannot make these executive decisions for ourselves.

Philosophers call this line of enquiry the 'brain in a vat' scenario. Ignoring the medical complications for a moment, could our brain be removed before death, kept alive in a vat, and its thoughts read, allowing us still to communicate with others? By the reverse token, could an artificial brain with no body parts assume selfhood and the status of personhood? Many of us are already starting to have this kind of relationship with our electronic devices.

The deep self
We know that our body changes over time, but we also know that, although we lose our looks, fleetness of foot, speed of reaction and perhaps our sense of humour, we retain continuity of identity. We remain 'essentially' who we are. Even if we are stricken by dementia, our 'self' is that part of us that doesn't disappear even after everything else has been lost.

113

Mountains of the Mind

This suggests that the self, whether judged to be deep or shallow, is indivisible. In Lonely Hearts ads we list the six things we want to 'sell' about ourselves, but when we meet a potential partner in the flesh, the 'parts' that define us coalesce as a whole person. When we sign our passport, we cannot say whether it is our hand, eye or brain directing the pen. The signature appears anyway, but only as an outward symbol of who 'we' are.

Thinkers of all persuasions have proposed their own models of how the self is brought into being, rather than just 'happening'. Plato saw it in moral terms, as a battleground between desire, reason and will. Jean Piaget saw through the eyes of biology: the same developmental processes that increase our height and weight also direct our mental growth. The psychologist Abraham Maslow disagreed: our self does not automatically emerge, it has to be consciously 'actualised' by our uniquely personal endeavour to flourish as an individual.

We begin to individualise and socialise ourselves
through our interactions with other people.

Intriguing as these models are, they are metaphors and descriptions, not causes and explanations. Whichever model we choose, our journey towards selfhood starts as children, when we learn how to control our moods and temper tantrums, training our neocortex to get a grip. Then, slowly, we begin to individualise and socialise ourselves through our interactions with other people.

On one core point, all agree: the self is not fixed, but constantly on the move, with no promised perfection awaiting us at the end. In that sense, the flat mind theorists and evolutionary psychologists are right. Whatever self we adopt, we sit astride a dual nature in adulthood. Though we have the neuroplasticity to master trigonometry and send a space probe to Mars, we are also capable of tribalism, genocide and suicide. We can be very smart and very stupid in the same moment.

Given that we must have a 'deep self' as a repository for our beliefs, we might as well make it a reasonable one. We crave a narrative to hold body, mind and soul together, and a vision of the kind of future we want for ourselves. These needs are not optional extras, but are as necessary as the roof we build to keep the rain off our head, or a sacred canopy for those who believe in higher powers looking down. They make life tolerable, and give purpose to our actions.

114

Mountains of the Mind

History gives dire warnings of what follows when the self is abolished: respect for the person, civil liberties, even life itself disappears. People denied their selfhood and personhood, whether shallow or deep, real or imagined, become expendable ciphers of the state or the machine.

Self belief
Our strong cultural perception of the self, the foundation of our self belief, has its roots deep in the human past. At the start of the Western tradition, we are introduced to powerful tragic egos strutting the across the stage, heroically resisting the destiny that the fates have decreed them. These are self-proclaimed *individuals*, grandly marking themselves out from the crowd and defying what the gods throw at them.

The Eastern sensibility is closer to comedy than tragedy, the individual seen as part of the whole, accepting life's ups and downs, smiling at its absurdities. The self we possess is only temporary and mostly illusory, not destined for heaven or personal glory, but likely to be anonymously recycled, enfolded back into the ceaseless round of birth and death.

The clearly defined Western ideal of the liberal self, which John Locke declared four hundred years ago to be 'a thinking, intelligent being that has reflection', is still on full display in our novels and films. Their heroes either already know who they are, or find their 'true self' by the end of the story, without which they cannot be a 'me' in relation to 'others'. In real life, this transfers into talk of 'reinventing' ourselves, or taking on a new persona when we get tired of our old one. In practice however this is hard to do, and few of us have the psychological resources to pull it off.

It doesn't help that the way we talk about ourselves is often ambiguous. We say 'I couldn't get myself to do this' as if there are two of us. We struggle to differentiate 'my self' with 'myself'. The first is the self seen from the outside, bearing our name and giving us our voting rights; the second is who we feel we are as we look from the inside.

This confusion arises because the self is not a singular essence, but always relational, or socially realised. We present different faces to the world, and play different roles. Behind them all is our sense of 'what it feels like to be me', so personal and vague that it is unanalysable, beyond scientific investigation.

115

Mountains of the Mind

Flat mind theorists are not surprised by any of this, because in their view we are not captains of our soul anyway. Therapists belonging to the 'positive' school of psychology bubble with optimism, encouraging us to 'find ourselves', as if there is a true self waiting to be found. Existential therapists are much more cautious about the pitfalls and perils of self-making. We are forced to be free, but there are no fixed meanings to mark out our course. Our 'self' is what we establish by our choices, and a life well lived is judged by what we deem to be important in our short time in the sun. Death constantly hovers, even in the flush of youth.

There is no locatable centre where 'I' happens.

Neuroscientists pour cold water on both of these schemes, pointing out that, though we might *feel* that we have a historical 'me' that anchors us in a particular life, and an 'I' that writes new diary entries every day, it is our brain that calls the shots, and our sense of a 'self' is a fiction, little more than a neurochemical hodgepodge of distributed multiselves, with no locatable centre where 'I' happens.

They are right in the sense that, through our life, we try on new identities and try to cast off old ones. As children we learn to develop different personae for home, the playground and the classroom. If we suffer abuse or have bad childhood memories, we have the option of writing a new version of ourselves, obliterating the old one so it cannot come back to haunt us. When we make a romantic connection, we initially fall in love with our own reflection, not always progressing through hard experience to see the 'self' that our partner sees in us, who is a different person altogether.

We are not therefore proud monarchs of an inviolate kingdom called the self, because like Shakespeare's kings, we discover that our sovereignty is not absolute. As with royalty, our self is not a possession but a process, a role we play out and an act we perform, no more substantial than the escutcheons that adorn the palace walls.

Our self resides not in what we are but what we do, which is to invent ourselves constantly through custom, language and ritual. We 'are' the words we choose to frame each thought, the succession of voices in our head, the stories we fabricate to match our intentions, the faces we put on to greet the faces we meet, the reflections of what we choose to look at.

116

Mountains of the Mind

Such a teaching is not new. Buddha preached that our sense of self is what we cling to, the aggregates of our body and mind, a constant arising and subsiding of thoughts. Freud characterised the self as the uneasy facade we present to the world to mask our roiling desires down below.

Postmodernists take a slightly different approach: our sense of self is like the front page of a newspaper that gets blown away by the wind every day. We are creatures of habit and fashion, and what we see on the surface is only the show of a false self. They follow Karl Marx in portraying the self as the site of culturally specific signifying activities, while evolutionary psychologists dismiss the notion of the self as a parasitic meme in thrall to the blind replicators of the genes.

The absent executive

Flat-minders are in good company therefore when they insist that, by the time we reach adulthood, our brain has constructed so many deceptions and models of how the world works that it is the true protagonist of our drama, always on stage but never seen, quietly moulding our perception of reality to its algorithms and processes. Abstractions like the self and the mind are too shallow to resist the emotional currents and psychological distortions that overwhelm us. Against such heavy artillery, we can hardly claim to be who we think we are.

Social psychologists add their two penny worth by revealing our inability to live with uncertainty and doubt. We'd rather contradict ourselves than live in a state of cognitive dissonance. We are so desperate for integration that we block out any challenges to our fragile ego, never admitting that the pattern we've imposed on experience is randomly chosen. We invent a credible past, build a future on slender hopes, persist in our beliefs despite evidence to the contrary, ignore our own ignorance, and fool ourselves into false confidence.

We are stuck in a hallucination masterminded
by the black box inside our skull.

We may have the illusion of being in control, but ultimately we are stuck in a hallucination masterminded by the black box inside our skull. We do what our brain prompts, what our subconscious urges, and what our ego insists upon. In other words, we barely know our own thoughts, and if we have any claim to being the author of our lives, it is only in retrospect.

We do something, and then wonder why we did it, because we lack conscious access to our brain's hidden neural machinations, making us the last 'up top' to know what our brain is up to down in the bunker. As a result, we operate under several delusions: we perceive accurately, process information logically, act rationally, form reasonable judgments, have a stable sense of self, can be sure about things we are largely ignorant of, and always know what is good for us.

We cling to these delusions because we are profoundly disconcerted by the idea of subsystems in our brain doing our thinking for us, functioning without central control and perhaps even being totally random. We convince ourselves that we are the chief executive of our own minding. Increasingly however philosophers, psychologists, brain researchers and cultural critics have eroded our confidence that we are fully in charge, and the humanist illusion that we know our own minds has been shattered.

There are so many unseen forces at work that only our unconscious is real, or what neuroscientists have relabelled our default network. Our brain is a bottom-up confection of tricks, controlling us psychologically as surely as our sensitivity to pain controls us physically. New (as in later-evolved) top-down cortical software is awkwardly bolted onto old limbic hardware, full of repair patches, leaving us with not a purpose-built latest-edition executive operator, but a hairless primate with delusions of grandeur and a mind too big for its boots.

The idea of the sovereign self cannot however be entirely jettisoned. When we choose our politicians or friends, the 'character question' is usually uppermost in our minds. How can we trust what they say if there is no core self as bearer of truth, honesty and responsibility? Our estimation of maturity in those we claim to 'know' well depends on whether we feel they 'know' themselves, perhaps never fully, but enough to persuade us that they are prepared to change in the light of new experience, not forgetting of course that they are constantly making the same judgment of us.

Even Buddhist monks, who spend long years trying to efface their 'selves' by 'no mind' meditation, remain recognisable, quirky and individual personalities, not just 'bundles of perceptions'. The self is what integrates this bundle, greater than the sum of its parts. Without its executive authority we could not be put on trial for

118

our actions, or sign a legal document as the person bearing our name and wearing our face.

Even evolutionary psychologists are hoist by their own petard. If the mind is a potpourri of tried and tested 'gadgets' that solve separate problems for us, the self is also evolution's hard-won gift to us, without which we are blind automata, not sighted individuals able to contemplate such thoughts as these, or to expose our 'selves' to scrutiny.

The progress trap

If we do lack a central executive in our brain, this has deep consequences for our species. The human cognitive revolution happened over thousands of generations, with untold contributory factors, and as far as we know, no other species has matched our progress.

But such planetary domination is a double-edged sword. It might have led us into the progress trap. Traits that served us well in our evolutionary childhood, such as gorging on rare treats of fat and sugar when we could get them, and fearing all non-kin, are now burdens to us, leading to modern epidemics of drug abuse, obesity, depression and anxiety, as well as fuelling populist politics.

Our brain evolved to get us safely through to the next day, with no long-term goal in sight. It had no way of seeing where it was going, or second-guessing the law of unintended consequences. Similarly, our serendipitous social organisation provided no forums for appraising the long-term impact of each technological leap forward as it appeared. As a consequence, we face the spectres of nuclear Armageddon, planetary combustion, polluted oceans, superbugs and machine minds that can outwit their programmers.

Something of a myth prevails that our hunter-gatherer ancestors were careful guardians of their environment. Piles of fossil bones of bison and auroch at the foot of cliffs suggest otherwise. Our forebears did not take just what they needed, but drove whole herds to destruction, taking species to the edge of extinction, just as today the craving for shark fin soup in some parts of the world is wiping out shark populations ocean-wide.

From the outset, and even now, we have not been wise stewards of natural resources, but greedy and thoughtless. Time is almost up for the orangutan, panda,

119

tiger, lemur and pangolin, their forest homes chopped down to make way for cattle farming or palm oil plantations.

This encroachment on nature, on which the health of all life on earth depends, has been going on since the agricultural revolution of ten thousand years ago. After an eternity of hunter-gathering, it seemed an inevitable and obvious progress to tame some oxen, use them to till the soil to grow domesticated crops, store the grain in a specially built settlement, and raise more children as a result.

What our ancestors could not foresee in this profound change of lifestyle was a less varied diet, greater exposure to disease, more mouths to feed, vulnerability to drought, back-breaking work in the fields, the loss of long leisurely afternoons, and eventual subservience to a priestly caste who demanded endless quantities of surplus grain to sustain their idleness, feed their mighty armies and build huge monuments to their gods, thus cementing their power and privilege over the masses.

We innovate and invent without the slightest idea
where our ingenuity is taking us.

Some social commentators see a parallel in the present digital revolution: we innovate and invent without the slightest idea where our ingenuity is taking us. We see only quantity of goods, not quality of life, speed of gadgetry, not depth of communication. In our drive for efficiency we sacrifice job satisfaction and meaning. Meanwhile the very institutions that are meant to save us, such as our parliaments, schools, law courts, hospitals and police, seem overwhelmed by inexhaustible demand, exploding data and declining trust.

Easter Island
If the secular Myth of Progress is squarely in the sights of flat-mind theorists, the Delusion of Religion is even more so. Easter Island is frequently put forward as a prime example of religious superstition triumphing over common sense, showing how belief in local gods can become a catastrophic tyranny.

The conventional explanation for what happened on this small island in the Pacific is that, between 1400 and 1650, the native population became so obsessed with erecting *moai* or huge stone statues of giant heads that they chopped down large numbers of trees on the island to manoeuvre them, thereby initiating an ecological disaster. As they fought fiercely to be the ones to cut down the last tree, they were also precipitating their own extinction.

When the first Europeans arrived in 1722, they found many of the statues toppled, though fifty have been re-erected in modern times, if only for the tourist trade. They stand as gaunt reminders of collective delusion, mass stupidity and ideological obsession. Scholars cannot agree whether the megaliths are monuments to local deities, chieftains and ancestors, or potent symbols of human folly. All we can be sure of is that they were not erected by gods. Thor Heyerdahl showed in the 1940's how simple mechanics with elementary tools and lots of manpower can account for their erection.

There is however a much more plausible explanation for what happened to the megalith culture on Easter Island that is a testament to human adaptability, not religious ideology. Climate change had already reduced the number of trees on the island when the first white colonisers arrived, and there was evidence that the indigenous inhabitants had shown great resilience in developing alternative methods of agriculture in their now treeless island.

They were far from being reduced to starvation, or living as 'savages'. Their toppling of the statues was probably brought on by the gradual decline of their culture, precipitated by slaving raids, introduced diseases, plagues of rats and theft of their land. Superstitious idolatry was the last thing on their mind.

The fate of the Easter Islanders nevertheless symbolises what for many thinkers down the ages has been the 'problem' with religion: it is a grand illusion which holds us in thrall, a social toxin, an unresolved neurosis, wish fulfilment, a cry of the oppressed, an unsatisfied longing for the mother, a sublimated fear of the father, a comfort blanket for when troubles beset us, a mask for our prejudices.

Any kind of religious creed is a 'disease of the intellect'.

These armchair theorists about religion try to consign it to the childhood of the human race by 'explaining' it as tricks of our perceptual system, vulnerability to magic, an invasive parasite in our brain, or a 'God spot' somewhere between our ears. It might be a drug-induced dream, primitive nature worship, our eternal craving for solace, or our need for group solidarity. Ralph Waldo Emerson cut to the chase by describing any kind of religious creed as a 'disease of the intellect'.

Evolutionary theorists are divided over whether religion enhanced survival prospects by favouring 'procreative' genes, or wasted vital resources that could have been put to better use. The difficulty with the latter argument is that, if religion is a bad hangover of genes that should have been weeded out, why do they still flourish?

These 'origins' of religion do not account for the fact that some belief systems such as Buddhism, Marxism, existentialism and market capitalism ask for no belief in God at all, but are firmly grounded in the material world. Nor is the concept of God a childish fiction: most theologies are as full of sophisticated and subtle reasoning as anything science can offer.

Easter Island
The moai of Easter Island in the Pacific still stand as stark reminders of the danger of allowing an idea to become a destructive ideology. Or is there a more rational explanation?

Nor does history show that replacing God with the human intellect, or worshipping our own ingenuity, has provided a surer route to peace, justice, happiness or harmony. If we are to thrive beyond the predicted mass extinction of the Anthropocene, our species needs an ethical revolution, or changing of hearts and minds, which reason and science alone will not be able to bring about.

Religion nevertheless is attacked as the quintessence of flat-mindedness, feeding off several evolutionary gremlins in our brain: our addiction to seeing faces in clouds, fear of predation, craving for protection, loyalty to the group, desire to expose cheats, miscalculation of risk, misattribution of causes, superstition about the evil eye, hankering for meaning at the expense of reason, putting belief before fact, self-deception, ancestral guilt at having to kill to stay alive, and our childlike wish for something to be true even when we know deep down it cannot be.

These failings are not however unique to religious believers. They are human foibles that expose a much more ancient conflict between thought and feeling, or analysis and intuition, by no means confined to places of worship. We are just as likely to encounter them in the debating chamber, the science laboratory and internet chat rooms.

Terrible things have been done in the name of religion, but so have they in the name of just about every other cause that humans espouse. Religion has greater potential to inspire togetherness and healing than division and aggression. Violence is human, not divine.

Born superstitious
It is religion nevertheless that evolutionary psychologists have in their sights when they point out that we are born superstitious, prone to believing in things with no evidence for doing so, indeed believing even more fervently when evidence is denied. On the surface for instance, and taken literally, the Biblical account of Abraham's readiness to sacrifice his son on the altar is an act of gross superstition, irrationality and barbarity.

Religious language however works through symbol and paradox, not amenable to rational binary deconstruction. Abraham and Isaac are only partly recognisable as modern characters gifted with free will and self-consciousness. Neither assumes he has a choice: their God has spoken. What strikes us is not their individuality or existential angst, but their obedience and trust.

Abraham's readiness to sacrifice that which was most precious to him was testimony to the strength of his faith. Furthermore, it was rewarded. God accepted an animal in place of a child. Human sacrifice was common in ancient times, so on one level, the story of Abraham and Isaac is an allegory about our progression as a species from superstition to reason, from external ritual to inner vision, from bowing down before graven images to understanding God as both an immanent and transcendent spirit.

Such an intellectual leap was a vital precursor to our modern understanding of the forces that hold our minds together, and the laws that underpin the revolutions of the stars. The story of Abraham and Isaac foreshadows our progress in scientific knowledge, moving away from authority, superstition and certainty towards enquiry, abstraction and scepticism about the 'common sense view of the world'. Without these, the hidden laws that govern nature would have remained a mystery to us, because the truth lies beyond what appears to our senses.

Religion and science are often set against each other, but they both emanate from 'belief' modules that evolved around the time our brain doubled in size on the African savannah two hundred thousand years ago. Our mind ever since has struggled to integrate them, seeking a lost sense of oneness with our surroundings and each other. We have evolved to crave answers, whether as a sense of belonging 'in here', or an understanding of how everything fits together 'out there'. Our imagination wants to trace every event to its cause, while also reading meaning into everything we see. This explains why we can study theology without being religious: knowledge *about* God is not the same as knowledge *of* God.

Some see modern eco-spirituality as the product of this psychic double-act. It has all the trappings of a religion which may yet save us from our own ambition: a deep sense of connection to Mother Earth, a common sense of purpose, a call to atone for the guilt of ravishing our planetary paradise, anxiety over the Armageddon we are storing up, and a call to make sacrifices in the present to bring about a better future.

The new science
The modern scientific quest in the West began with Thales in Ancient Greece. He saw the world as a combination of inert matter and moving spirits, though other than speculating imaginatively, he explored neither matter nor spirit in any depth. Five hundred years later, on its adoption in the West, Christianity largely ignored intellectual enquiry about matter, substituting God as the Prime Mover. The salvation of the eternal soul eclipsed curiosity about the ephemeral world.

By the Middle Ages however, St Francis of Assisi was spending as much time using his earthly senses to notice birds and flowers as he was poring over the Bible for spiritual enlightenment. 'Scholastic' churchmen such as Roger Bacon and Duns Scotus began to apply their considerable intellects to the scope of reason, largely with the approval of the Church. They are often accused of fretting too much about logic, but their musing laid the foundation for scientific method.

Mountains of the Mind

St Thomas Aquinas saw how faith and reason might start to pull in different directions, so he laboured to integrate them through the notion of 'natural law', reconciling the observed facts of physics and biology with the idea of divine creation. This posits that as both faith and reason emanate from God, the two cannot be in conflict.

Aquinas's attempted synthesis makes a strong case for attributing our present prowess in science, democracy and the rule of law as much to what Judaic, Christian and Islamic scholars taught as to Enlightenment Reason. Rationalists trace the rise of the modern mind back to the seventeenth century scientific revolution, but there is an unbroken thread of rational enquiry and scholarship stretching back to ancient times. Both rationalism and empiricism grew out of a core religious teaching that the world is ordered and comprehensible. Also, rationalism and empiricism were able to flourish only because society was held together by mutual bonds and shared values that owe more to faith than to reason.

It is too simplistic therefore to say that Christianity blocked the progress of science for fifteen hundred years, or that religion is an atavistic throw-back. From the earliest days, believers and sceptics were in constant dispute, creating a moral and intellectual climate that enabled science to flourish. Where there can be differences of opinion, there can be new adventures in thought. Not every heretic was burnt at the stake, and when they were, the charges were usually motivated by tribal passions, not intellectual arguments. Bigotry and envy are human failings, not solely religious in their motivation.

Despite their differences, believers and sceptics adhered to a common conviction: the world is a cosmos, not a chaos. Reason is our birthright, knowledge is attainable, and truth is a goal worth pursuing. Our modern scientific understanding is a direct descendant and complement of the Judaeo-Christian tradition, not a rejection or contradiction of it. Both are natural expressions of the Western mind, a joint legacy of our religious culture and secular history.

Just as over two thousand years of Confucianism have seeped into the Chinese mind, so has Christian culture pervaded the Western mindset. Capitalism is often presented as secular self-interest, but at its heart is the language of morality, which has biblical roots: a fair day's pay for a fair day's work, plain dealing, 'clean' money, good character, honest profits, justified rewards, and earned holidays enjoyed with a clear conscience.

Mountains of the Mind

The stories we lap up in our novels and on our cinema screens are soused in penance, steeped in retribution and marinaded in redemption. An evil pollutes the body politic, a good person arises to cleanse it, demons are exorcised, the culprits are hounded down, restoration is made and the status quo restored.

We are inheritors of a world that is at once sacred and profane.

This lingering legacy suggests that there has been no clean break with our Christian past, nor can there be, because although we cannot say that the Christian 'story' invented morality, it closely shadows our moral progress as a species. Altruism was a winning strategy long before a lawgiver god arrived on the scene, and if God did not descend from the clouds, he was already in our dreams. We are embodied souls, convinced of our agency. We are bound together morally, inheritors of a world that is at once sacred and profane.

The sixteenth century statesman, counsellor and later to be made saint Thomas More encapsulates the marriage of faith and reason. He was a lawyer, convinced that reason can complement revealed truth, but also a devout Christian, prepared to die for a principle. His religious beliefs rooted him in the past, but his forensic intellect foreshadowed the scientific revolution that was about to happen.

By the seventeenth century, the 'new science' had increasingly squeezed faith into a tight corner. After centuries of believing in witches, hobgoblins and demons, more rational explanations were being sought. Although Isaac Newton dabbled in religious speculation, his theories of light and gravity were pure feats of reason.

And yet in a strange way modern science has come full circle. In an unexpected coming together of the religious and the scientific quests for truth, quantum theory reminds us that we are simultaneously players and spectators, participants and observers. On the one hand we are animists, believing nature is alive with spirits, on the other we are materialists, cutting nature at the joints to see how it works.

We are natural dualists, convinced there is a reality beyond what we see. We are also determined monists, desperate to find a theory of everything that binds all phenomena together. If the first question our ancestors asked was 'Where does the spirit go when it dies?', the second was 'What is the world made of?'

Mountains of the Mind

In that sense religion and science, as well as art, are feats of the imagination, or bold stories aimed at addressing our ultimate concerns. They answer our emotional need for belonging, but they are also triumphs of the intellect, seeking rational answers to profound questions about unseen worlds.

We see this drama played out most clearly in the earliest cave paintings, cosmologies, burial rites and religious visions. The plot might have begun with magic, sorcery, witchcraft and divination, but these were necessary preliminaries to alchemy and all our subsequent attempts to control nature, not to mention our personal destiny. We might think we are nearing the final revelation, but we have merely replaced one form of oracle with another.

Defining religion

Religion is a catch-all label for a wide range of practices and beliefs that evolved over tens of thousands of years, not a single mass delusion that entered the human story at a fixed moment. There are so many 'explanations' of religion's origins, causes and varieties that pontificating about them has been likened to three blind men placed beside different parts of an elephant. When asked what is before them, the first describes a sinuous trunk, the second a bristly hide, the third a stiff tail. None of them sees or understands the whole animal.

Evolutionists cannot account for religion as a biological adaptation, as it is too expensive, with no obvious gain. Cognitivists see it as a hijacking of neural processes intended to explain mundane causes, not miraculous interventions. Sociologists suggest that, rather than dropping down from some sacred realm, religion had secular origins, as a bonding mechanism to ensure social cohesion and solidarity through ritual and culture.

Psychologists hazard a guess that, given our tendency to find what we seek, trusting in a greater force can provide an anchor in a storm, and consolation for underserved suffering. The faithful insist that the world is not all there is: the truth is out there, for those who know where and how to seek.

The problem all these blind men face in classifying religion is that not all religions are founded on supernatural creation myths, belief in an afterlife, the teaching of a semi-divine founder, faith in a particular divinity, or the performance of sacred rites. Religion cannot therefore be shredded down to a few definitions which can be rationally dismantled one by one.

127

Mountains of the Mind

This means there is no magic bullet of description, let alone explanation. Do we define 'religion' as attending a religious site, worshipping ancestors, believing in a sacred text, sensing a divine presence, trusting to a personal saviour, adhering to a particular moral code, practising mindfulness, having an out of body experience, appeasing the spirits of the forest? Only a few of these apply to Christianity, and even fewer to Buddhism.

Nor can scholars agree on the purposes and functions of religion. Is it to console the masses, reward goodness, strengthen mutual obligations, ensure social stability, enforce taboos, guarantee salvation, justify the ways of God to man? Why do people *believe*, and more importantly, why do they give credence to these *particular* beliefs?

Amid this flurry of unanswered questions, there is one feature common to all the great world religions: the quest for goodness, justice and truth, in a world where these things are in short supply. These are works of the moral imagination, deriving from our social nature, for which a materialist explanation provides no rationale or model. No amount of fact and information translates into value and inspiration.

Science lays a strong claim to seeing the whole elephant, but only by narrowing its scope. There is only one theory of gravity, not a Russian, Chinese or American version. A stone falls to earth in the same way, whichever passport it holds. Religion is not like this. As on Easter Island, it always has a local name, worshipping its own idea of the elephant. The theory of gravity is universal, but no-one bows down before a generalised theory of religion.

Despite their local origins, some religions have shown universal missionary potential. Abraham was the leader of a local tribe intent on marking out its identity from neighbouring tribes, by bloodshed if necessary, going on to found the faith of the Jewish people. Christianity and Islam are evangelical in outlook, able to plant their flags far from home, but Hinduism is tied to India, its country of origin.

It is a religion's teaching that marks it out from its neighbours and rivals. Taoism is barely a faith at all, more a set of self-help principles than a religion, asking of us only that we see that there is nothing beyond the pleasure of what we are doing right now. Buddhism and Sikhism are comfortable with the idea that there are many pathways to enlightenment or God.

Mountains of the Mind

The idea of being specially chosen is particularly divisive.

This is a wise approach, because those who try to nail their dogma to the deck end up splintering into schisms, sects and cults at the first sign of a doctrinal dispute. The idea of being specially chosen is particularly divisive, because it automatically excludes everyone else.

As our ancestors established farming and started to build the first cities, religion had to become organised. This meant superimposing local gods on pre-existing intuitions about how the world works, reinforced by priestly teaching. Religion in this sense is not a 'designed' product of biology or culture, but an evolved social practice that, like language and mathematics, piggybacks on brain operations and intuitions evolved in very different times for very different purposes.

This makes for difficulties in a brain that evolved simply to get us through the day. On the face of them, 'It is raining today', 'Two plus two equals four' and 'God made the world' sound like simple claims about reality, but our brain has to process them in radically different ways. Similarly, our brain must be able to play different language games. 'Coal *is* black' and 'God *is* love' share a common grammatical form, but in our brain, that little word *is* requires very different semantic interpretation.

Religion and morality

Some insist that religious injunctions bind us together morally, others that we are better off without them. Two-year-olds are born with moral intuitions. They exhibit a strong sense of right, wrong and fairness long before they are told *why* they should be good, though parents are equally aware of the need to mould these instincts into shape.

*No known human society has evolved
without some form of religion.*

Humanists rightly point out that modern secular societies are perfectly capable of practising morality without shamans, priests and imams to preach to us and at us. At best, say its critics, religion gives us bad reasons for doing good things, so we might as well ditch the religion, and do the good things anyway.

We will never know however whether secular society is capable of generating moral harmony from scratch, because while religion is written deep in the human story, secularism is barely a couple of centuries old, and limited to relatively few countries. No known human society has evolved without some form of religion.

On the other hand, evolutionary psychologists point out that religious 'commandments' merely piggy-back on the social contract of self-evident truths that our ancestors thrashed out on the African savannah: treat others as we ourselves wish to be treated, or as game theorists would have it, avoid zero-sum confrontations. A society of psychopaths could not survive beyond the first generation.

What we find across all cultures is an endless variety of solutions to the challenges of human flourishing: a balance of rights and responsibilities, mutual safeguards, common rights, shared goods, protections of the vulnerable and defences against the greedy. We might no longer live in Eden, and will never create an egalitarian utopia, but our laws and ethics do their best to guarantee the birthright that, in an ideal world, we are all entitled to.

Another core intuition is our sense of agency. Perhaps our ancestors entertained several theories of what causes a tree to sway in the wind. It might be the tree god expressing displeasure, or a sign of an approaching storm. African tribes are often held up as examples of 'primitive' believers, but they are as rational as the rest of us, offering a dual explanation for why a branch might fall and kill someone.

They know there are physical causes, such as trees getting old and breaking under the strain. But they also want to know why this particular branch fell at this particular moment, killing someone who matters to them. This second question is much harder to answer, with no help forthcoming from evolutionary strategists or game theorists.

Our ancestors were not stupidly superstitious. They knew that a shadow in the grass is not the juju man stalking them, but a warning that a predator is about to pounce. Such thinking is not primitive, but the foundation of our scientific search for causes and effects, to which we owe our technical mastery of the world.

Nevertheless, in the nineteenth century there was enthusiasm for the idea that religion has evolved through animist, polytheistic and monotheistic stages. This

130

Mountains of the Mind

theory was easily converted into an ideology for propping up white imperialism: believers in one God are intellectually and morally superior to idolatrous infidels and fetish-worshipping savages.

But the theory is deeply flawed. Our Western concept of a superior God has developed very slowly from humble beginnings. First there were earth gods, mostly pregnant women with obvious sexual organs, more fertility symbols than deities. Then there were sky gods, looking largely like grisly old white men. From a pantheon of many gods presided over by One God to Rule Them All (henotheism), who still looked like granddad, emerged a non-human 'One' (monotheism), so remote and abstract that it was a sin to mention his name or make an image of him.

James G Frazer
1854-1941
Frazer strongly believed that religion progressed from primitive belief to scientific rationality, a view now challenged by anthropologists and evolutionists. All forms of belief are simultaneously present in all cultures.

In addition, anthropologists have shown that all forms of religion are present at all times in all cultures. When we look at our modern beliefs honestly, we realise we are still as superstitious as ever, occasionally sneaking a look at our horoscope. Seen in this light, 'primitive' belief systems are not just 'God of the gaps' guesses, but rational attempts to explain phenomena that have not yet been understood.

Mountains of the Mind

Primitive or evolved, religion draws much fire from flat mind theorists, militant atheists and impartial sceptics for its failings. Like all things human, it can provide solace, inspire love or evoke fear in equal measure, which means it has many sins to atone for, especially hypocrisy. Paedophile priests have abused their positions of trust, and the Church has consistently put its own reputation before the shattered lives of their victims. Some conservatives and evangelicals readily espouse obnoxious far-right ideologies merely to further their own anti-abortion or anti-gay prejudices.

Religion can be a whited sepulchre, paralysing through reproof, cursing through voodoo or controlling through the Evil Eye. It can make people hate themselves, feeling eternally burdened, having to atone for imaginary crimes, living a life of guilt for sins they never committed. It can set up scapegoats, victimising vulnerable groups to keep them trapped in the faith.

Religion can force a closing of the mind, bolstered by the prescribing of dogmas, the declaring of fatwahs and the launching of holy crusades. These create sycophants who desecrate each other's temples, churches and shrines, claiming exclusive revelation and absolute knowledge, unable to tolerate difference in their midst or at their borders. This tribalism contrasts strongly with scientists who neither blow up rival laboratories nor kill each other for their beliefs.

Born spiritual
For every martyr or jihadist however who is prepared to sacrifice others in the name of their god, there are countless believers who selflessly sacrifice themselves, devoting their resources, time and energy to making the world a better place, or alleviating the suffering of others. What they exhibit is not religious zeal or doctrinal purity focused on the next life, but spirituality and compassion grounded in this life.

Spirituality offers wide secular benefits too, without signing up to the articles of a particular faith. Declining numbers profess a religious faith, but many practise a religion-less form of spirituality, a long way from religiosity, which is uncritical enslavement to a particular creed. Those who pronounce themselves atheists can continue to enjoy the artistic and cultural legacy of faith and spirituality, such as sacred architecture, holy music, religious painting and devotional literature.

Mountains of the Mind

Spirituality is not concerned with inquisitions and indulgences, but renewal and insight. It is a way of seeing the world sacramentally, not instrumentally. This is not to forego rational integrity, bow down before relics, recite mumbo jumbo or buy into New Age mysticism. It is to sustain a sense that nature and the life within it is sacred, not profane, something to be stewarded, not trashed.

Passion to save the planet has become the new 'green' spirituality.

This practical and humane approach is encapsulated in the teaching of the Quakers, whose only dogma is to improve human flourishing, not to dispute the wording of a creed. We see this broader spirituality manifesting itself in a growing understanding that the oceans, forests and the species they support are not mere resources, but a delicate ecosystem of which we are a part. For many young people, their passion to save the planet has become the new 'green' spirituality.

And yet admitting to 'being spiritual' remains awkward because, following the decline of traditional religion and belief systems, we struggle to find a language to express our spiritual affinity with each other and the living world, not to mention what we see and hear when we explore our own experience.

Words such as prayer, praise, soul, meditation, devotion, surrender, worship, service, transcendence, even love in its broader sense of fellowship, now form a forgotten language, or lost way of seeing the world, no longer coming easily to our lips. In his poem 'Church Going', Philip Larkin bemoans not only the fact that the churches are emptying, but also that we have no unifying rituals to put in their place. No-one as yet worships at the altar of technology, bows down before a book of logic, or consults the spiral helix for solace in the face of life's tribulations.

Faith instinct
Holy and sacramental objects have been found in human burial sites going back at least a hundred and fifty thousand years, so we have served a very long religious apprenticeship, suggesting that we are 'naturally' religious, or that we inherit a 'faith instinct'.

According to evodevo theorists and flat-minders, we should have out-evolved this by now. Faith is superstitious, and should be giving way to a scientific mindset, which is the opposite of instinctual, overwritten and cultivated by hard

133

intellectual effort. Just as we come to understand that our biological father is not omnipotent, so we must come to accept that there is no 'big daddy in the sky'. The authority of the father figure is a superstition that we must grow out of, and replace with a rational worldview.

Religious faith however, just like any other artefact of the human mind, also evolves. There is no doubt that its back story includes human sacrifice, infanticide and cannibalism, and even the Old Testament is replete with genocides, murders and betrayals. In this sense, religion has undeniably been used as a pretext to get good people to do bad things, but it is facile to blame all the moral evils of history on religion. The flaw lies much deeper, in the human heart. When we look at incidents of militaristic religious violence in the name of some heavenly cause, there is always a worldly potentate behind it, using the idea of a wrathful god to foment tribal enmity, not the brotherhood of man.

The Evil Eye
The sense of being watched, like all superstitions, is hard to shake off. In Voodoo, the Evil Eye is a curse. In Christianity, it is the Inquisition reading our every thought. In Islam, it is Fatima watching over us for our protection. In the street, it is the surveillance camera, from which no secrets are hid.

The New Testament was meant to set up a new covenant, but we have since seen the stoning of sinners, torturing of heretics, burning of martyrs, drowning of witches and honour killings, all to protect the purity of the faith, though these acts of violence are often more motivated by secular xenophobia than religious zeal.

For these reasons and many besides, evodevo thinkers insist that we still carry the heavy evolutionary burden of being superstitious 'automatic believers', our pre-scientific mind clouding our reason and swaying our perception: that lucky charm round our neck protects us because we *believe* it will. We are 'instinctive god-makers', attributing agency where none actually exists: that thunderclap is our tribal deity expressing displeasure with us. We are 'natural religionists', suckers for fairy tales and just-so stories: that charismatic preacher is our Messiah. Like the crowd in the film 'Life of Brian', we are so desperate for deliverance that the more strongly Brian denies his divinity, the more fervently we worship him.

These charges set up a series of puzzles however. If the idea of a presiding spirit in nature, or God, is as intrinsic as knowing our 'up' from our 'down', buried deep in our DNA, why is one a toy we must put away, while the other is the sign of sanity? If our desire for emotional communion is as strong as our craving for rational sense, who is to say which is our better guide through the human journey of birth, death and suffering? If religion is merely superstition, fear of the unknown, 'licensed insanity' or bad science, why do so many bold, intelligent and rational people continue to profess a religious faith?

The answer is complicated by the fact that religion, like any other human institution, has two faces. It can be used as an instrument of repression or liberation, to cover up injustice or to expose it, to worship false idols or to set the mind free. Paradoxically, in tandem with reason, a faculty it has nurtured more than repressed, it has played its own role in warning us not to trust those who claim that God is on their side, or that they possess infallible knowledge.

Despite the attacks by its critics, on balance religion has taken us more steps forward than backward, and it is certainly not going away. Rather than being deselected from the gene pool of human mind-worlds, it is showing remarkable staying power across the world, not as bigotry, indoctrination or superstition, but as a spiritual discipline, and the lifeblood of a community.

There is another unresolved conundrum in evodevo and flat mind logic. If we are hardwired for spiritual experience, religion must once have possessed important survival value. If religion kept the group together on the African savannah, or helped us bear the burden of existence, it still has the capacity to do so now, perhaps in a new form.

Evolutionary biologists like to point out the extent to which we are still the playthings of our primate sex drive. By the same token, if our spiritual 'drive' was a powerful motivator in the childhood of our species, we need to allow that it too still runs like a golden thread through our cognition and understanding.

Mountains of the Mind

Also, speculation about our ancestral beliefs can point in either direction. We can argue for instance that we evolved as meaning-seekers long before we became explanation-givers. Myth, ritual, poetry, song and dance preceded science by many millennia. We were participants in life's mystery long before we were its spectators, and to this day our choices are governed as much by moral as natural laws.

Spirituality grows not on a private ladder to salvation,
but in the public spaces between us.

Even with our expanded neocortex, we are as intent on deciding whether life is worth living as on fathoming how things work, because the mind has purposes and needs other than explanation and investigation. For most believers, the argument is not about whether God exists, looking vertically to the sky for an answer. More important is the horizontal plane, where spirituality grows not on a private ladder to salvation, but in the public spaces between us.

The common feature of religions throughout history has not necessarily been the idolisation of some remote transcendent deity, but the desire to comprehend the unseen order behind everything. This is of course also the prime goal of scientists, but they did not invent curiosity, reason and the search for meaning: they inherited them from the founders of the world's great faiths and belief systems, which is why modern scientists are increasingly unafraid to sound notes of wonder, mystery and the unity of everything in their writings.

Darwinism grew from what the Book of Genesis leaves unexplained, evolutionary psychology is a continuation of the thoughts of the Buddha under the bodhi tree, and sociology, economics and politics are continuations of the Confucian search for 'the mandate of heaven', or what makes for a harmonious society.

Religion and science

Religion means 'that which binds', and its critics are right to attack religion when it privileges tribal thinking over intellectual enquiry. Faith becomes anti-intellectual when it claims absolute knowledge by elevating dogma over fact, such as denying the truth of evolutionary theory, or the efficacy of vaccines. Faith as

136

honest doubt however is the driver of progress in both science and religion. If this were not so, our knowledge could not advance.

We believe, but need help with our unbelief.

'Believing in' quantum theory demands as extraordinary a suspension of belief as expressing faith in the idea of a personal God, albeit activating different circuits in our brain. Both require trust in counterintuitive truth and ability to embrace abstract reality. To that extent, we are all like the father in the Bible story, witnessing the miraculous recovery of his son from illness, believing but needing help with his unbelief. This cuts both ways. For both the scientist and the spiritual seeker, there is always something new to discover, and always the possibility that others know something we don't.

Some scholars bemoan the day when the God of Abraham triumphed over the God of the Philosophers, the dark spell of Jerusalem dimming the light of the reason of Athens for nearly two thousand years. This is however too glib an account of the history of ideas in the West. As we discussed earlier, as well as using reason to justify dogma, theologians also promoted the application of logic to human thought processes through the so-called 'Dark Ages', keeping alive the spirit of Aristotle until the intellectual climate was right for modern science to blossom. The monastic minds that had been sharply trained to dispute the finer points of Bible verses were well placed to debate the niceties and nuances of material causes.

Christian teaching was however for too long over-concerned with giving proximate explanations of which direction to face while praying, rather than seeking ultimate explanations of how matter behaves, not to mention offering practical measures for relieving suffering in this world. It is hard for us to understand from our rational post-religious vantage point how appeals to the supernatural suppressed the search for natural causes for so many centuries, or deflected attention away from earthly explanations to heavenly aspirations.

Religion's opponents criticise the way religious leaders have presumed to pronounce on all things animal, vegetable and mineral. Clerical insistence on divine authority coupled with lack of curiosity about the physical world has been a block to progress, because religion on its own is ill-equipped and too other-worldly

137

to solve real-life technological and environmental challenges. It is too local and divisive, setting one truth-system against another. Only the universality of science guarantees clean water, life-saving medicines and practical solutions for all. History teaches that highly religious societies have not been as able as secular ones to raise the average wealth and living standards of all their citizens.

Religion acts like a cloak over the intellect, but even when this cloak is removed, a scientific understanding of the world does not automatically pop into our mind. Thinking according to scientific method is a demanding cognitive feat, the accumulation of centuries of mental acrobatics, activating a different 'belief system' altogether.

Then, once we absorb its facts and procedures, we have to take on trust its assurances that there is a world of molecules, particles and quantum waves emanating from the Big Bang. They power the internet and our mobile phones, even though we can't see them. In the natural world, these facts offer us our best mechanical explanation of how things work, more reliable than anything faith can offer.

This dependable way of taking nature to pieces does not render religion or spirituality redundant, because the personal realm is no less easy to navigate, making very different demands on our cognitive and emotional capacities. While science satisfies our intellectual curiosity, religion addresses our ultimate concerns. Where science gives us the meaning of molecules, religion gives us the meaning of existence. To be fully a person in the world, we need to nourish both forms of enquiry.

Ways of knowing

Our 'knowing' is provisional in both realms, though our 'believing' operates differently. Once science has been explained to us, and its findings laid out rationally, it is no longer appropriate to say we 'believe in' it. Either we accept it, and see its truth, or we don't.

The personal and interpersonal realms are not like this at all. They call on faith, which is needed when we can't be sure of an outcome, or don't have a theory which explains why everything doesn't always work out as we want or expect. We have to live with anxiety and loneliness, we crave meaning, and we spend every day in the shadow of death, even as a child.

Mountains of the Mind

Learning to be a person in the world is a hard apprenticeship.

So whereas there is no need to 'believe in' electricity, we do find ourselves 'believing in' each other, because human life always carries the heavy weight of uncertainty. Tomorrow might bring unexpected joy or angst. A stranger might save our life, or a friend betray us. We might become seriously ill, or a loved one might die. Learning science at school is hard, perhaps even unnatural to our way of thinking, but learning to be a person in the world is an even harder apprenticeship.

Religion and science are both products of the human brain, sharing many features and rituals which direct the human quest. They are driven by a natural tendency to see faces in the embers of a fire, an intuitive motivation to find out how things work, an urgent need to connect with the natural world, a deep desire to feel part of the flow of life.

Nevertheless, there is one sense in which the scientific worldview has an edge over the religious mindset, and that is in its sourcing of information. It relies far more on empirical enquiry than divine revelation, which means that, though it has many blind spots, it is faster than religion to acknowledge and correct them. Not only can it go back to check on its sources, it can change its mind when the facts change. Religion can't do this, or at least not in the same way.

Religion is good for addressing some of our urges to know and understand, science for others. Often they overlap, integrating thought and feeling, but the key is to grasp how each speaks to a different spiritual or intellectual capacity of mind. Science is a much more recent way of knowing, but this does not mean that it must call into doubt or render obsolete all the knowledge and experience that went before it, nor does it need to.

Religion, philosophy and science have all had their heroes, their ideas changing how we appreciate life, comprehend reality and understand nature. What we need is a new generation of visionaries, thinkers and innovators, practising an integrated faith based not on local differences but on global stewardship of the Earth, better informed reasoning, longer term planning and more humane technology. We need new commandments for the twenty first century and beyond, teaching us how to care for our planet, live with our differences, and protect the human essence from the encroachment of the machine.

139

It doesn't help therefore to bundle spirituality, faith, superstition and religion together and pit them against science, reason, scepticism and progress. Each gives us a different kind of truth, one about people, purposes and suffering, the other about things, processes and substances. Not all religious believers hand over their rationality to a supernatural intelligence. Like scientists, they probe the 'big' questions, and as the gaps in our knowledge narrow, often the two complementary worldviews draw closer in their answers.

On the African savannah, understanding other minds and second-guessing an uncertain future mattered more than putting nature on the rack to determine cause and effect. Long before they needed to calculate formulae for how things work, our ancestors needed to plumb the depths of other minds, and establish the complex rules of peaceful coexistence.

This means that spirituality, faith and religion, despite dismissal by humanists, atheists and rationalists, will never become obsolete, because although reason is always eager to advance, the roots of human nature remain firmly in place, not holding us back, but reminding us where we have come from. We might dismiss religion as a pre-scientific or pre-rational way of knowing, a cognitive precursor to our modern materialistic explanations of what makes things 'tick'. It evolved however as an emotional primer for how we make our personal relationships work, and how we accommodate pain and suffering, and these are daily challenges we have by no means solved or out-evolved.

Also, mankind cannot live by rationality, logic and mechanical explanation alone, essential though these are. Unless we rewrite the human genome, we will still be prone to believing in ghosts, ghoulies and things that go bump in the night. These are not childish neuroses or optional fancies, but seeds that eventually grow into our adult appreciation of theatre, art and carnival.

Religion and hypocrisy

Religion is too often a thin veneer for self-justification. In the nineteenth century the philosopher Søren Kierkegaard castigated his fellow Danish citizens for merely playing at being Christians. They wanted the comfort of religion without the inconvenience. They practised a pick and mix version of Christianity, welcoming the angels but ignoring the demons, preferring absolution to penance, winning eternal salvation without any of the sacrifices demanded by the gospels. He was just as hard on himself, always feeling he was falling short of an impossible ideal. Perhaps, he concluded, there has only ever been one true Christian, and that is Christ himself.

All we can do therefore, to avoid hypocrisy, it to put our convictions to the test. This calls for a leap of faith. He didn't pretend for a moment that this is a rational thing to do. The fact that there is suffering in the world, but that God loves us unconditionally, is as irrational and paradoxical as it gets, but to find out more, we have to make the commitment. It's no good simply attending the church fête once a year. If we want to know what the cake on the cake stall tastes like, we have to put it in our mouth and swallow it. By changing our belief, and acting on it, we change who we are, and what is shown to our mind.

If Kierkegaard were still with us, he would be scathing about the self righteousness of the evangelical right in the USA, who vote for any candidate who promises to ban abortion and gay marriage, regardless of their moral probity or stance on global warming. They don't care, because in their theodicy they have already booked their place in heaven. They are saved, but the sinners they condemn will burn in hell for eternity.

As if these criticisms are not ammunition enough to sink the good ship religion, evodevo theorists also have a theory to explain why religion has so often been linked to bigotry and bloodshed. It oversees our vital rites of passage: birth, marriage and death. It assumes responsibility for controlling reproductive rites, the education of children and the passing on of core teaching. It corroborates our belief that our tribe is the chosen one.

These things are worth dying for, even killing for, and that is what makes devout 'religionists' such willing recruits in the fight to defend their own. The secular belief systems of communism and fascism are frequently condemned for their 're-education' of dissidents and executions of defectors, but they learned these dark arts from the shunning, excommunication and persecution visited on religious unbelievers and heretics in times past.

And yet, however we tally the appalling toll of those killed in the name of religion, that figure has been dwarfed at the hands of the 'atheistic religions' of communism and fascism. We might add the millions of slaves who have died under the aegis of capitalism, eager to expand its colonial influence, maximise its profits and commandeer natural resources. More have died in the name of the secular gods Commerce and Profit than Jehovah and Allah. Also, it is too facile to blame radical militant fundamentalism on religion. We could just as easily link it to poverty, social exclusion, political extremism and, for some, a university education.

Religions of all hues have contributed to
the slow march of social reform.

In drawing up their charge sheet against religion, critics often overlook the debt of modernity to the people of many faiths who have bequeathed us moral codes, political reforms, humanitarian ideals, schools, hospitals and charitable foundations. Religions of all hues have contributed far more to the slow march of social reform than they have taken away or denied.

While it is true that some religious leaders have abused their power and squandered their trust, scientists also have occasionally been embroiled in questionable eugenics policies in the past, or are caught today in races to the finish line in bio-engineering, pharmaceuticals, military technology, artificial intelligence and space tourism. It is the winners who get the profits, not those who pursue knowledge for philanthropic purposes.

Religion as cash value
Another approach to religion is to contemplate the *effect* of what we choose to believe, or its 'cash value' for us. Rather than seeing religion's beginning as some grand spiritual illumination, clan cult and attempt to take things apart, it makes more sense to consider how it kept things together, underpinned social solidarity, and worked as a guide to practical action.

At this level, our beliefs are interest-based: are they good enough to get us safely to the end of the day? If not, we soon revise them, because what we believe about reality shapes our actions, not the other way round. Many Londoners resisted on principle the idea of a traffic congestion charge, believing it was unfair. After its introduction, they faced a problem called cognitive dissonance: what they believed no longer matched what they saw, which was the practical benefit of cleaner air and clearer roads. The only resolution to this dilemma was to change their minds, which meant changing their belief.

Mountains of the Mind

At a higher level, beliefs can still have very practical consequences, such as binding society into a single community. This was the view taken by the nineteenth century sociologists Émile Durkheim and Karl Marx. Whether as a vertical transcendent reality providing such unifying rituals and symbols as the Cross, the Lotus or Diwali, or a horizontal social force applied through such structures and hierarchies as schools and the class system, both theorists viewed religion functionally, in terms of its capacity to mould individual consciousness and communal identity. Durkheim saw nothing spiritual in religion at all, merely a capacity to foster a sense of belonging, which is essentially secular.

On this grander scale, beliefs are institution-based, bolstered by religious creeds, political loyalties and club rulebooks, directed at deeper questions about 'the point of it all' or 'where do I fit in?' Our membership of these communities, consciously or otherwise, gives us ready-made guidance on big questions that are often too complex to think through for ourselves every time.

With these arguments in mind, the psychologist William James took a pragmatic approach to religious belief. He did not judge between religions, but saw each as a way of life, not devotion to a particular Supreme Being. This makes sense, because some religions have no beliefs in supernatural gods. Also faith, as in believing in the unseen, can be secular as well as religious. Politicians believe in a fairer society, and scientists believe in a final theory, though neither has arrived yet.

James understood that religious experience provides no empirical evidence or external court of appeal, except for its impact on our feelings. But that is precisely why our feelings evolved: to help us make sense of our sensory inputs, value one thing over another and sweep us along in a collective story. So rather than analyse what religion *is*, James considered what religion *means* to those who adopt it, or how it provides 'cash value' for them. We should look not at what sacred texts or religious leaders *say*, but at what religious followers *do* as a consequence.

He realised that the myths of religion evolved not to satisfy the intellect, but to assuage the heart and satisfy the imagination. They must be judged not by the objective measures of truth or falsehood, or as scientific theories, but by their *lived* truth: how do they help us make sense of our lives, console us when things go against us, prepare us for our death or persuade us why we should value truth in the first place?

143

Mountains of the Mind

William James
1842-1910
James was wise enough as a psychologist to realise that people believe not principally for dogmatic reasons, but because their beliefs help them make sense of their lives. In other words, their beliefs have 'cash value'.

As our ancestors toughed it out on the savannah, and societies became more complex, religion proved to be a vital cultural asset. It did not 'teach' us the benefits of cooperation over competition, because these were already self-evident. Instead, as society became more complex, it was used to amplify the virtues of empathy and caring.

In a small group, thieves could be quickly identified and dealt with, but in an anonymous crowd, a moralising god who could see into the heart proved to be a useful invisible policeman. Not all religions took this route however. For many millions, their religion is not about what they believe but what they do, not what they fear, but what they freely choose. They do not need the stern voice of a wrathful god or the baleful stare of a security camera, because small acts of kindness have become second nature, in the form of the little civilities that make the wheels of society turn more easily.

Railing against religion is a bit like complaining
about our hair colour.

If we live in a community where it is customary to say please and thank you, to help someone in need, to give up our seat to an older person, to feel safe when we walk the streets alone after dark, we are the beneficiaries of religion in its original

144

sense, as the daily observances, decencies and courtesies that bind a society together, passed down the generations, regardless of belief in a supernatural deity.

Seen in the long view, we cannot doubt that the great religious belief systems of the world encapsulate something lasting, moral and deeply human, informed by compassion, not violence. The names of hundreds of local deities might have vanished, but their legacy remains deep in our psyche. Religious beliefs might be 'emergences' from selfish genes learning to cooperate, even cultural parasites that claim to be the only cure for their own virus, but they are no less real or keenly felt for that. Railing against religion is a bit like complaining about our hair colour. Both are realities in the world, and both are here to stay.

Religions seek to understand human experience as part of a cultural story, not to explain the nuts and bolts of how the world works. Our yearning to plumb the depths of the soul, reach out to 'otherness', and feel significant in 'the eternal silence of these infinite spaces', is as essential in the grand scheme of things as any attempt to 'see into' the mysteries of matter. This is why religious education is as important as the rest of the curriculum. We need to understand how religion has contributed to the totality of our knowledge and experience, not as an aberration in human evolution, but as part of our ascent to rationality.

Religion as rationality

Religion is as verifiable a 'social' fact in our history and culture as any 'material' fact established by science, as any glance at our language, rituals, calendar or city skyline reveals. But what if its main characters exit the stage? In the nineteenth century, Friedrich Nietzsche proclaimed 'God is dead', interred by the same human beings who invented him in the first place. The tide of the 'Sea of Faith' was withdrawing across the Western world. We're on our own now, responsible for our own actions, with no comforting myths to cling to. It is not Providence that rules over our lives, but brute necessity.

For many, the departure of the traditional God of Christianity left a spiritual vacuum, leading Max Weber to express concern that scientific rationalism has 'disenchanted' the world, emptying not just our sacred spaces of believers, but also our minds of awe.

Scientists do not see things this way, insisting that their revelations open up wonders of a natural kind. Some of us however find science's confidence and optimism intimidating if not hubristic, especially when our own nature is made part of its grand experiment. Awe at nature's wonders is a powerful emotion, but it does not answer our need for belonging and interconnectedness. In fact it can be quite alienating, inducing irrational anti-science sentiment.

Others have turned to agnosticism, atheism and secular humanism as new orthodoxies which, although claiming to be more rational, are nevertheless still belief systems, placing their faith not in supernatural deities, but in earthly reason and scepticism.

They cannot however claim definitively that there is no God because, despite centuries of debate, there are no killer arguments for the existence or non-existence of God. Science cannot 'prove' that God does not exist, nor can the Bible 'prove' that he created the world. To make such claims is to misunderstand the nature of theory, the foundation of knowledge, the fragility of certainty, the psychology of belief formation, and the role of the mind in making judgments based on experience.

If God is outside time and space, knowledge of or about him/her (sorry about this awkward nod to gender sensitivities, but it is indicative of the nature of the problem) by definition transcends the empirical purview of science, and 'proof' cannot be attained by this measure. In a further difficulty, 'God exists' and 'God does not exist' are both axioms, and no axiom can put itself to the test of its own logic. If we insist that there is no meaning without God, we are appealing to God as the backstop of what meaning means, which makes for a circular argument.

It is not rational to claim to know what cannot be known, but it is rational to accept that there is more than one way of knowing, if only because that shields us from over-confidence in an entirely materialistic explanation of the world. When we look at our progress as a species in the round, we realise that we need different but equal reasons for 'believing in' goodness and each other with one part of our mind, and in 'accepting' the workings of gravity and genes with the other.

Some fault religious claims to knowledge on the grounds that, unlike scientific hypotheses, they are incapable of being falsified. We can't for instance falsify the claim 'God is Love'. A religious believer might reply that we don't need to, because it is verified every time we witness an act of kindness. Not so, says the sceptic: it is falsified every time a child dies from disease or torture.

146

Mountains of the Mind

According to the philosopher of science Karl Popper, falsifiability is the first principle of scientific method, the engine which drives science forward, away from false towards true knowledge, or at least fuller knowledge. A very small number of skydivers have survived jumps when their parachute has failed to open, but we don't take that as falsification of the theory of gravity, or verification that humans can fly.

Scientific knowledge, to be knowledge at all, must be repeatable: we can't form a theory that humans can fly like birds until everyone regularly survives a fall of ten thousand feet without a parachute. Perhaps unsurprisingly, those who walk away from such freakish accidents tend not to want to repeat the experience.

Science versus religion does not have to be a fight to the death.

Belief in God and the truth of science need not be treated as binary opposites. In what is a complementary process, not an adversarial one, faith takes into consideration everything that science claims, and then theorises about the things that science cannot tell us. Science considers the claims of faith, then without necessarily negating them, offers alternative explanations. It does not have to be a fight to the death.

More than reasons

Believing or not believing is generated by our perceptual system, which has evolved to notice difference and fill in gaps. This means it is not only 'reasonable' but also inevitable that some see evidence of intelligent design when they gaze at the night sky, while others see the afterglow of the Big Bang. The only way of eradicating this choice of optics is to redesign the evolution of the human brain, which apart from being impossible, is hardly desirable. Our multiple ways of seeing, like the mountains of the mind, make us who we are.

Absence of evidence is often taken by sceptics to be evidence of absence: if God leaves so few visible signs, why should we believe in him/her? Not seeing something is not proof that something is there, only that it is clever at disguising itself. If we claim we regularly see UFO's, the burden of proof is on us, not on our incredulous listener.

Mountains of the Mind

Our values need to be grounded in causes
beyond our own limited perceptions

There might well be aliens out there, but we can't prove it by the strength of our conviction. On the other hand, we do need to fire up the feeling part of our brain if we are to find meaning, fight injustice, defeat poverty, defend rights, chase down scientific truth or overcome prejudice. These ends require more than arguments and reasons: we have to be emotionally persuaded they are worth devoting our lives to. Whether we build our values on a religious or a secular foundation, they need to be grounded in causes beyond our own limited perceptions.

Science does not require a declaration of atheism from its devotees. Many Nobel Prize-winning scientists profess a religious faith, so there are no grounds for insisting that belief and intellect are mutually exclusive. Some scientists believe not in spite of but because of what science has revealed to them. Their adventures in science are the inspiration of their faith.

Most scientists err towards a materialist explanation of the world, but they still feel as great a sense of wonder about the preciousness of each human life and the uniqueness of our universe as any religious believer. Albert Einstein referred to a 'cosmic religious feeling' that unites and inspires both the scientist and the religious seeker after truth. Carl Sagan described science as 'informed worship', convinced that science, as powerfully as religion, can give each of us, made up as we are of billions of atoms of stardust, what William James described as 'the feeling of being at home in the world'.

Faith can be rational, as Thomas Aquinas tried to show with his five arguments for believing in God. He was wise enough not to present these as proofs, because he realised that God cannot be known by intellect alone. Faith comes first, and what we experience after we have chosen our beliefs becomes our means of understanding. We believe *in order that* we may understand.

Faith is therefore necessarily *un*reasonable because, as the later theologian Martin Luther observed, there is no rational explanation for why, despite our many failings, God loves us. Like a parent, his love is free, undeserved and, after a sleepless night nursing an unsettled baby, downright irrational. But we bring children into the world anyway, because the eye of faith sees love as a miracle that reason alone cannot account for.

Finally there is the old chestnut about religion and morality. Primates in the wild and in captivity have been seen to protect and care for wounded or orphaned individuals. We are primates too, and altruistic people walked the earth long before religion became organised, or God was 'invented'. It is perfectly possible therefore to be a moral person without being a religious person. Interestingly, when we pray or meditate, we fire the same areas in our brain that help us to distinguish between good and evil.

Love among the chimps
Like us, our nearest primate relatives can show each other affection, or treat each other violently. How influential has religion been in promoting altruism and quelling aggression? We cannot rerun evolution, so we will never know.

This does not mean that 'good' equates to what is good for me. If this were so, we would be incapable of acting selflessly. What it does show is that we can't read morality, compassion, altruism, belief or faith from a brain scan, only from how we treat each other in specific social situations.

Religion as reality
It seems more 'reasonable' therefore to view religion not as a function of the flat mind, but as a natural expression of the human mind. It evolved as a way of binding society together, making sense of randomness, and lightening the burden of pain and suffering.

From our enlightened modern vantage point it is easy to forget how religion was a light in the darkness for our ancestors, providing much needed meaning in

149

an otherwise brute world. Their consciousness was steeped in myths, symbols, rituals and taboos that are largely lost to us today, but linger in our unconscious. Religion infiltrated so much of their thinking that our modern split between what is religious and what is secular meant nothing to them. It was much more important to be able to navigate what in their world was sacred and what was profane, which usually revolved around what was deemed clean or unclean.

Given this deep history, it is not surprising that the ancestral memory of living life under the aspect of religion leaves strong traces in the modern psyche. Some write this off as an atavistic throwback, but it is a core ingredient of our mental health. Just as some opt for a 'paleo' diet to keep their body healthy, so we need to acknowledge our 'paleo' spirituality. The religious sensibility might have held up the advance of scientific thought for many centuries, but it has also been an inspiration of great art and a guardian of learning, without which science could not have flourished.

Religion is not a lumpen mass, characterised only by bell, book and candle. It is as diverse as art and culture, with many manifestations. For some it is deeply personal, calling on the God of Abraham to justify the ways of God to man, for others it satisfies an intellectual need, calling on the God of Philosophy to explain the Cosmos as the work not of a Divine Magician, but of a Celestial Architect. Many, with no trace of cognitive dissonance, are able to combine the two, and not a few scientists see the laws of the universe as evidence of an overarching intelligence.

The Easter Island statues hark back to a primitive or idolatrous form of religion, not the later 'religions of the book' which have more to say about compassion, spirituality and the interconnectedness of life. The civilising influences of higher religion and its benefits to the believer tend to be glossed over, even though we see their legacy in our cultural and social practices.

The great cathedrals of Christendom bear no comparison to the towering blocks of glass and steel that dominate our city skylines. Sacred buildings are not brazen temples of corporate finance, but joyful answers to the call for transcendence, even though they were funded by the meagre gifts of the poor. Evolutionary psychologists can't have it all their own way. If sex, altruism, aggression, jealousy and technology are naturally evolved traits in our genome, so is our yearning to create beauty and seek a higher meaning.

150

Mountains of the Mind

It is true that religion has many dark sides: the cruel suppression of heresy, the exploitation of believers, the vanity of its institutions, the abuse of its authority, the insistence that we are miserable sinners, the millennial outbreaks of panic and hysteria that the end of the world is nigh, the use of sacred texts to justify barbaric practices.

It has also however expanded our consciousness by emphasising the importance of undertaking a personal journey, replacing external ritual with working out our own salvation, getting to grips with the distractions of our mind, finding a reference point outside our own desires. It has insisted on the sanctity of life, drawn our attention to the needs of the downtrodden, and preached non-violence, though critics point out that no Christian country has yet banned nuclear weapons or unilaterally disarmed.

Religion cannot however be held responsible for the failings of realpolitik. Religion's faults and failings are human ones, not unique to our addiction to any kind of god. Political ideologies, patriarchal power structures, technocratic monopolies, even 'scientific' practices such as untested medical treatments, behaviourism, eugenics, sterilisation programs and transhumanism, have all shown they are equally capable of inflicting outrages against human freedom and dignity.

For all its philanthropic credentials, science has too often become mired in misanthropic research, whether with deadly military hardware, dangerous pharmaceutical compounds or invasive digital technologies. On this score, if religion is a neurosis, so potentially is everything else we believe and do.

Religion may well most directly satisfy our yearning to believe, but not all of its beliefs are wrong or harmful, and nor is it the only claimant on our credulity. It is *people* who believe, whether in a sacred text, national sovereignty or gene editing, and it would be rash to jettison our spiritual inheritance with no guarantee that we have something equally cohesive and life-affirming to put in its place.

Atheism and agnosticism
Atheism has neither put religion to flight nor written a 'better' chapter in the human story. It might regard itself as more honest or empirical, but it gives us no surer a vision of what is 'real' in any sense. Also, insisting on a secular explanation for everything can become as dogmatic as any religious teaching, though we go too far if we accuse atheism of being just another cult based on a belief in non-belief.

151

Mountains of the Mind

There is no 'church of atheism', because it has no sacred texts, agreed rituals or reliance on transcendent beings. Most of us settle not for atheism but for agnosticism, or not knowing enough to be sure one way or the other. If nothing else, this saves us from cognitive dissonance, because we don't have to commit to either.

Any sect that hoards its wisdom is the antithesis of science.

Agnosticism is preferable in its open-mindedness and suspension of judgment about 'ultimate concerns' to Gnosticism, a second century Christian heresy. Gnostics saw us as trapped in matter, but they claimed to possess esoteric knowledge of an ultimate reality denied to the rest of us. Any sect that hoards its wisdom and boasts a monopoly on truth is not only a potential threat, but also the antithesis of science, which openly airs its disputes in public, acknowledges its errors and changes its mind, qualities which instil trust and inspire confidence.

Atheists reject supernatural explanation. They accept that religion has bequeathed us art and ideals that are beautiful and noble, but deny that religion has an exclusive claim to morality. Some of them are proud to be labelled 'militant', but their claim to absolute certainty of the non-existence of God falls by the same logic they use to attack the total conviction of the believer.

A more satisfying and productive opposite of theism is not atheism but humanism, a vote of confidence in the ability of human reason to work out its own place in the grand scheme of things without recourse to the supernatural. Its first manifestation in the Renaissance saw no conflict between science and religion, only a deepening confidence and pride in human potential. The early humanists still saw reason as a reflection of the divine mind, but like Adam and Eve, they also felt an overwhelming urge to bite into the apple of forbidden knowledge.

Humanism reappeared in the nineteenth century, this time minus faith in the transcendent. We have to go it alone, firstly because God has been exposed as a human artefact, secondly because we owe it to each other to adopt a rational and ethical approach to life. We must treat each other fairly because it's the decent, even the 'logical' thing to. There is however no 'church of humanism' either. Instead we have to find our own special sites, myths and rituals as foci for our communal life, whether in the football stadium, on social media, in our service to each other, or in the quiet of our own minds.

Reasonable beliefs

We are born believers. Our brain has evolved to make maps and establish patterns based on probabilities, and where these are uncertain, it makes them up. To put it another way, we cannot *not* believe. Our beliefs motivate us, ward off anxiety, guide our actions, and give us foundations in which to frame our life.

Research shows that a healthy brain is one that sees the world whole, without lots of gaps. People with conflicting or disordered beliefs struggle cognitively and spiritually, but those who subscribe to a clearly defined worldview, religious or secular, are generally happier and longer-lived, their positive beliefs eliciting affirmative responses in the reward centres of their brain, acting like a buoyancy device.

No mind is born as a flawless rational processor.

Unfortunately this 'like' response is not an indicator of whether these beliefs equate to anything objectively real. Whether the belief is rational or weird, secular or sacred, certified or wishful, the same neurons receive a little dopamine hit, and the same brain areas light up. This means that what is a meaningful belief to one may be meaningless to another, or what is considered plausible to one mind might elicit only ridicule from another. All we can say with any certainty is that no mind is inherently immune to believing in witches, nor is any mind born as a flawless rational processor.

The evodevo explanation for this is that our perceptual pathways are riddled with gremlins, our reality-formation mechanisms are flawed, and we are automatically given to magical thinking. There might even be a 'gene for' belief in supernatural agency. We should not be surprised therefore that the world is full of popular delusions and temporary insanities, because we are all born dreading being abandoned to wolves, terrified of being eaten by a predator, and petrified of being contaminated.

These atavistic fears 'out' themselves in various ways. We have a tendency to believe against the odds. Being told evidence to the contrary does not weaken but

153

strengthens our convictions, especially if we have invested our life purpose in them. We can't let them go. Despite defeats, we still believe that our team is worth supporting. Such beliefs are expensive to maintain, despite being regularly dashed, so they must have a value to us beyond mere rationality.

This is doubly true when our chosen beliefs unite us with a community of believers, compatriots or fellow fans with shared values and rituals. The 'truth' of our beliefs emerges from the way they integrate us with the group, and answer wider questions for us without having to think too hard about them. This is how ideologies and dogmas work. On the salami slice principle, we start by signing up to one article of belief, and end up eating the whole sausage.

This was particularly true in mediaeval times. If there is only one Theory of Everything, maintaining that God rules over all, and we accept it totally, there can be no crisis of faith, because all is explained: this is how the world and the people in it fit together.

This was the case for Gerard Manley Hopkins too. Having chosen the path of Catholic priesthood, he did not need to thrash out how God could be three in one, or how humble bread could be transubstantiated into the body of Christ. He had only to accept them as mysteries within a wider system, and wait for understanding to come slowly. Possibly less than a tenth of his faith was rationally calculated: the rest welled up from his wordless unconscious.

Hopkins belonged to a tradition in which a world without God was literally inconceivable. There was no mind space for atheism, and no word for it. His faith permeated every aspect of his life from individual salvation to group solidarity. Its appeal on the private plane was that he could create the Beloved in his own image, without the exacting demands of a flesh and blood relationship.

Such devotion to the divinity pays off if our God's principal attribute is Love, but this has not always been so. There have been many failed gods, most of them cruel and unapproachable, their effigies buried by desert sand, their names blown away on the wind. Where now are Zarathustra, Marduk, Ahura Mazda and Zeus?

In search of answers, religion has been put to the same sword as mind and consciousness: what is its likely evolutionary back story, and what developmental patterns can be observed? One theory is that the religions of the Old World grew out of dependable harvests, so their gods are largely those of fertility, and an assumption of a cosmic order. The New World, sitting largely on the Pacific Rim, was characterised by volatile events such as volcanic eruptions, earthquakes and tsunamis, so their gods need to be placated. In the case of the Aztecs, this could involve the sacrifice of hundreds of prisoners, their blood spilt to provide fuel for a ravenous and capricious sun god.

In a further consideration, those who live in a harsh climate find themselves bowing down to a male god of strictness and retribution, but those who live amidst plenty can afford a more generous and forgiving female spiritual overseer. Some deities were stern warrior gods of vengeance, others were forgiving peacemakers. As the historian Herodotus remarked, those who trade in horses end up worshipping a god that is horse-shaped.

Taboos and rituals
The challenge for historians of religion is that, while they can catalogue the taboos and rituals dating from ancient times, they can only guess at their meanings. They are not amenable to rational analysis, because they are deliberately irrational, more intent on marking out their performers as chosen or different, not on offering reasoned responses to reality. We see this kind of logic at work today in initiation ceremonies and hazing rituals. The more painful and bizarre they are, the more effective they are as proof of membership. The principle is: the greater the pain of entry, the less likely the risk of desertion.

When populations started to live in cities, their gods migrated with them, but increased numbers changed religion's role from local cult to state orthodoxy, with much higher levels of control, reflected in our modern urban communities. We are anonymous, so out on the street our conduct is no longer shaped by the watchful eyes of those who know us. We are kept in line by a different kind of God, no less stern, who monitors us and keeps a record of our misdeeds. We call it the police.

Religion offers us a 'one size fits all' explanatory system.

We need to remember that our ancestors lived amidst much greater uncertainty than we do, worrying about attacks from neighbouring tribes and predators, fluctuating supplies of food and water, and the vagaries of climate, disease and death. This lack of control was fertile ground for superstition. When the unexpected happens, it is easier to believe that the stars above govern our fate than to expend brain power looking for natural causes. Religion offers us a 'one size fits all' explanatory system, and some degree of control over uncertainty. For hunter-gatherers, it was never certain where prey would be, or other predators. For farmers, sporadic rains could result in starvation.

Religious rituals were not therefore irrational, but quite the opposite: they were based on observations of nature's regularities, and offered a kind of risk management, or way of controlling anxiety levels. Also, as acts of thanksgiving they bound the tribe together, providing better stability than the irrational ups and downs of modern stock markets.

Magical beliefs

For most of our history, there was no distinction between magic and nature. Our ancestors lived on the edge of the unknown, and with no way of knowing why storms roared or tsunamis rolled, nature was magical, and magic was natural. There was little or no understanding of things happening by natural causes.

Theory-making was at best approximate. Without any way of recording seasonal migration, it was assumed that birds disappeared into the mud in the winter, flew to the moon or changed into another species. Geese that flew off in the spring to breed in the Arctic spent the summer underwater as shell fish, hence their name barnacle geese. Mice emerged spontaneously from old clothes, and flies from rotting meat. Disease was not understood as infection by bacteria, but as a curse by a witch, or possession by some unseen force. Cures were based on the principle of similarity: a potion made from the pansy, or heartease, makes a good tonic for the heart, because its leaves are heart-shaped.

True magic is invoked when empirical explanation runs dry.

Anthropologists note that magic prevails where outcomes are precarious. Primitive magic works on a much deeper level than stage conjuring, which dupes our senses and exploits our credulity with tricks and sleights of hand that can be learned by anyone. True magic is invoked when empirical explanation runs dry, which for our ancestors was quite often. This explanatory chasm created a role for the juju man, who could exploit subjective beliefs in the absence of objective reasons.

156

Mountains of the Mind

The argonauts who navigated huge distances across the vast expanse of the Pacific Ocean were pre-scientific in their thinking, which is not the same as saying they were ignorant. They knew how to read the winds and the waves, but they also knew they could not control them. Their charms and incantations began at the point that their science ended, which was the moment their lives were thrown to the mercy of the ocean currents.

In the seventeenth century Western thinking took a 'scientific' turn, but it was a long, slow conversion. Alchemy still lingered, 'natural philosophers' were still regarded as magi, and witches were burned well into the next century. Today we persuade ourselves that science has banished the need for magical explanations, but our understanding of digital technology is so slender that it is only one step away from magic. How can all the world's knowledge be inscribed on something no bigger than a pinhead?

John Dee
1527-1608
Dee was a gifted mathematician and advisor to Elizabeth 1, bestriding the age of magic and science in equal measure. He dabbled in astrology and always carried with him the 'philosopher's stone', the potent symbol of the alchemists.

For all our modern advances, we are still prey to illness and mortality, worried about new types of Armageddon and unstoppable pandemics. The juju man is still out there. No wonder science's very success in providing a rational explanation for everything fuels a counterculture of occult sects, crazy superstitions, weird cults and conspiracy theories.

This phenomenon also explains why, despite intense efforts at suppression, religious faith continues to thrive across the world, and in many places is increasing, though for secular reasons as much as spiritual ones. Religion offers a convenient cover for reactionary politicians who conflate it with national identity and 'traditional values' that are perceived to be under threat.

Purpose and meaning
As a species, we continue to yearn for purpose and meaning above and beyond the daily grind. These are emotional and psychological needs, so it makes no sense to question whether the beliefs we adopt to satisfy them are factual, or match reality. What matters is their role in creating a metaphysical reality of loyalty to a team, nation, flag, cause, fraternity or higher calling.

Modern religious affiliation has moved a long way from the 'enthusiasm', 'temple madness', fanaticism and intoxication that swept away the reason of the believer in ancient times. Those who make a commitment of faith often do so against powerful rationalist arguments. They are free minds who make a conscious choice from all the options.

Not so, say the militant atheists, critical of religion's insistence on blind faith in strange gods and unseen rewards, manipulated by a scheming priesthood. Women who are told by the voodoo man that the child they are carrying is a cursed guppy are victims of sinister superstition and cruel misogyny. Believers are brainwashed with patent falsehoods, their minds infected with parasitic memes. They are dupes of a religious mindset that renders the brain vulnerable to self-deceit and irrationality.

Religious believers have failed to apply critical reason and rational scepticism, which alone have the power to demonstrate that water cannot be turned into wine, because nature has never been observed to deviate from her course. Taking their cue from the arch-sceptic philosopher David Hume, critics fault miracles on the grounds that it would require a greater leap of faith to believe the unreliable 'witnesses' to such wonders than the miracle itself demands.

The challenge for atheists in their determination to vanquish superstitious faith is that logical argument is useless against belief in a non-rational transcendent reality. Also, religions vary enormously, evolve in their own way, do not necessarily appeal to the supernatural, and do not usually offer an easy way out. Faith that entertains honest doubt, weighs all the options and then makes a moral commitment is not blind and stupid, but clear-sighted and smart.

It baffles atheists that religion survives in
an age of technological advance.

Material progress has brought obvious benefits: we can jump on a plane, chat on social media, buy fresh strawberries at any time of year or receive instant medical assistance. Science has reduced the God of the gaps to a thin sliver. It baffles atheists therefore that religion survives at all in an age of technological advance.

Religion is not however intrinsically anti-progress or retrograde in its thinking, and we may yet need its ministrations. As the age of biotechnology, superintelligent machines and transhumanism looms, we have absolutely no idea where our current technological advance is taking us. It might turn out to be another progress trap, or a new god of Mammon, less forgiving than the old.

Our brain evolved to invent ever-smarter solutions, not to keep us spiritually healthy, bind us in mutual ties, or teach us why we should care for each other. We might be able to jettison some of the trappings of our old gods and beliefs, but not the substance of their message. As our machines accumulate the power to shape their own destiny, perhaps only religion will save us, not as a series of mutually exclusive creeds, but as a spiritual attitude towards the sanctity of life, the inviolability of the human form, and the full expression of creativity.

The religious impulse as part of a new humanism can guide us through our integration of the speed and efficiency of our technics with the slow and complicated demands that other minds make upon us. Our machines can speed up our communication with each other, but only we can explore more deeply what we have to say to each other, make the best of who we already are, and celebrate our differences.

Mountains of the Mind

The anatomy of belief

We are born to believe, though not in anything in particular, or even an objective reality. In fact most of our beliefs are in things unseen, though this does not mean that they are superstitions, which are beliefs without evidence. We can't see justice, but we believe in it, because it helps us create social realities that cohere over time, and provides continuity for human communities.

In these instances our brain presents the world to us so persuasively that it doesn't occur to us to question it. Once we've settled on our beliefs about how the world works, true or false, we tend to stick with them, because it's too much cognitive effort to change our minds.

Beliefs are not however intrinsically beyond change, or irrational. Our only way of responding to the outside is what we 'get' inside, or what is 'real' to our senses. We believe, therefore we are, and what we are is what we believe.

This does not leave us at the mercy of random impressions. The science of phenomenology and the practice of meditation show how we can learn to introspect carefully, subjecting the objects of our thought to the standards of reason. We can also trust our mind when we feel it points to realities beyond our senses. If this were not so, we could not make any sense of mathematics, let alone art or religion. A perfect circle, a perfect beauty and a perfect God are all conceivable by the human mind, and each is a reasonable proposition. Whether we will ever see them in our lifetime is a different question.

There is a very fine line between a belief and a delusion. If a man stands up in the market place and claims to be the Son of God, we dismiss this as a delusion. He is locked in a private truth, or a sect of one believer. He might however have experienced an epiphany or moment of enlightenment, even a bang on the head, changing his brain and person in equal measure. The seeker has found what he is looking for, and his life is transformed from that point.

If he builds up a wide following, his belief might survive for several centuries. If whole communities erect buildings based on his teaching, his belief becomes a social fact, determining moral, legal and political structures across the social spectrum. His belief is no longer a delusion in the sense that, by being shared by many, it achieves critical mass in the annals of history.

It is hard to disprove or dislodge a social, cultural and historical belief of this kind once it has taken root and achieved momentum. But some beliefs can and should be challenged, however intuitive they seem, if and when new evidence emerges, usually from scientific investigation. It is difficult for instance to cling to a literal account of the world being created in seven days, or the existence of an Intelligent Designer standing outside the system, in the light of the evidence of fossils, extinctions, and the match of living organisms to their environments, not to mention genetics and DNA.

There is no loss of face in changing our minds in the light of new evidence. It was believed for centuries that letting anger out was a kind of cleansing: it's better to vent our spleen and get it out of the system. Brain scans show that the opposite is true. It is better for our health and those around us, when we feel about to explode, to do all we can to defuse and deflect our fury, however vindicated we feel in our wrath. We have not evolved as pressure cookers that need to let off steam every now and again. Behaving aggressively, where it is tolerated, is a cultural norm, not a biological necessity. It makes it more likely we will blow up faster next time, doing violence not just to ourselves but also to those nearby.

It is a problem when a personal belief impinges
upon the mental wellbeing of others.

Challenging such a belief might be hard, but not impossible, because it doesn't go far beyond our own self. The problem arises when a personal belief impinges upon the lives, rights and mental wellbeing of others. How do we tackle a conviction that women and rape victims should be denied abortion rights, or that homosexuals and transgender people should be forcibly subjected to aversion therapy?

Conspiracy theories
Conspiracy theories are equally hard to challenge, especially in an internet age where we can find support in the online echo chamber for whatever we choose to believe: the apparatus of the 'deep state' is drugging our food so that it can steal our minds, the Moon landings were faked, the world is being run by a financial cabal of Jewish child molesters, phone masts give us cancer, the Holocaust is a hoax because the emaciated bodies in the photographs taken after the liberation of Auschwitz in 1945 belong to American actors.

161

Mountains of the Mind

Some object to the phrase conspiracy *theory*, on the grounds that this devalues the hard intellectual work that needs to go into justifying our beliefs and establishing true knowledge: accumulating data, sifting evidence, checking our sources, staying as close to reality as possible, taking the emotional heat out of an argument, revising our opinion when necessary. Conspiracy 'theorists' tend to do the opposite, doubling down when challenged, seeing only the positives that support their cause, ignoring negatives, putting feeling before fact, always seeking to add to their trove of dangerous nonsense, never to eliminate the dross.

It is easy to dismiss conspirators as crazy coots, not like our sensible, rational selves, but sometimes they may be right. We must therefore hold ourselves to the standards we expect of them, and work twice as hard to show where they are being more than economical with the truth.

It's also worth remembering that our brain doesn't specially care what beliefs we choose, so long as they cohere in a workable system. We often blank anomalies that don't square with our principal conviction or belief system. We get away with this sloppy habit because no belief has a logical back-stop: all we find behind it is an earlier belief, or a foundation-less conviction about what is best or right, usually for us, not for other people. Ideologies don't show up on a brain scan. They are only attitudes that trigger activity in the 'tough' or 'tender' emotional areas of our brain.

Mountains of the Mind

When the facts change, why don't we change our minds too?

We are all conspirators of one kind or another, seeing only what we want to see, fighting our own war against reality, under the spell of the picture our mind paints for us. This is especially true of our political convictions. They are particularly hard to shift, usually fixed for life, as if drunk in with our mother's milk.

If we're conservative at heart, we accuse liberals of soft-pedalling on law and order, creating a culture of self indulgence, with attendant high crime rates, broken families and spoilt children. In reply, liberals charge conservatives with a mean-spirited view of human nature, motivated by belief in a gospel of fear, inequality and selfishness, filling the prisons to overflowing.

At election time, we can become so locked in our tribal enclave that we don't even hear opposing views, and it seems impossible to change a person's thinking by rational argument alone. This is quite a depressing thought: when the facts change, why don't we as readily change our minds too?

And yet we are capable of switching allegiances, and quickly at that. When we put on a different uniform, take on a new job or join a rival team, we begin singing the new corporate song as if our life depended on it. Suddenly we find fifty different reasons why the outfits we have thrown off are so embarrassing, behind the curve, the wrong colour or ripe for takeover.

But that's not the same as subscribing to a conspiracy theory, or allowing ourselves uncritically to be taken in by one. True conspiracy theorists rejoice in our confusion about what a conspiracy is, how it is formed, and how to get rid of it. They thrive on disruption, half truths and misinformation. They prefer bloc loyalty to thinking for themselves.

Their agenda isn't to support a cause or defeat an enemy, only to get a buzz from seeing everyone at war with everyone else all the time. Conspiracy 'theorists' respond to the same imperative as terrorists. They are driven not to defy rational argument and offend reasonable moral sensitivities, but to stick two fingers up at what everyone else cares about. They want revenge against a world that doesn't think like them, or pay them enough attention.

163

Mountains of the Mind

Claiming that a pandemic is a hoax is much more exciting than reading a text book on epidemiology, and shouting that an accredited election has been rigged is much more fun than quietly reading our country's constitution. The standard advice for resisting conspiratorial thinking is to find out who is telling us something and why. This sounds fair and rational, but it cuts no mustard if we don't care for the truth, or can't be bothered to stand on our own feet.

Living with duplicity

Democracy has arisen from a growing belief that individuals have a right to a say in the running of their lives. This may seem an obvious entitlement to the Western mind, but it is very recent, and much blood has been shed to get this far. For democracy to work, and if we are to make a free choice at election times, we need an ability to flip between contradictory ideas about loyalty, or conflicting visions of justice.

Such duplicity enables us to live with our own hypocrisy, by presenting a different public front from our private agenda. We might insist on liberal freedoms in the presence of our friends, but turn a blind eye to the illiberal operations of our state secret services. We might preach a doctrine of educational excellence based on selection of the brightest, until our own child doesn't make the cut. Then we bend every rule in the book to secure a place at the local grammar school.

Somehow, whatever our political persuasion, we manage to square our inconsistencies with our conscience and sleep soundly in our beds at night, because we can't bear cognitive dissonance, or having to entertain contradictory ideas in the same mind space.

We have a capacity to pretend not to know what we do know.

This makes us inconsistent in our rationality. We parrot the evolutionary theory of ruthless natural selection that we learned at school, while also believing we are specially made for each other. In the pub, we stand under the 'Don't drink and drive' sign, avoiding mental conflict by telling ourselves another shot won't do us any harm. If we've got a drinking problem, we seek the company of fellow-drinkers who help us to hide from our weakness. We think we are Teflon-coated: we never admit we are fat, only joke about how much we love our food. Somehow

164

we have a capacity to pretend not to know what we do know, when it suits us to do so.

Darwin and Freud, not often thought of in the same breath, come together in a powerful science-plus-psychology combination to suggest we are more of a biological brain than an essential mind. There are strong drives (biological needs and evolutionary gremlins) and deep urges (psychological wants and unconscious forces) operating below waking awareness that shape our behaviour and thinking. We think we are the jockey, but too often we are the horse bolting out of the stable without a rider.

Biologists, sociologists, economists and advertisers believe they have our measure when it comes to explaining our 'rational' or 'free' consumer choices. They know that our retail decisions are not rationally or freely made at all. Our genes or desires (which amount to the same thing) lead us into conspicuous consumption: flashing the bling attracts a better mate, gains more social prestige, wins more friends, displays our success in life.

No wonder shop windows are set up to appeal to our vanity, concupiscence and status anxiety. Such a dim view of our motivation does not however account for the story of the widow's mite: though she had little, and wasn't of noble birth, she willingly gave a share of it to those who had even less. She made a free choice. Or had she been indoctrinated to respond like this? Was she pushed by forces unknown to her? We consider the nature of free will and memory in the next chapter. To what extent can we call our choices and memories our own?

How free are we?

Free will – types of freedom - the art of the nudge – advertising –
memory - nostalgia – history – recovered memory - trauma

- Our core beliefs and values are grounded in our freedom to choose.
- This act of faith is undermined by the 'flat mind' charge that free will is an illusion, and the mechanistic view that nothing is uncaused.
- And yet, however events may be predetermined at the synaptic level, in the cut and thrust of life, we are forced to be free.
- We need therefore to be clear about where we are free, and where we are unfree.
- We are more gullible and biddable than we think, with no simple nexus between wishing, willing and doing.
- We don't mind being nudged towards a better choice, so long as we feel we are left with the final say.
- Advertisers like to leave us feeling free to choose, but their motives are far less pure.
- Our memory is also not as free as we like to think.
- We assume it gives us an accurate record of the past, but it evolved to help us make sense of the future.
- In addition, we recreate each memory every time we recall it.
- Nostalgia is a rosy recreation of the past, often a defence against an uncertain future.
- The past stays the same, but history changes, because it is a reflection of our priorities in the present.
- This explains why judges advise juries to exercise caution with eye-witness testimony, and extreme caution with 'recovered' memories.
- Trauma however is usually based on real events, which is why it is so hard to free ourselves of it.
- There is much we can do to stimulate, improve and make better use of our memories.

166

Mountains of the Mind

The paradox of freedom

The idea of freedom is woven into our every thought. Our language rings with words like might, should, could, ought, will, shall and maybe. Whether we approach freedom politically, legally, morally or existentially, we start from a simple premise. *We* make our choices freely, of our own volition. *We* take responsibility for our actions, *we* choose our pleasure, partner, career path, political allegiance and which team to support. Don't we?

Yes and no, say flat-minders and cognitive scientists. Our much cherished sense of being a free agent in charge of our life is an evolutionary trick of our brain. It's no use turning to moral philosophers for support, because in two and a half thousand years they have failed to 'prove' that we are free. The only consolation is that they haven't proved that we are automata either.

Can neuroscience settle the argument? Research by the neuroscientist Daniel Libet has revealed a microsecond delay between an impulse to act in the nervous system (body) and our conscious awareness of making a free decision (mind). Cricket bat in hand, our brain strikes the ball before our arm does because it knows what we are going to do before 'we' do. In more complex decisions, the time lapse can stretch out to several seconds.

Libet admitted that this might simply be a case of our brain gearing up before 'going public'. It doesn't mean we are neural puppets controlled by cerebral strings in our preconscious that we know not of. We might not 'know' what 'we' have just decided until a split second after our brain has, but we still know. The timing of our nervous impulses hardly matters, because in terms of what appears to consciousness, there is only one 'now'.

We all live slightly in the past, or not simultaneously with reality.

There's also neuromechanics at work, subject to the arrow of time. If an electrical impulse travels at thirty metres per second along a nerve, there's bound to be a time lapse between departure and arrival, no matter how small, even in the brain, creating a delay until signals in our prefrontal cortex reach a tipping point, making 'us' realise in the global workspace of our conscious awareness what we

167

are about to do next. In that sense, we all live slightly in the past, or not simultaneously with reality.

Our brain has evolved as a predicting machine. When we reach out to pick up an object, it has already calculated distance, its likely weight, the strength of grip required, not to mention what we want it for. It reacts when things turn out otherwise, and has to send quick adjustments to the muscles. It is surprised when somebody creeps up behind us, because this event was not on its horizon. But it is not surprised when we tickle ourselves, because it knows what is coming.

Not only does our brain like to know what is coming next, it also relies on feedback, and once again, nanoseconds of delay are involved. Bat in hand once more, our brain has to signal to our hands how to angle the bat against the expected flight of the ball, then calculate how many runs there might be in the shot, having felt the strike through the gloves.

When we get to the sharp end of deciding whether to hit the ball or let it go for a bye, even whether to play for the local team in the first place, nothing is forcing our response, except our skill level or personal preference. There's an unfree stimulus of a bouncing ball, or the local side just happening to play at home this weekend, and then our free response to hit a six or settle in for the afternoon.

If we hand decision-making over to our brain completely, we lose our mind's power of veto, and accountability for our actions. If free will resides anywhere, it is in the split second delay between the synapse and the decision, or the stimulus and the response, without which we would not be 'responsible movers', but automata, zombies and moral wantons.

We are not, because 'willing' happens in two stages. The first is a wish, which is generated by our emotions, or appetite. We really do want that second drink with friends before we drive home. The second is the flexing of our will, which is the strength of our resolve, the expression of our values, and the exercise of our rationality: is this a *reasonable* action, given our understanding of how the world works, what we know about ourselves, and the outcome we desire?

If we're arrested for drink-driving, we can't plead with the judge that the alcohol was to blame. The judge will refer us to the moment when we were still sober: that was our chance to *choose* whether to allow a wish to become an action.

168

Mountains of the Mind

The jury aren't interested in debating whether there is a steady jockey called reason battling it out with a highly strung filly called emotion inside our head. Their only concern is whether we were free to choose whether to have that second drink, regardless of the 'readiness potential' that triggered our arm to lift the glass to our mouth. We cannot plead that 'my arm' or 'my brain' poured the drink down our throat, denying us volition, as if we are unable to control our body.

Libet's research does not deny metaphysical freedom of choice, but it does explode the myth of the self as an 'uncaused causer'. Our sense of 'deciding' comes at the end of a long chain of mechanical operations in our brain. If we put our hand on a hot surface, the chain is very short: our hand withdraws in quick reflex, with no time for deliberation of 'yes' or 'no'. When we decide to drink and drive, the chain is much longer and more complex, with as many links to 'free won't' as 'free will'.

The moment of choosing
There is little agreement about whether our actions are free in any meaningful sense, though many have nibbled at the philosophical problem of free will. Aristotle guaranteed it, but only if we apply our reason. This didn't help Oedipus, cursed by a prophecy at his birth that he would kill his father and marry his mother. His father paid for the child to be killed to thwart fate, but guess what, Oedipus survived, returning as a young man to the city of his birth, ignorant of his past, to carry out what had been foreordained.

For Oedipus, regardless of his good character, destiny could not be denied. In fact, the irony runs even deeper. He knew of the prophecy about him, and by travelling to what he thought was a different part of the country, far away from his birth place, he thought he had done everything in his power to nullify the curse. He believed he could cure the plague ravaging his adopted city, without realising he was the cause of it.

This is a warning against going to see the fortune teller. In what is known as the Cassandra paradox, our efforts to foil a bad prediction about the future might lead us inexorably to the very consequences we are so desperate to avoid.

There is an even deeper irony at the heart of fate and fatalism. The Ancients were given to Amor Fati, or loving what befalls us, since we can't stop it happening anyway. And yet common experience convinces us that our actions *do* make a difference, both in what we decide, and in the influence we have over others. Our thoughts and feelings have evolved for precisely this reason, to help us make informed and reasonable decisions beyond choosing which television channel to watch. In that sense, evolutionary logic supports the idea of free will, even as neuro-determinism denies it.

We don't feel fated in any sense, if only because we have no way of knowing what forces are working on us from above or below, or the thousands of micro-events that have brought us to this point. Life is full of accidents, but these are random. Fatalism is the opposite, a kind of grim determinism, which not only doesn't suit the modern temper of liberalism and individualism, but also strikes at the heart of being human, a cut above the rest of the animal kingdom. We don't knowingly set out on a road journey expecting it to end in a car crash. If we knew that, we wouldn't set out in the first place.

John Calvin
1509-64
God knows the future, so he knows who will be saved, and who won't. So much for free will. Calvin didn't seem too concerned over the confusion this creates about responsibility for our actions. If our salvation is already determined in the future, why bother to behave ourselves now?

Stoic philosophers, generally convinced that life is fickle and justice is arbitrary, offer the cold comfort that the future is as the gods wish it to be. The Eastern doctrine of karma sees us not just dragging baggage from the past but also hauling it out of the future, in a kind of reverse causation.

Christianity fares little better in 'explaining' free will. John Calvin, based on the biblical verse 'God will have mercy on whom he will have mercy', concluded that, if God knows our actions before we do, it has been determined in our cot through the doctrine of predestination whether we are 'elected' for heaven or hell. The priest Nicolas Malebranche came up with an ingenious compromise. When we decide to raise our arm, at that very moment God lifts it for us, so both parties are satisfied.

We think we are free, but those nasty controlling
thoughts just can't be kept down.

Secular explanations haven't fared much better, or been much more logical. Freud suggested that our actions are controlled by our unconscious. We might think we are free, but those nasty controlling thoughts just can't be kept down. Biologists look to the genes, endocrinologists to the hormones, neuroscientists to neural networks, physicists to atoms colliding in the void, quantum theorists to the collapse of the wave function.

These materialist explanations fall some way short of the metaphysical reality of what we feel when we make a decision, and our existential need to claim responsibility for our actions. How do we get from the superposition of particles to our conviction that when we choose, we somehow change a little bit of our life world?

Not easily, say philosophers of mind. Free will may be a trick of experience. Our conviction that we can explain our lives backwards gives us the illusion that our future must be all to play for. Neurologically, it might be the alternation between two systems in our brain, the autopilot that regulates our body, and the manual control we switch to when we want to change speed or direction.

So, when we decide to wriggle our toe, who is 'we' and how do we 'decide'? The physiology and the phenomenology flummox us equally. We are only just at the beginning of understanding how a biochemical message is fired by a neuron through a synapse down an axon to cause a muscle to contract, and perhaps we will never fathom which part of us decides to do such a thing, or not to do it, or how, or why.

Determinists insist there are causes we are not aware of, millions of chemical dramas down in the basement of our brain for which our mind is only the viewing gallery. One day, if we can establish all the starting conditions, and go back down the chain of causes far enough, we will be able to predict all the outcomes, or at least calculate their statistical probabilities.

171

Mountains of the Mind

Or will we? In the chain of causation, there's many a slip twixt cup and lip. Physicists have shifted from a static and linear view of nature to a fluid and dynamic one. As things become smaller, they become more complex, and much less predictable. Brownian motion shows us that there is no way we can predict the movement of trillions of molecules of water when we boil our kettle. Inside a cloud, motion is stochastic, or a blend of randomness and probability. Will it rain or won't it? This is not to say that weather is uncaused, only that it is not determined, or forecastable down to the last drop of rain.

There is also the world of counterfactuals, where a small change at the start of a process causes very large changes at the end. Had one of the universe's 'six numbers' been one decimal point to the left or right at the Big Bang, a different species might have risen to evolutionary dominance on our planet, or not at all. Had one extra butterfly been crushed underfoot in the Jurassic Age, democracy might now be overwhelmed by fascism. If Cleopatra's nose had been shorter, the entire history of the world might have been changed. Had one tiny strip of DNA unravelled differently during our gestation in the womb, we might now be an introvert, not an extrovert, a genius, not a duffer, a conservative, not a socialist.

Open futures
From an evolutionary perspective, the growth of our neocortex, which is the seat of our conviction that we are free, has left us in a double bind. Thousands of default networks coded in genes and proteins do not allow us to defy the laws of nature: every neural event must have a naturalistic cause.

At the same time our frontal lobes persuade us that we have an open future: I think I will dress in blue today, to suit my mood. That's *my* decision. We are all existentialists at heart. Out of all the calls I might have made in all the lives I might have led, *this* is the one I am making right now. I might be an automaton at the molecular level, ignorant of my 'causes', but up top, I'm a conscious self-organising biological system, constantly interacting with my environment. I am not closed and determined, I am open and self-determining. My spontaneity, novelty, rationality and omnipotence of thought guarantee my freedom.

Such reasoning has led many evolutionists and neuroscientists to consider that caused choice is not an oxymoron. In a compromise called compatibilism, determinism and freedom are seen as complementary, not cancelling each other out. In fact, the one enhances the other. Determinism on the lower rungs of the ladder guarantees a 'free' outcome at the top, especially for creatures with highly evolved brains like ours. 'All is determined, yet permission is granted', wrote the philosopher Maimonides. The very constraints on the first rungs of the ladder of complexity are what give us our elevated and limitless view from the top.

We operate in a universe of strict physical laws, as we discover when we drop our cup of coffee, but through a process called emergence, those very laws make creativity possible. Poetry and music achieve their magic and beauty because they are shaped by laws of prosody and harmony, not constrained by them. Chess has fixed rules, but an almost infinite number of moves.

At the level of neural processing, our sense of 'freedom' may well be an illusion, but at the level of *experience*, we make our choices *as if* we live under the aspect of free will. If we sit and theorise about free will, we paint ourselves into a deterministic corner, but when we go out onto the street, we fly free like a bird. We *can't* be running on fixed algorithms. As William James remarked, his first act of free will was to believe in free will. The apple might have obeyed the laws of necessity in falling from the tree, but Eve *chose* to bite into it.

Compatibilism suggests that although events in our brain have physical causes, our will is not necessarily determined. Our brain is *both* programmed to process input in a certain way *and* primed to respond openly to change and opportunity, otherwise we could not learn, or find reasons for our actions. Survival depends on having enough fixed algorithms to cope with everyday needs, but enough flexible programs to adapt when the going gets tough, or we need to move in a different direction.

We are capable of change, and taking responsibility for what we do.

Without this scope, and the possibility of growth, there would be no incentive to teach children to show manners, no need to apologise for what we have done, no guarantee of keeping a promise, and no point in praising someone for doing well. Discriminating between good and evil, or a beautiful and an ugly painting, would become meaningless, because in a fully determined universe, things could not have been otherwise. Criminals would have no fear of the police, and there would be no comeback if we shouted 'Fire!' in a crowded theatre.

173

Mountains of the Mind

In reality, our interactions with other people are nothing like as 'free' as doing as we please. That is mere wantonness. Our moral assumptions, and the very fabric of the social contract, are premised on the belief that *we could have acted otherwise*. We are capable of change, and taking responsibility for what we do.

Human decision-making is not a binary choice between 0 and 1 with nothing in between. These algorithms work well in our computers, and if we're in a hurry, they can help us choose quickly between tea and coffee. They do not upscale or map easily onto the complexities we face in our personal and social lives, which call for not for conviction or insouciance, with no stations in between, but a 'fuzzy' logic of fudge and compromise.

Our life is branched, not linear, more like a sprawling tree reaching for the sun than a maze of forked paths, where we don't know which road to take. If ever we get to a dilemma or crossroads where all we can do is toss a coin, it is not because we don't care about the outcome. It is because we cannot reconcile conflicting goods.

Dare to be free

The philosopher Immanuel Kant intuited the ambivalence of free will a century before Darwin and two centuries before brain scanners, based solely on his power to think the issue through from the comfort of his armchair. As a prime mover in the thinking that drove the eighteenth century Enlightenment, he urged his readers to dare to know, which amounts to daring to be free. If no-one had taken up this challenge, doctors would still be bleeding patients as a way of curing disease.

He reasoned that 'imponderables' such as free will, mind, justice and truth can't be proved or disproved, because we can't step outside of ourselves to appeal to a higher court of judgment. Free will and other 'mind realities' are constitutive of what it means to be human, because that's the way our mind has evolved to process reality, just as we intuitively know the difference between up and down. Between what our senses give us, and what our thoughts reveal to us, we don't have the intellectual apparatus to see things any other way.

To possess a mind at all is premised on a loop we cannot escape from: we are free because we are programmed to feel as if we are. The self, free will and morality are part of the physical world, but also something new in nature. Nothing 'causes' them, and they cannot cause themselves. Our bodies inhabit the Realm of

Mountains of the Mind

Necessity, where causes reign supreme. But our minds belong in the Kingdom of Ends, where we are not only free to choose how we treat each other, but also obliged to face the consequences. We inhabit a metaphysical sphere of human ends, not biological means.

We might not be conscious of all the causes of our choices, but we are utterly persuaded of our agency. We are acted upon, but we also act. We act on our beliefs, which are free creations of the mind, only contingently related to the world of matter. Every time we act, we engage with other minds in some way, which influences what we are likely to think, believe and do next.

To accept necessity is to achieve perfect freedom.

Paradoxically, Kant believed we are most free when we accept the constraints upon us, rather than fighting them. Obeying the moral law, which essentially means treating others as we would wish to be treated ourselves, is the most rational thing we can do. Accepting this as the way things are is not subservience, but mastery, of the kind advocated by the great religions of the world.

In that sense, monks who devote themselves to a daily regime of service and meditation are the freest people on earth. By dulling the sharp pricks of want and desire, they liberate themselves to enjoy life's simple pleasures. By accepting necessity, like water running downhill, they achieve perfect freedom, leaving them free to do as they will.

This approach can of course be taken too far. We are not natural ascetics, and are entitled to enjoy our pleasures. Nor do we like anything that smacks of fatalism. The philosopher Spinoza remarked that we act freely when we couldn't have acted otherwise. This suggests a kind of resignation, or exhortation to become a hermit, but it's more to do with recognising how little control we have over events, and teaching ourselves to be content with what we have, 'moving comfortably in harness', as the poet Robert Frost phrased it. We are most free when know the true reach of our mind, understand its limits, and live our lives accordingly. Flat mind theorists couldn't put it any better.

Our brain does not work on linear code, nor can it be reverse-engineered into strips of protein, despite the enthusiasm of tech wizards. The gift of language is our best proof of this. Our brain possesses an underlying grammar, but within it,

Mountains of the Mind

our semantic choices are infinite, as the linguist Noam Chomsky showed in his example 'Colourless green ideas sleep furiously'. Language, like music, is combinatorial, and any child is capable of generating a thought or humming a tune that no-one has thought or heard before. Art depends on the free flow of ideas, woven infinitely into new patterns.

Noam Chomsky
b 1928
The linguist Chomsky showed that our use of language is a mixture of the fixed and the free. We are primed with the rules of word order, but can combine words in an infinite number of ways. Colourless green ideas sleep furiously.

Determinism and creativity are not mutually exclusive but yin and yang, each powerful in its own frame of reference. Determinism is a useful tool when we apply it appropriately as a single explanation, which is usually in the material world, where truth can be absolute (though even this is hedged with provisos). Accepting that we can't put spilt milk back into the bottle is plain old common sense, not fatalism.

In the personal and creative spheres, truths are multiple and relative, occasionally divisive, and we rue the fact that we can't recall words spoken in haste or anger. The arrow of time is a one-way ticket. Self-determination is a different kind of determinism altogether, with the chance of a return ticket if we want it. Without it, most of the core assumptions on which liberal democracy is built, such as freedom of thought, political preference, individualism, agency, responsibility and the right to change our mind, would come crashing down. There would be nothing to stop society from being totalitarian or utopian, as there would be universal acquiescence that things cannot be other than the way they are.

Political theorists have long realised that society is determined by forces very different from pulsars and quasars. Towards the end of the nineteenth century, anthropologists and social scientists began to discover that variety and unpredictability in human affairs are the norm. Put simply, they were astonished by the diversity of religious beliefs, cultural practices and political systems they found in societies outside their own. The only thing that was universally 'determined' was that there would be local unpredictabilities, understandable only from the inside, not explainable from the outside.

Even if we manage to trace an individual thought right back down the chain of causes, we end up with the eternal regress of an apparently free choice preceded by a neural correlate fore-ordained by a synaptic neurotransmitter anticipated by a protein manufactured in the nucleus controlled by a particular gene. On this basis, there is no need to choose, because the future is already decided.

Determinism also ignores chaos theory, with its potential for 'leakage' at any link in the causal chain. Even the reliable silicon-based algorithms of the smartest computer crash now and then. This is even truer in a dynamic system such as the brain, made of flesh and blood. As with attempts to forecast the weather, simple, tiny and local changes such as the flap of a bird's wing in the Amazon can result in massively diverse outcomes.

Causal chains
Historians are familiar with the dilemma of finding the 'causes' of a historical event or movement. They have to distinguish between two types of cause, proximate and ultimate. A proximate cause for a declaration of war might be an invasion by a neighbouring country. The ultimate cause will lie much further back, and is not likely to be reducible to a single trigger or specific influence: a centuries-old grievance, a broken treaty, more aggressive leadership, a hunger for resources, the desire to expand the empire, behind all of which, even more 'ultimate', lies a fault line in the human psyche: ancestral animosity towards the out-group, whoever they are.

Biological causal chains are no less complicated than historical ones. Both disciplines make it clear that chance and necessity, plus time, create many possible openings, of which only a few can be explored. By the time we add will, intention and action, we come up with a very complex formula indeed.

Some of the outcomes, by occurring more frequently, wear grooves that we are consciously aware of as 'experience', and which operate below the radar as tacit knowledge. The cumulative weight of all our previous choices and discoveries means that we never choose 'blind', but always through the prism of prior learning. In the garden of forked paths, all choices point to the future, but only as probability, never certainty. There can never be causal chains stretching into the future, as the future hasn't happened yet.

Much that happens in our grey matter is contingent, not necessary, as unpredictable as the colliding ripples of two stones dropped into a pond. We can at least see these ripples on the surface, but we never get to see the billions of similarly contingent quantum effects deep below. No wonder the human sciences of psychology, sociology, history and creativity constantly intrigue us and defy augury. Even the natural sciences cannot always guarantee us the outcomes we predict.

The noise and bustle of the stock market looks random, but from it emerge clear trends and patterns. As in the brain, the dice are being rolled millions of times a second, but the end result is not chaos. There may be a few surprises, but there is also interconnectedness, from which come purpose and meaning.

For these reasons, and more besides, few biologists are rampant determinists, and even physicists hedge their bets. The tree of life is not singular, but made of many living organisms, each nestled in a delicate ecosystem, not a machine enacting automatic routines. Evolution is as unlikely to have produced a totally determined brain as a totally random one. Metaphysically, the thought that everything we do is totally random, and therefore unpredictable, is as unsustainable and scary as the feeling that we are zombies, or totally programmed.

Some neuroscientists get round this impasse by limiting determinist explanations to what happens lower down the chain of causes in the brain, while accepting that, as we climb the ladder of neural complexity, new realities come into play, such as choice and creativity. In other words, there is a point on the causal ladder where determinism morphs into a freely choosing individual.

In search of where exactly this rung is, neuroscientists have identified two areas of our brain that interact to give us freedom of choice. When we are driving,

Mountains of the Mind

we often drift into autopilot, until suddenly there is a red light, or a busy roundabout, or a dog in the road. Our anterior cingulate cortex fires a warning shot, switching on a higher level of consciousness, preparatory to making a decision. Our ventromedial cortex responds by 'deciding' which action to take.

How and why some messages win out over others remains a mystery, and yet this is the very challenge faced by designers of artificially intelligent software for self-driving cars, raising as yet unanswered metaphysical and moral questions. At the moment, what distinguishes humans from zombies is our ability to change the future. If we program human-style decision-making into our machines, however fallible or error-free, we make them responsible for their actions, or give them agency, which presupposes a kind of awareness that equates to human consciousness.

Quantum theorists add a further twist: our mind is constantly on the edge of chaos. When an electron passes between two locations, it makes use of all possible trajectories, with no way of predicting which one it will 'choose'. It moves like a wave, going in all directions simultaneously, passing through solid objects as if they are not there. This explains why our mind, with all its imaginings, has such quickness of thought, and why, from a cloud of choices, we suddenly arrive at a moment of decision.

If we add that events in our environment, or decisions we make, reverse the whole causal chain and trigger in response the making of new proteins in neighbouring neurons, we realise that our first decision changes the conditions in our mind for all the decisions that follow. In other words, we create our freedoms as we make our choices, and vice versa. We talk back to our genes as much as they talk to us.

Parallel worlds are unable to contact each other, so
there is no risk of waking up in the wrong bed.

If we want an even more complicated account of freedom, we can always opt for the 'multiple worlds' hypothesis: the universe splits at every decision point, anything that can happen will happen, particles can be in different places at once, and their exact location is not fixed until somebody turns the light on and looks at

179

them. This explains why every life is different, how God can be in every church, and why Father Christmas comes down every chimney.

It also means that what we reject in this world doesn't matter because it gets chosen in another world. Although we choose to live with Tom, parallel versions of ourselves are playing their lives out in an alternative universe with Dick or Harry. It is merely a matter of debate whether we have chosen the best of all possible worlds, or been dropped into the worst. Fortunately these parallel worlds are unable to contact each other, so there is no risk of waking up in the wrong bed.

Freedom evolves

Whether or not we understand such abstruse physics, when it comes to accounting for human behaviour, determinists must learn to live with two paradoxes. Firstly, even in a deterministic world, freedom has evolved. Secondly, irreducible complexity does not deny free will, but makes it inevitable.

The proof of this is that I am under no obligation to give you a reason for making such a claim, so I won't. But I might change my mind. As the libertarian said to the determinist, if you want to know what I'm planning to do next weekend, you can always ask me. What you can't do is rely on what I did last weekend, because there is nothing written in yesterday that obliges anything to happen tomorrow.

The opposite of determinism is randomness: if a meteor strike hadn't wiped out the dinosaurs sixty five million years ago, we wouldn't be here now. But we might not have been. How can freedom emerge from an evolutionary process driven by chance and necessity in an unexpected universe? Randomness offers no basis for something as deliberate as free will to emerge.

Not so, say evolutionary theorists. Evolution defies randomness and entropy by storing winning strategies in DNA and passing them on to the next generation. There is no going backwards. Extinction is final for individual species, but in our case the ever-forward trajectory of evolution is our guarantee of freedom and intelligence, because both have had to keep pace with the dynamic growth of our neocortex over the last ten thousand generations. Not only are we as free as our ancestors ever were, but our technological progress makes us more free, in ways they could not imagine.

180

Mountains of the Mind

*If we're too confused whether to eat the carrot or the parsnip
for lunch, we end up going hungry.*

Richness of choice can however create a reverse effect. Faced with every possible choice, whether of menu, partner, worldview or identity, we end up like a child in a sweet shop, not knowing what we want any more, confronted with what is at once the comedy and tragedy of the human condition. We are like Buridan's Ass, so confused whether to eat the carrot or the parsnip for lunch that we end up going hungry.

Opting between types of root vegetable should be quite straightforward. Fashion choices are a bit more complex: shall we dye our hair black, or have a tattoo? Much more complex are the big decisions: what do we *want* out of life? This isn't about reasons, it's about emotions, which *motivate* us to choose our values. As the philosopher David Hume pointed out, reason is the slave of the passions. If this were not so, we would feel like Hamlet, forever stuck between 'To be or not to be?'

When our choices overwhelm us, they all look the same, none obviously morally superior to any other, or able to give us lasting satisfaction. We might be tempted to throw all our freedoms to the wind by allowing a narrow-minded demagogue to make our decisions for us, if only because this relieves us of the burden of choosing.

Forced to be free

Jean-Jacques Rousseau's take on this was that we can't sit back and allow this. We are forced to be free. We are not animals, able to fall back on instinct, but humans confronted with the dilemma of freedom. If we pass up our power to dissent, defy, assume responsibility and think for ourselves, we might buy ourselves a quiet life, but we cannot claim to be free in any meaningful sense.

This theme was picked up by the Russian writer Fyodor Dostoyevsky. Jesus came to set people free, but what they really want is bread and security. Life is much simpler if we surrender our will to a higher authority. If our wishes chime with their wishes, our life is free of friction and care. Rousseau insisted however that such a life is as unfree as it gets.

181

Mountains of the Mind

The later French thinker Jean-Paul Sartre saw us as being forced to be free in a different way, more personal than political. Freedom means nothing except in the context of hard private choices for which we alone are accountable. We are the only species for whom freedom is an existential problem. We have to grasp it, otherwise we are merely existing, not living, but in doing so we generate anguish. Standing on the cliff edge of life, we have to choose whether to jump, when to jump, and having jumped, bear the consequences. We should not however fear this existential anguish, but welcome it, because it proves that we are free.

Jean-Paul Sartre
1905-1980
Sartre saw freedom not as a moral abstraction, but as a reality we make for ourselves by our daily choices. In other words, we are forced be free, because life imposes freedom upon us.

We start life as biological creatures in a random world, but the moment we take our first breath, we have to begin creating ourselves and imposing some order, defining who we essentially are. Life is contingent, a series of unrelated happenings, and if it is to assume a meaning, and our life is to be authentic, it can only be by our taking personal responsibility for it.

In other words, we have to turn a mere 'situation' into a life that is going somewhere. Given that we start off with no defined nature, and no idea who we have it within us to be, we must rise to the challenge of finding out. This involves many failures, but unless we impose ourselves on the radical uncertainty of things, and accept life's necessities, every action we take is only one step away from absurd.

His catchphrase for the human predicament was 'existence must precede essence'. He had survived the Nazi occupation of his country, so he saw freedom in terms of a quintessential choice: submit or resist. The deepest unfreedom is to fail to make this decision.

Freedom is meaningless unless we *feel* free. If we merely accept being hemmed in by negative freedoms (all those things we cannot or are not supposed to do), and fail to engage our positive freedoms (all those things we could or would like to do), we might as well be zombies, not even noticing when our freedoms are taken away from us.

Choosing to be free makes demands of us, beyond passively accepting the conditions of our culture, class, gender or job. One day Sartre observed a waiter in a Parisian cafe, routinely moving from table to table. He wondered if all our lives are like this, merely playing a part to avoid the burden of being free, or adopting a role instead of discovering our true self. He called this fear of risk, change, honesty and uncertainty 'living in bad faith'.

Half a century before Sartre, in a world where freedom of the will was no longer circumscribed by belief in God or the power of the state, several other existentialist thinkers threw down the challenge of living out an authentic freedom. Friedrich Nietzsche saw freedom as heroic self-creation through the will to power, resisting what he called the 'slave morality' of those who turn the other cheek or opt for an easy life by going along with things. Søren Kiekegaard advocated a dangerous personal leap of faith, not hiding behind cosy groupthink or second hand doctrine.

> *Freedom is a necessity, an essential act of mind*
> *and achievement of consciousness.*

Existentialist thinkers are sometimes criticised for paving the way for the simplistic self-realisation therapies and hippie 'do your own thing' fads of the 1960's, and to hell with everybody else, but none of them promoted freedom as self-assertion at the expense of the freedom of another. On the contrary, freedom imposes a heavy moral responsibility, and the moment of decision can be

183

terrifying. In the act of choosing, we determine not only what sort of person we are, but also our commitment to others, and the sort of society we want to live in.

History gives plenty of warnings of the political dangers of denying freedom in theory: it is soon denied in practice. Even so, determinists still insist we cannot claim free will in any meaningful sense. They are not making a moral or political point, simply suggesting that, if our mind is flat, or if we can never know it fully, freedom becomes impossible. As Sartre showed however, from the perspective of our own brief lives, and our wider political liberties, freedom is a necessity. As a device for pulling together all the loose threads of experience into a single strand, it is an essential act of mind, and achievement of consciousness.

Free won't

Understanding free will depends on what kind of freedom we are trying to explain. We can't equate our freedom to choose which film to watch with the necessity of rain falling downwards. A circle is not free to be a square, the Earth is not free to reverse its orbit, and the elephant is not free to fly. The bird is free to fly, but only by relying on the resistance of air against its wings. It is not free to live beneath the sea. Seen this way, freedom is not the negation of the laws of nature, but what happens when we act in accord with them.

Another way of looking at this is to say that we are free to choose our actions, but not our desires. The cat may choose between whether to chase the rat or the mouse, but it can't resist the urge to hunt. The addict is free to decide which drug to take, and where, and who with, but not whether to take it.

So is the addict free in any meaningful sense? Yes, because even the most inveterate habit creates only a probability for what happens next, not an inevitability. If that were not so, rehab clinics would be out of business. The only sense in which our future is already laid out is the pattern we create by our previous actions, which we are free to change. We tame our animals, but they do not *know* they have been tamed. The addict *knows* what freedom felt like before it was stolen by the drug habit. The only genuinely unfree person is a slave, a condition of physical and mental subjugation from which every fibre longs to be free.

There are other journeys into freedom that we can make. Pre-diabetics are free to reverse their prognosis through taking control of their diet, and racists are free to learn to see *untermensch* as fellow human beings with equal rights. Victor Frankl, who survived Auschwitz, pointed out that our ultimate freedom is to choose our attitude in any set of circumstances, regardless of the injustices inflicted upon us.

We live our lives somewhere between automatic reflexes and an extraordinary capacity to defy expectation through our determination and imagination. We shape our lives by the choices we make, and our brain is fashioned by what we set our mind to. Neuroscientists have dubbed these qualities neuroplasticity and neurodiversity, but 'up top' they amount to the same thing: we are free to self-direct.

This is not the same as saying that freedom knows no bounds. Each living organism, including human beings, has evolved a set of flexible responses, otherwise it could not move into a new future. At the same time it must defy entropy, holding its molecules together as long as it can before decay sets in. The price of survival is that it must work within strict constraints.

In nature, absolute freedom is as meaningless as music with no structure or harmony, the individual sounds scattered with no organisation or finale. Aleatory music, based on the idea of rolling a dice and 'playing with' the repetition of a random phrase, like a snatch of birdsong, is still a *composition*.

Music that is well-written sounds at once bound and free, or free *because* it is bound, each phrase enjoying a perfect freedom: it can sound no other way, and how it sounds is just right. Many couples claim to enjoy such perfect freedom. This is achieved by knowingly rejecting all other distractions, so that they can feel the security of commitment. Unfazed by the negative aspect of freedom, or the affairs they cannot have, they have made a positive choice of each other. This does not halve their freedom, but doubles it.

Negative freedom

The historian of ideas Isaiah Berlin defined negative freedom as what we are free *from*, as in the limits we voluntarily accept to our freedoms. When we keep to our side of the road, don't speed and keep our vehicle roadworthy, we do so because we wish others to do so too: everybody benefits. It is an enforced negative freedom when a government denies a whole population access to the internet in the name of 'security'.

Mountains of the Mind

Berlin reasoned that the happiest and most democratic society is one where we enjoy positive freedom, or the freedom *to* choose for ourselves. We can become a rally driver, smoke, volunteer for a charity, eat red meat, go vegetarian, attend political rallies, watch pornography online, and no-one will stop us, unless we break the law or harm others.

Freedom comes in several flavours. If we're locked in a prison cell, with only one hour a day in the exercise yard, we're left in little doubt what it means to be denied the liberty of our body. In Roman times, the *liber* was a free man, not a slave. In political terms, imprisonment and slavery are severe cases of negative freedom, or what we are not permitted to do.

In this sense, the opposite of freedom is coercion, or constraint. Most of us hope we will never end up as a prisoner or slave, but we regularly accept limits on our freedom: we mustn't force others to act against their wishes, or to conform to ours. We mustn't take what is ours, or drive while intoxicated.

If we are caught breaking the law in this way, no court is likely to throw the full weight of punishment upon us unless we were not free to act otherwise, or capable of seeing the impact of our actions upon our victims. The judge must be sure we were not acting under duress, or suffering from some kind of neurological impairment. We can only be found guilty if the court judges us to be *mens rea*, or in our right mind at the time of the deed.

The flip side to this is that total freedom implies total responsibility. We might be shown leniency if there are mitigating circumstances such as poverty or bad company, but a cornerstone of the law is that all are treated equally without fear or favour, and it is a dangerous precedent to suggest that some are more free than others.

If we are given a prison sentence, there is still an important sense in which we remain free even while our cell door denies us liberty. We might show remorse, persuading the prison governor to release us early on the grounds of good behaviour. If we've been imprisoned for paedophilia, we might volunteer for chemical castration in return for parole. We might learn through a restorative justice course after our release to live a better life, or to work with young people who would benefit from what we have been through.

186

Mountains of the Mind

Positive freedom

The political philosopher John Locke was more interested in positive freedom. If the door of our cell were left open, would we walk through it? The answer seems obvious, but it raises a fundamental question about the nature of human freedom. For us to make a decision of this magnitude, electrochemical events must happen in our synapses. If our legs are to stride out to liberty through the prison gates, the messages that control muscle movement must be physically generated in our brain.

So what part of us 'decides' to grasp this great opportunity of freedom? If it's activity going on below our conscious awareness, without our say so, the opposite of freedom is not imprisonment, but determinism. We are not free to walk at all, but merely following our programming. Seen this way, positive freedom is a clanging cymbal, making lots of noise but having no substance.

The experiences of hostages and prisoners of conscience suggest otherwise. They say that freedom of thought, or keeping their minds active, is a positive freedom that sustains their spirits while they are denied their liberty. Some keep their will free and their mind alive by writing journals and reading books. Those condemned to solitary confinement invent games and people their inner world with imaginary characters to retain independence of mind, if only to deny their captors total victory.

The higher our sense of positive freedom, the greater our happiness.

Hostages are taken against their will, but the rest of us avoid incarceration by sticking to the law. We can exercise as many positive freedoms as we like, so long as we obey the essential negative ones, especially 'Don't cause any harm to other people'. It's worth sticking to society's rules if it means we never get in trouble with the law, because we can go about our lives unhindered. Studies show that the higher our sense of exercising our positive freedoms, the greater our happiness and optimism levels.

Our parents limit our freedoms when we are children, but not because they are control freaks. They give us time to learn how to self-regulate. By the time we leave their care, we become truly free on the basis that we can self-govern, balancing our negative restraints with our positive opportunities. Bad parents are not the ones who spoil our fun by sending us to bed on time, but those who let us play with sharp knives before we are ready.

Gaming our freedom

Mulling over free will is all a bit irrelevant unless we *believe* in it, despite all attempts to debunk it or persuade us that we are unfree. We help ourselves greatly if we learn to 'game' our freedom, in the first place by identifying our frailties, then practising how to strengthen them, mindful that free will is not an infinite resource.

Experiments show that after a sustained period of self denial, our 'free will' muscle gets tired, and we become more likely to *choose* to make that secret late night trip to the fridge. Whether we reward ourselves at the end of a long day with a stick of carrot or a slice of cheesecake is entirely up to us, our own free choice. We can make the choice even simpler by not buying cheesecake in the first place.

As well as believing in free will, we need also need to be good at exercising free won't. Going back to Daniel Libet's discovery of tiny delays between input and output in our brain, our power to say yes or no may reside in that brief moment. Instead of contracting out our responsibility to our brain, or nervous system, or unconscious, *we* choose from the maelstrom of stimuli or 'exciters' which ones are saying something important to us.

We fire 'inhibitors' that enable us to eliminate bad options, and single out the right or best response. The only exceptions are if we suffer from an addiction, or a neurological disorder such as Tourette's. The road we *don't* choose to go down can matter more than the one we eventually do.

Free will is not an infinite resource.

Free will is not therefore a switch that is either on or off, or a gift that some possess and others lack. It has to be cultivated by diligent practice. It is not an infinite resource, as Odysseus realised when he asked his crew to tie him to the mast of his ship, so that he could not be lured by the Sirens. If we're controlled by a craving, the first thing we have to learn is how to deliver ourselves from evil. Our free will, which is the regulating valve of our appetites, is under constant attack.

Mountains of the Mind

Each choice we make is in a particular context, with different temptations to 'just say yes', or support systems to help us to 'just say no'
.

Contaminated thinkers

As we all know, resisting temptation is more easily said than done, because it always lurks. Also, denying ourselves any treats at all errs too far towards asceticism. Obesity has become a serious problem in the West, but we don't want our government to ban cheesecakes, or to insist that our hands are tied behind our back as we pass the cake counter. These draconian measures might reduce our waist line, and give us an extra year or two of life, but they are negative freedoms. Self-regulation is best.

> **Hamlet**
> Like Hamlet, we hate the thought of being 'played upon', but we are not always as clever as we think at knowing when we are being 'nudged' in a particular direction.

Expressing our positive freedoms is not however always entirely our own affair. Advertisers have some very clever tricks at their disposal to persuade us that cheesecake is one step away from nirvana. We are vulnerable to their magic, because they target the hit-seeking biases in our reptilian brain, and the heat-seeking sensors in our nervous system, prioritising images over words, and immediate reward over tedious waiting.

Like Hamlet, we don't like the thought of being played upon like a flute, and yet, in what is known as the name-letter effect, our name might have a secret hold over us. Greenwoods are more likely to become gardeners, Kates are more likely to donate to Hurricane Katrina, and Davinas are more likely to be attracted to Davids.

In other words, our thinking is contaminated, albeit at a subconscious level, before we start. This makes us biddable and gullible, not just to the obvious shove, but also to the subtle nudge. If we are 'primed' by being shown lots of words about age, illness, aches and pains, our movements afterwards might reflect these qualities, whatever our age. We haven't been hypnotised or brainwashed, merely nudged. We are free to respond, but our choice is no longer quite free.

Advertisers know that if we are approached directly, our reason resists. So they creep up sideways on us, looking for cunning ways to modify our behaviour. We are more likely to buy a product or pay our taxes if we are addressed personally, spoken to by a named official, greeted with a friendly face or given a 'free gift', which is already costed into what they are going to charge us.

There's a greater chance we'll pay a tip if everyone
else around us is doing so.

There are other ways in which our response can be primed or our thinking contaminated. We'll laugh more at a television sitcom if it's accompanied by 'canned laughter'. We'll buy French goods if an accordion is playing in the background. We'll give kinder responses if we have a warm drink in our hands, and harsher if there is a bad smell in the room. There's a greater chance we'll pay a tip if everyone else around us is doing so, and an even bigger tip to avoid being seen as measly.

We're more likely to agree to water-saving measures if the Water Board offers to put a sign outside our home praising our eco-credentials, so that we can be admired by the neighbours. We're more likely to study the boring statistics on our water bill if we're given a 'smiley' emoticon when our consumption is economical.

In other words, we are not as free as we think. We are suggestible, and our generosity is open to manipulation. If we're asked to donate £10 to charity, we're more likely to give £9 than £1, because the higher figure was 'planted' in our subconscious, so our response is 'anchored' before it is allowed to drift away from its mooring.

190

Mountains of the Mind

Another trick charities play is to capitalise on the power of the image: we are more likely to donate to the schooling of one smiling child far away in Africa than an abstract appeal for funds to raise academic standards for all at home. This masks a blind spot: having made ourselves feel better about something far away, we obliviously walk past the food bank for the hungry children just round the corner.

Positive nudgers

We don't mind a positive nudge towards a change of habit such as using our own coffee cup or shopping bag to save the planet from plastic overload. We might value a fitness tracker that monitors our calorie intake and gets us a discount on our health insurance. We can live with higher taxes on red meat and dairy products, steering us towards buying more fruit and vegetables, if the health and environmental benefits are spelled out to us.

Change through voluntary response is better than forced legislation.

These are more subtle strategies than the simplistic behaviourism of the early twentieth century, when humans were routinely treated as salivating dogs or pecking pigeons. It is better if our actions come from inside, rather than be imposed from the outside. Change through voluntary response is better than forced legislation, and fact-based advice is better than skewed manipulation, especially in matters relating to our health, financial security and the care of the planet.

This does not mean that the nudge alone can make us better humans or free choosers. It's not a case of which neurons get switched on, or off, but what motivations we find to change our behaviour, remembering that we never fully escape the influence of those around us, good, bad or subtly manipulative.

Behavioural economists, rational choice theorists, neuromarketers and the designers of social media algorithms spend millions to discover the best way of getting past our rational resistance (I don't need a new car) to gain access to our biddable wants and desires (but it would be cool to be the first in my street to own an electric car). Car dealers know that we're much more likely to buy a car if we're allowed to take it for a spin.

Mountains of the Mind

Credit card companies know only too well how to find our weak spots, persuading us that we don't need to wait for things we really want, which is not to be confused with what we really need. It's not their fault: they, like us, are playing the system. As we get better at resisting, so they must increase the temptation, and refine the nudge. In a society built on easy borrowing, our only choice is to develop the mental muscle not to flash the plastic every time we see something shiny. We have to become our own nudgers.

Biddable choosers

We don't mind being nudged if it is in our interest or directed towards the public good. Plato defended the use of the Noble Lie, such as the myth of national unity during wartime to keep morale high. We are less comfortable when this becomes PsyOps (psychological warfare operations), or coordinated attempts to bombard us with leaflets from the air, spread conspiracy theories or target our computer inbox.

We like the idea of a litter bin that plays us a tune when we throw something into it, or a stairway in a train station being painted like a piano keyboard to encourage us to walk up it rather than take the escalator. When we view a property for rent or sale, we don't object to the owner filling the place with the aroma of coffee to make it more inviting to us.

We accept these as good-humoured ruses that don't compromise our right to choose, because they emanate from the Ministry of Love, not the Ministry of Fear. When such tactics are ramped up to state level, they can still be 'freedom preserving', or examples of responsible libertarianism, so long as we don't feel coerced. We can walk away if we want to. Some however regard any such meddling as social engineering, or the nanny state at its worst.

What do we feel for instance about becoming an organ donor by default? Our recycled body parts can be used to save a life, not because we have made a conscious decision to opt in to the scheme, but because we haven't made a deliberate choice to opt out. Do we feel that making the wearing of seat belts and crash helmets compulsory, or mandating the use of surgical masks during a pandemic, are infringements on our liberty, or the least that can be expected of a responsible member of the community?

We find out we have been paying into a pension scheme to provide for our future long after we wise up to the fact that we can choose to withdraw all our money to go on a spending spree next week. We've not been denied the freedom to choose, but empowered to make a more informed choice later. Governments are happy to provide short term tax relief for this long term game plan, because they don't want a generation of retirees who can't support themselves.

Minor changes in our environment can and do 'cue' healthier behaviour: give us smaller plates and spoons in restaurants to encourage us to take smaller portions, serve green vegetables to children on a light-coloured plate, place the fruit and veg at the front of the supermarket, take the tempting chocolate and sugary drinks away from children's eye level at the checkout, put traffic calming measures on residential rat-runs.

We need these well-meant nudges, because we often overestimate our ability to change our own behaviour, or we underestimate the power of habit. This is especially true when we are younger, before our cognitive 'system two' reflection mechanisms are strong enough to resist the impulses of our 'system one' gut responses.

This applies particularly to the obesity crisis. Some advocate outlawing the sale of high-calorie snacks in schools to 'protect' children. Adults too are 'protected' by the banning of 'three for two' offers on junk food in supermarkets and fast-food outlets. It will be interesting to see what mix of positive and negative incentives governments adopt to get millions of us to switch to generating solar power, driving electric cars, flying less, and eating laboratory-grown meat.

Our thinking is easily contaminated.

We generally comply, but we react badly if we find out that we've been 'had'. Not that we always wise up to this: our brain is highly suggestible and our thinking is easily contaminated. The Soviet filmmaker Lev Kuleshov established that our response to an image can be determined by what immediately precedes or follows it. By using juxtaposition, he showed that once an idea is put in our heads, it is hard to ignore it, like a tune that won't go away. If we are told not to think of pink rabbits, all we can think of is pink rabbits.

This makes us vulnerable to the 'mere exposure' effect, which is the secret of advertising, branding and electioneering. A steady drip feed of images and words eventually seeps into our subconscious, until we feel familiar and comfortable with it, part of our mental furniture, making us more likely to buy it next time, our will no longer transparent to ourselves. This makes us especially amenable to pre-Christmas advertising when we are young: if we see a toy often enough, we end up clamouring for it in our Christmas stocking.

Problematic memorisers

Not that we are likely to remember doing so. We don't lay down memories in our first two or three years because we have not yet grown the appropriate neural circuits. This cognitive boost coincides with our ability to recognise ourselves in a mirror, and the arrival of language. Only then do we possess the necessary inner speech to write the story of our autobiographical self. Those who claim to remember things happening to them in the womb have good imagination, but poor understanding of cognitive biology.

Around the age of ten, apart from a few stand-out moments, we forget most of our childhood memories as the major brain reorganisation of adolescence gets under way. We generally have lots of memories from those exciting years, when everything is new, disconcerting and embarrassing.

Our adult memory starts to get filled up, but it resembles nothing like a photograph album, filing cabinet, archive or wax tablet. These are merely metaphors for a process that is invisible on a brain scan. Despite decades of research, neuroscientists are still baffled about what memory is, how it works, and what happens when we remember something.

An important step towards solving the puzzle was taken in 1970 by Eric Kandel. A snail's memory is relatively easy to study, because its brain contains only twenty thousand neurons in nine clusters. Kandel was able to detect chemical changes in the synapses when the snail makes a foray into the world. These constitute learning because, through sensitisation and habituation, the snail is able to 'remember' whether an object is safe, a threat, or potential food.

As we ascend the ladder of biological complexity, the feats of memory become ever more remarkable, always linked to survival challenges faced in the wild. A wrasse earns its living by serving as a 'cleaner' for larger fish. It may have thousands of clients, some of which are more cooperative than others, so it pays to keep a virtual list of favourites.

Mountains of the Mind

A scrub jay not only forms a spatial map of where it has cached thousands of acorns, but catalogues how long they have lain buried, not bothering to return after they have rotted. It also makes sure that other scrub jays don't see where its favourite hiding places are.

A chimpanzee has a photographic memory that puts humans to shame. It can remember the location of a sequence of numbers after less than a second's exposure on a screen, probably a throwback to its need to recognise and remember the location of ripe fruits high up in its tropical forest home.

Starting with the humble snail's rudimentary brain, Kandel made a good start in understanding how memory works, but human memory, operating within a brain of a hundred billion neurons, presents puzzles, paradoxes and problems of a totally different order, such as control, selectivity, storage, accuracy and efficiency.

Memory evolved to serve not as an accurate data base of the past, but as an inventory of strategies to help us respond fluidly to future situations. It's pleasant to recall all those holidays in the sunshine, but that's just an unlooked for extra. Principally, we remember the past so that we can make a better plan for the future.

Our brain doesn't get 'full', but it does need to stay efficient.

Counterintuitive as it sounds, we remember to forget. We can lay down new memories right into old age, possibly accumulating as many as six hundred million memories in our lifetime, but we can't remember everything, because we don't need to. Evolution has built forgetfulness into the system, as the price of flexibility and complexity. In order to make and store new memories, there must be a facility to throw out the old ones, not because the brain gets 'full', but because it needs to stay efficient.

This entails physical and biological constraints. If memory were infinite and super-fast, we might be able to learn to play the guitar in a day, but we would forget everything we learned on our cookery course last week. Our most efficient memories are those that are well organised, steadily accumulated, and regularly curated.

It would be a curse to remember what we had for lunch every day of our life. Some people have 'photographic' memories, able to redraw a whole cityscape after one glance. Mozart could play back an entire concerto after one hearing. Such skills are however very rare, and are usually 'paid for' somewhere else in the brain.

When we recall a memory, it's not like visiting a bookshelf and blowing off the dust. Memories are laid down by one batch of proteins, and recalled by another. Every time we trawl up a memory, we subtly change it, and it changes us. In other words, memory is not consistent. After hundreds of call-ups, that childhood memory on the beach at Blackpool falling off that donkey bears little resemblance to what actually happened.

It is no longer accurate, not because we are dishonest or negligent, but because it's our favourite memory: we've changed it substantially by frequent use, retranscribing the neural tissue each time, if ever so slightly. We're made aware of this when a sibling reminds us that we *did* fall off an animal on holiday, but it was at Clacton, and it was a model horse on the merry-go-round.

Memory might *feel* persistent, but that doesn't mean it's accurate. We are convinced we remember it well, and it's unsettling to be told that things happened differently. We have conflated several events into one, and tinged our memories with our feelings in the present, which in this case is the warm cosy glow of a happy childhood.

Storage capacity is essential if we are to have a sense of the timeline of our life, but there is no single place in the brain that acts as a memory warehouse. The neurosurgeon Roger Penfield discovered that he could activate specific memories by stimulating different parts of the cortex, suggesting that memories are stored in an associative network, not a series of labelled boxes.

Some rats had the 'memory part' of their brain removed after running a maze several times, but days later they remembered the route, proving that memory is spread right across the brain, not just in the hippocampus, which has long been regarded as the seat of memory. Wide distribution is a clever evolutionary failsafe: it means integrated networks, faster recall, and less likelihood that vital memories will be wiped.

Random memories may pop up now and again, perhaps triggered by a smell, or rummaging through an old drawer, only to fade from view almost as quickly. This suggests that, though most of the past is wiped, a few essential moments and images are cached, but they stay active only if they regularly sound an echo in the chamber of the present.

Mountains of the Mind

Certain cases of brain damage in humans suggest that some memory functions and data can be lost, but memory is rarely destroyed completely, because there are different types for different functions. A bang on the head might erase our short term memory temporarily, but our long term memory stays intact. This phenomenon explains why traumatic memories are so difficult to erase: they are buried deep, leaving scar tissue not just in the amygdala, but all over the brain.

We are left with many questions. If our brain is our memory-minder, what is 'our' role in selecting what personal memories to keep, and what to let go? What powers do we possess to rewrite, improve or enhance our memory? Is it possible to 'recover' memories of abuse, pain and suffering from an unhappy childhood, decades after the event?

Nostalgic dreamers

Our brain relies on up to five thousand proteins in the synapses to store memories, possibly different ones for good and bad. Once it has decided it wants to keep a particular memory, it deploys the enzyme kinase to transfer it from the body of a neuron into its nucleus, where it is 'safer'. Other chemicals give each memory an emotional 'tag', storing it alongside the event that caused it. This is why, when we are in a good mood, we tend to recall more positive memories, making us feel more or less kindly disposed to ourselves and those around us. Bad moods have the reverse effect.

For these reasons, it is highly unlikely that we will one day be able to download our memories into a digital avatar of ourselves. Even if the facts of our life survive the transfer, our feelings, which are the true indices of who we are, will be lost in translation. Our avatar will not cherish the little mementoes and keepsakes that mean so much to us, but nothing to anyone else.

Our important memories are not banks of catalogued data, but personal associations and feelings, usually sorted out during our sleep, when our brain consolidates what it has learned during the day. This includes motor skills. We might struggle over a new piece of music during our piano lesson on Monday, only to find that we play it better on Tuesday. Our brain has installed 'muscle memory' while we slept.

Long term memory helps us to store important names, faces and incidents as the tracks of our years, but only selectively, and not always reliably. Memories are

Mountains of the Mind

sorted into different 'drawers' for quick retrieval, but this system only works well if we remember which drawers we put things in, and we inspect them regularly.

> **The Persistence of Memory**
> In his painting of that name, Salvador Dali (1904-1989) suggests that memory is anything but persistent. Time bends, space warps, and accuracy is negotiable.

This applies to short term memory too. Sometimes we forget what we went to find upstairs. The solution is to go back downstairs, because in our memory, upstairs and downstairs occupy different 'drawers'. Going back to a place we visited long ago can also jog our memory, because memory is highly associative. Police take potential witnesses back to the scene of a crime and recreate the details of the incident as closely as possible, hoping that a key memory will be reactivated.

Both long term and short term memory can let us down, because our memories seldom work in isolation. They are combinations of time, place and sensory input, stored in different neural circuits. Gremlins and glitches can be caused by mechanical stutters or by emotional contamination.

This explains why we might struggle to remember people's names if we meet them out of context. We recognise their face, perhaps even the sound of their voice, but until they remind us when or where we met them, the jigsaw pieces of memory scattered across our brain are slow to remake the original picture on the lid.

Or the jigsaw can remake itself involuntarily, through the power of association. Not only do smell and taste communicate fastest to our hippocampus in the present, they are also able to trigger our earliest and deepest memories. The scent

198

and flavour of a particular cake, or the echo of a long-forgotten tune, can take us instantly and effortlessly 'back down the vista of years', as D H Lawrence put it.

We feel the hold that the past has over us most strongly in our predisposition for nostalgia, which literally means 'pain for the past'. 'Where are the snows of yesteryear?' pined the French poet François Villon. We spend countless hours lost in the past, going over words we wish we hadn't said, or actions we might have performed differently.

As the joke goes, nostalgia is not what it used to be, but it can make some of our oldest memories shine more vividly than something we did yesterday. As the song 'I remember it well' reminds us, we don't remember well, because we recreate the past we desire, and we invent the childhood we always wished we had. As we age, nostalgia becomes a foretaste of death, not as anxiety about what we might lose in the future, but as sadness about what we don't want to lose from the past.

The past tends to look more beautiful than it was in reality, casting a shadow over the present. But we are deluded to think that we were happier back then, or that life was more meaningful. Nostalgia helps us to gloss over the challenges we faced in those times, sweetening our good memories and blanking our bad ones.

The past appeals because it has already happened, and is therefore much more controllable than the future. A fantasy country of the mind in the never-never of the past allows us to escape, albeit temporarily, the reality of what has become of our body in the present. Similarly, clairvoyance, horoscopes and palmistry offer us only mirror images of what is behind us, projected into what lies before us, like time repeating itself backwards. As T S Eliot wrote, time that is eternally present is 'unredeemable', and time future 'is contained in time past'.

The Roman writer Cicero knew that our memorising abilities alter as we age. His solution in his senior years was to use his memory as a 'running track for the mind'. This was wise, because as we age we experience two phenomena. Firstly we suffer age-related memory loss, the result of a gene that is expressed less strongly with the passing years. Secondly, in our dotage our memory starts to feel like a film played backwards.

As we get older, our memory slows, not necessarily because we are 'losing it', but because we have far more to remember than in our salad days. We are still making new memories every day, and we need to keep our filing system in order.

Mountains of the Mind

As the past recedes, it becomes an inverted pyramid, the top much wider than the base.

The top is populated by incidents nearer in time, most easily remembered because most frequently recalled. There's no surprise in forgetting the name of someone we last had dealings with forty years ago. Even the squirrel sometimes forgets where he has hidden his nuts. The base of the pyramid will remain firm, because our brain has identified a few precious memories as the 'origin story' of our life. They are like the badges we sew onto our rucksack to show where we have been.

Our earliest memories are usually the last to go.

Our first memories are buried deepest, almost indelible, mere handfuls of proteins coded as 'engrams' or units of information. Flushed out and renewed over and over, they somehow survive for eight decades or more, even half a lifetime of coma in the case of those who contracted 'sleeping sickness' in the 1920's pandemic. If we suffer from dementia and start to lose our mind, our earliest memories are usually the last to go. We pine for our 'land of lost content' or, like Citizen Kane, mysteriously mutter 'Rosebud' as our dying word.

Fractious forgetters

Whichever way we look at it, remembering is a 'big ask' for our brain. Even healthy brains struggle to remember, and lapse into forgetting, for several reasons. Storing a memory and then finding it again is an intricate process of making, encoding, filing and retrieving, all of which require attention and effort, because memories are symbolic representations of events, not snapshots of anything that relates to the real world.

As our time-travel agent and guarantor of personal continuity, our brain has to recall memories not just of what happened in the past, but of appointments and events that lie in the future. It pays to be good at looking both ways, because evidence suggests a strong link between accurate recall and good foresight. Our brain has to distinguish between primacy, or when we first encountered an experience, and recency, or when we last did so. It might store hundreds of tunes in our head, but lose all track of where we first heard them.

Mountains of the Mind

*Keeping a careful tally of who is our friend was potentially
a matter of life and death on the African savannah.*

Our brain has to be good at forgetting. We have about a thousand dreams a year, but most of them are scrubbed. If one or two are remembered, or reactivated in our waking moments, it has to be for a good reason. By contrast, we build up a store of hundreds of faces (though not necessarily their names) because keeping a careful tally of who is our friend, or who owes us a favour, was potentially a matter of life and death on the African savannah.

What our brain remembers is a function of our powers of attention, or the extent to which we notice things. Psychologists distinguish between lantern and spotlight attention. We need the more distributed glow of the lantern when we are trying to place a memory in a wider context.

The spotlight comes into play when we have to concentrate, making us more likely to remember specifics. This is especially true in the phenomenon of a 'flashbulb' memory, which burns itself onto our retina. This is a happy gift when it's an image of us crossing the winning line first, but not if it's a distressing sight we would dearly love to forget.

The stronger stimulus of spotlight memories might lead us into the error of 'revisionism', compounded by suggestion, bias, distortion and plain misattribution. We might *want* to remember that our boss said we are due for a rise, but in fact she didn't. In such cases, our feelings of how things *ought* to be override our brain's attempts to keep an accurate record of how things *actually* happened.

Memory boosters
In the nineteenth century, Hermann Ebbinghaus showed that learning small amounts at regular intervals, interspersed with self-tests and review, allows us both to learn more, and to remember it for longer. Revision for an exam is better performed a little and often over several weeks, rather than trying to cram everything in the night before. There may even be a degree of fetishism involved. By the law of association, if we wear a lucky charm while revising, wearing it on the day of the examination might prompt us to remember more.

Mountains of the Mind

It won't pay us to do random memory exercises for fun, such as learning by heart the first page of the telephone directory. Learning and memory aren't like muscles that can be made fitter by exercise. They are skills that need specific applications, so mugging up on how to service our car won't help us to make a good job of hanging the washing out.

We remember more when our flow is interrupted. This sounds paradoxical, but it is better to leave our learning circuits open, because they shut down when our brain feels a matter has been resolved. Research with waiters suggests that as soon as our meal is served, or we have paid our bill, they forget about us. Without closure, unfinished orders stay in the forefront of their mind. We might forget that we haven't paid, but they don't.

Those who achieve most highly are those
with the best working memory.

Short-term memory is vital for efficient day to day functioning, but it's good for only a handful of items, and it lasts only about fifteen seconds, its duration short because its circuits are short. Now where did I put those keys a moment ago? Short-term memory works on a 'magic seven plus or minus two' basis, which is why we struggle with long phone numbers or shopping lists. We find it hard to recall more than seven of the twenty items on a tray before it is removed from sight.

Whether we can recall them ten minutes or ten years later is a different matter. What such a memory test can't reveal is the quality of our working memory, or our ability to juggle several tasks simultaneously, like a good chef keeping on top of a busy kitchen. He might forget the names of kings and queens he was taught at school, but he needs to remember the timing of each dish, which customers need a follow-up, and what supplies need ordering for tomorrow. Studies of schoolchildren show that those who achieve most highly in the long term are not the cleverest or fastest, but the ones with the best working memory.

We might be attracted to stories in the press about enhancing our memory. Our parents give us a good start when they go over the day with us, reviewing what we might have learned, and previewing the next day's activities. Memory is an art, and it repays diligence from our earliest days.

Mountains of the Mind

Students pay good money for the 'smart drug' modafinil, which might boost their memory for their final examination, but their extra knowledge might have disappeared a week later. Studies show that running a mild electric current through the brain can boost memory by up to thirty percent, but again, we hope that doctors, lawyers and pilots can do their job without the help of stimulants.

We're better at remembering long words, even nonsense ones, if we can somehow link the syllables together on the basis of sounds we already know. It's much harder to remember a series of random items, a novel with no plot, or a tune with no obvious melody, but there are various tricks we can play. Our memory struggles with unconnected bits, but not if we capitalise on our brain's natural strengths by making meaningful connections between them, visualise them or associate them in a story.

If we group things into categories, 'chunk' them as smaller but related items, or turn them into silly images in a daft narrative, they stick like cleavers to our clothing. Mnemonists, or people who win memory competitions, can remember a whole pack of cards, perhaps even two, by 'seeing' each card as a character performing an action in a specific place, all integrated into a personalised story.

We can play this game too. If we need to remember to buy milk, pick up a parcel and send our granny a birthday wish, we can picture a cow with a face like our granny wearing a postman's hat. The key point to remember is that our granny must not find this out.

In Ancient Greece, Socrates believed that certain memories are present from birth, like messages inscribed on the parchment of our mind from an earlier life. He took the fact that an uneducated slave could 'discover' arithmetical truths for himself through the power of logic as proof that the knowledge was already in his brain, just waiting to be activated. The modern view is that this is intuition at work, not memory. The 'knowledge' that three is greater than two is genetic, stored in our DNA. Even crows can 'count' up to ten, not literally, but sufficient to recognise quantity.

Remember (!) that our genes are in essence giant memory banks, each cell in our body harking back to LUCA, or the Last Universal Common Ancestor, linking us to the emergence of the first primitive life forms on our planet nearly four billion years ago, passed on as biological memory through each evolutionary leap forward. This might explain why we secretly enjoy wallowing in the mud: our brain stem, the most reptilian part of us, recalls the echoes of where and how it all began.

Types of memory

Our understanding of memory has moved on since Socrates. Cognitive scientists distinguish different types of memory, stored in different ways and for different purposes. Consider how we remember our way around our local area. Our brain has 'place and grid' cells that act as a neural GPS. In addition there are orienting, acoustic and iconic cells that relate to our sensorimotor capabilities.

Explicit memory is objective, because it regularly comes up against the reality test of things 'out there'. It is divided into episodic (dates, times and places) or semantic (the names of things). Implicit memory is 'in here', our subjective domain, of things that only we know, even if we're not sure how we know. Sometimes we get a question right, with no recollection how the answer found its way into our head.

This is not quite the same as having something 'on the tip of our tongue': we know the answer, but our access to it is blocked by another memory. Often the answer comes to us minutes later, when we've stopped thinking about it, or we can pump our memory by going through the alphabet or sequence of events for a cue or clue.

A third type of memory is procedural: once we've learned to ride a bicycle, it's impossible to forget, though we may get a little rusty. If we're laid up in hospital for a while, we may temporarily 'forget' how to walk, requiring occupational therapy to relearn the skill, which hasn't really gone away. Our brain still remembers, but our muscles need reminding.

Quizzers show off their prowess at explicit memory. We call such people 'eggheads', and there is evidence that the more they commit to memory, the more their hippocampus swells, which is the seat of memory. In the days before satnavs, London taxi drivers were famed for having an enlarged hippocampus, crammed with the layout of thousands of streets, short cuts and place names, though this finding has not been widely replicated.

When put on the spot, quizzers and taxi drivers might struggle to recall one vital fact, but there is a technique they can use called 'method of loci', invented in ancient times for remembering lots of information. This involves imagining a

204

house with many rooms. Each item is placed in each room in succession as we tour the house. This is 'our' house, so we know there is a lion in the first room, a clown in the second, and so on. If the first item to be remembered is a banana, we 'see' it sticking out of the lion's ear in our mind's eye, a bizarre juxtaposition which we are much less likely to forget. Then we move on to the clown.

Short term memory scores are improving, but
working memory is declining.

Some actors tasked with memorising hundreds of lines use such methods to 'locate' where they are in each scene, and to prompt their entrances and exits. Research shows however that, for all our rising levels of smartness and expanding digital databases, we are becoming poorer memorisers, because we are increasingly out-sourcing our explicit memories to our electronic devices.

Socrates made a similar argument against writing over two thousand years ago: it creates forgetfulness, giving us the show of wisdom without the reality. And yet spoken words have a habit of flying off on the breeze. Many writers keep journals and notebooks to pin their thoughts down, allowing them to revisit them months or years later.

Socrates may however have a point. Oral traditions, passed down the generations, are dying across the world. Also, school tests show that, although short term memory scores are improving, long term and working memories are declining, rendering children less able to apply their knowledge broadly and imaginatively.

Inventive historians

The only place the past exists is in our heads, and every time we recall it, we rewrite it to our own script. Once more we relive that happy childhood, or rehearse how kind we think we have been to our neighbours over the years.

This means that our memories are recreations, not historical documents. Repeated encoding, storing, calling up and decoding changes them subtly every time, even invents them. As our memories make our stories, so the stories we tell about ourselves remake our memories. Our acts of remembering change us, because we see the past through the eyes of our present experience or emotional state. The past stays the same, but our use of it changes, even in our history lessons.

Some people are compulsive fabulists, allowing their storytelling to invent their whole life. They write their biography as a succession of facts, but it is a work of fiction. They are so desperate to believe their own publicity, or in such psychological need of it, that their life implodes when their fabrication is exposed, genuinely shocked to be told that there is no truth in their tales.

We pride ourselves as a species on our good memory, but as we have seen, many animals outstrip us. There may however be a silver lining to having a relatively poor memory: it makes way for imagining the future, which humans excel at. Anticipation and flexible reasoning are more useful skills for a nomadic creature that has to adapt to a wide range of environmental challenges, not just remember where it has buried its acorns.

We define our identity as a nation, people or civilisation
by what we choose to remember.

Memory has been variously described as a library, sponge or CD ROM, but it is more fruitfully seen as a touched-up painting, idiosyncratic narrative or edited yarn, personally as a life narrative, and collectively as shared myth. We feel the weight of the communal past in the call to honour 'all our yesterdays' in our remembrance services.

We define our identity as a nation, people or civilisation by what we choose to remember, though in the case of colonial injustices and war crimes, it can just as easily be what we choose to forget. In the selective amnesia of election campaigns, the silence of the past can be deafening. Perhaps this is a good thing. The bloody Balkans conflict of the 1990's was a flare up of memories that had been festering for centuries, from grievances that no-one alive could remember.

Memory in this cultural sense is nothing like a computer which we can regularly upgrade with more RAM or a faster hard drive. Our brain is its own programmer, moving memories around, retagging them emotionally, deleting the ones it no longer wants, and rewriting ones that it does.

The past can never be repeated or revised, only acknowledged or denied. Historical memory is always a creation of the present, based on interpretation of

206

sources, seen through contemporary eyes. However much we like historical novels and movies, they are set in a world we have lost. Beyond the reminiscences of our grandparents, who at best give us a hazy view, we have no idea what life felt or smelt like in those days.

We realise in our history lessons at school that we are being given an edited version of the past, possibly a propagandist one, woven into a national, political and ideological narrative, however well or ill intentioned. When we walk our local streets, we pass statues of local dignitaries who contributed generously to their community, but they might also have made their fortune from running slave plantations thousands of miles away.

We then find ourselves called upon to review our attitude to the past in the light of what we today find objectionable. We might support an apology by today's leaders for crimes committed against indigenous peoples decades or centuries before we were born. This changes nothing in the past, but it does oblige us to interrogate our values in the present.

For Argentinian mothers seeking their twenty thousand or more sons who 'disappeared' around 1980, there are no graves, no bodies and no records to consult. For Chinese young people, the issue is not how many students were killed in the 1989 Tiananmen Square protests, or how many millions starved in the Great Famine around 1960. It's the fact that their government, by controlling access to the internet, prevents them from knowing that these things happened at all.

Questionable witnesses
There is no objective version of what happened, because memory is fallible and suggestible, which is a problem for 'sworn' eye witness testimony in a court of law. Things pop into our head unbidden, compromising our impartiality. Shown a video of two vehicles colliding, and asked how fast they were travelling on impact, we tend to exaggerate the speed if the question includes the words 'bumped', 'crashed' or 'smashed'.

Our memory is therefore impressionable, vulnerable to 'leading questions', never simply 'photographic'. Under the stress of a police line-up, when we're asked to identify 'whodunnit' from a range of stooges, we start to doubt our memory, even though we had a good look at the suspect on the day. If we're a key witness, we are asked not to watch or read any news during the trial, for fear our memory might be contaminated.

It's hard to hold our ground if everyone around us disagrees with us.

In an added complication, experiments conducted in groups recalling events collectively show that, if enough people around us are saying so, we can be persuaded to remember things that didn't happen, not because we're dishonest, but because we are 'revisionists', liable to conform to how those around us are seeing and remembering things. Peer pressure can persuade us to change our opinion about the length of a line, even though we were right in the first place. It's hard to hold our ground if everyone around us disagrees with us.

We operate on two memory systems, the immediate and the distant past, but one can invade the other. We forget what we had for breakfast last Friday, but we don't forget the moment many years earlier when we saw the Twin Towers burning. The adrenaline and dopamine fuelled emotion of the event ensures that we can even recall where we were when we heard the news, and who was with us.

But there is a problem. Many who saw the television footage of the incident say they saw a plane fly into the North Tower, and a while later into the South Tower. This is the sequence of what actually happened, but the memory of it is false, because footage of the first impact was not shown until the next day. Without their say-so therefore, their brain has rewritten its own version of events, or fused memories into a reality that they did not personally witness.

By the same token, distant and immediate memory systems can contaminate each other. A present anxiety or yearning can all too easily project itself onto the past, and unwanted images from years ago, perhaps ones we hadn't realised were buried down there, can flood our mind following a chance encounter in the present.

False rememberers
Can we have memories we have forgotten about? Yes, because sometimes a stimulus can jog us into recalling a memory from a long time ago. But there is a worrying flip side to this: our brain is just as good at inventing memories. In multiple personality disorder (MPD), several 'characters' can exist inside one head, with no access to each other's memory, or foundation in reality. Cognitive

scientists are divided over whether this is a psychological defence mechanism, a neurological disorder, a combination of both, or a made up condition by therapists to keep themselves in business.

A strong imagination is an asset for future planning and creativity, but not when it falsifies the past. False memory, or the tainting of memory with imagination, can have serious psychological consequences, especially in the case of trauma.

As a way of blocking bad things that happened to us, we can either bury them in the cellar of our unconscious, subconsciously rewrite happier memories to obliterate the nasty ones, or invent alternative personalities that can escape our troubling past, because they weren't 'there'.

In what is known as retroactive hallucination, some victims of childhood abuse create dozens of 'personae' with their own names and memories, but no foundation in reality. Their present may be so precarious and unbearable that they feel more comfortable living out fantasy-horrors over which they have some degree of control.

Over the years, various therapies have been developed to assuage such mental distress. Primal Scream Therapy invites us to bawl out the anxiety we felt during our difficult passage down the birth canal, or our panic at gasping for our first breath, even though the neonate brain has no mechanism for laying down memories about such experiences.

Recovered memory therapy is even more problematic, one step away from false memory syndrome. The neurological background is that our brain is constantly caught between making sense of the past and second-guessing the future. If pieces of this puzzle are missing, it sometimes invents them, without us being aware of it. Or have these repressed memories been there all along, just waiting to be triggered?

The same neurons fire in our brain whether we remember
a 'real' image or imagine it.

We might be convinced that a particular memory is genuine, oblivious to the fact that we have unconsciously adopted a memory that originally belonged to someone else. In a further complication, the rational part of our mind might be persuaded that a certain memory is false, while our emotional brain remains utterly convinced that it is true. This does not mean we are brazen charlatans, because we are not consciously lying. The same neurons fire in our brain whether we remember a 'real' image or imagine it, leaving us with oxymoronic true lies and false truths.

We know through the phenomenon of déjà vu that our brain can play tricks on us: didn't I have this thought a moment ago? Sometimes we have difficulty source monitoring: is that my own voice I hear, or someone else's? This doesn't mean we are schizophrenic, only that we need to perfect mechanisms for making sure that it's our own voice we are hearing, and our own memory we are recalling.

These quirks of the brain create complex dilemmas for the legal system. In cases of child abuse remembered years after the event, sexual or otherwise, how do we establish whether such memories are real, or 'planted' by over-eager social workers, investigators and therapists? The psychologist Elizabeth Loftus has shown how the memory of a trauma can be implanted, with appalling consequences for those wrongly accused.

'Recovered' memories were a problem during the 1990's in alleged cases of satanic child-sex rings. Children's memories are highly plastic, and a 'Salem Witch Hunt' hysteria was triggered where, the more children 'confessed' to being victimised, the more others became convinced it had happened to them. As a result, innocent parents and carers were falsely accused. Jurors are now advised to be on the lookout for memories that might have been planted by suggestion in the impressionable minds of children.

This doesn't mean that we can't trust our memories. All memories, short term and long term, leave a synaptic residue or structural change in the brain. Also, the formation of increasingly complex memories marks crucial stages and cognitive thresholds as our young brain develops.

Without this capacity to make a lasting record of reality, we would inhabit a world of constantly appearing and disappearing objects, with no sense of permanence, no parents to bond with, and no emotional tone. We would be permanent amnesiacs.

Mountains of the Mind

> **Elizabeth Loftus**
> B 1944
> Loftus's work on memory shows the danger of relying on 'recovered' memories, especially in cases of childhood abuse. Our memory is nothing if not suggestible.

Following a head injury in 1953, Henry Molaison suffered life-threatening epileptic fits, leading to a decision to remove his hippocampus. The fits stopped, and his personality and IQ were unaffected, but Henry paid a terrible price. He was stuck in an eternal present. Every five minutes, he needed to be introduced to the people around him all over again. He lost his anterograde memory completely, which is the ability to lay down new memories of what just happened. He even lost some of his retrograde memory, which is the scrap book of our life.

The good news is that it is very rare to suffer total memory loss, though a bang on the head might delete part of our archive. Cases are on record of amnesiacs who can recognise their house, but not the people they live with. Some suffer fugue, which is loss of identity that can be temporary or last years. It's not uncommon for sufferers to end up in a strange town with no idea who they are, leaving their loved ones to report them as missing persons.

Memory loss is distressing at any age, and a core symptom of Alzheimer's disease. No wonder Hollywood has shown so much interest in it. In 'Fahrenheit 451' (1966), books are outlawed, so they survive only as entire texts committed to memory by rebel readers, who then become political targets. Culture is nothing if not collective memory, which explains why, in order to build a brave new future in their own image, the first instinct of revolutionaries and ideologues is to rewrite the past, if not obliterate it completely.

In 'Blade Runner' (1982), humanoid replicants are not meant to have any memory of what it was like to be a real human. Those that do are hunted down and destroyed. In 'Total Recall' (2012), a factory worker agrees to have fake memories implanted as a lark, but the installation goes horribly wrong, and he ends up a wanted man. In 'Inception' (2012), the hero is a thief who can steal people's memories, making him the most powerful but also the most dangerous man on the planet.

Traumatised victims

When we are young, we are often frightened, but our mind is remarkably resilient. We might have the occasional nightmare of getting lost in a crowded shopping mall, but we are not left scarred by it.

Serious trauma however, burned in with the acid of cortisol, can overwhelm our filters and coping mechanisms. They are impossible to forget, lurking in our subconscious like a saboteur waiting for the moment to strike. In the condition known as post-traumatic stress disorder (PTSD), traumatic memories retain their potency, because they are not processed by the 'dreamwork' of sleep, or taken down into our unconscious where they are cloaked in more benign symbolism.

Our sleep plays a vital role in protecting us from routine harms, frights and phobias, by breaking the link between what is constantly present to our consciousness, and what has been squirreled away out of sight, in our deeper memory. Occasionally however, especially if we are an emergency worker or member of the military, we might find ourselves hounded by a shocking incident that engraves itself so vividly on the tablet of our memory, that sleep becomes a torment, not a balm.

If this vision of horror lodges itself in the 'top drawer' of our mind, stuck in short-term memory, it can shrink our brain and lower our resistance. By continuing to elicit the raw feelings it first evoked, unabated and unmitigated, it retains its immediacy, constantly breaking into our waking and dreaming hours, forcing us to relive it over and over.

All this suggests that accusations of childhood abuse by adults are seldom fabricated, and must always be taken very seriously. It takes great courage to come forward, and victims might have several reasons for delaying the telling of their stories. Abuse provokes stronger emotional attachment to the abuser, not less, which is why it can take the abused several decades to detach themselves from the experience, or come to accept that what was done to them was not their fault. They

212

might feel ashamed, or psychologically unable to face their demons, suppressing their painful memories until they are emotionally strong enough to bring them out in the open and deal with them.

The difficulty lies with those who claim to 'remember' trauma that they have seemingly 'forgotten' for forty years. Some psychologists point out that a genuinely traumatic experience is not likely to lie low. Unlike short term memory, which soon fades, trauma is chronic. It impacts for a lifetime, because it is designed to remind us on a daily basis to avoid a repetition of the abuse, or to save us from further harm. It refuses to be silenced, scorched deeply into our limbic brain, generating unrelieved distress for victims who cannot escape their torment.

They conclude that abuse recollected in tranquillity years after the event probably never happened, because trauma leaves enduring wounds or 'traces' in the synapses, not likely to lie dormant or be forgotten for decades. The idea of dark knowledge lying inside us without our being aware of it suggests a kind of dualism, a paradoxical remembering of memories we didn't realise we had.

Psychics like to entertain us with the idea of regression to former lives, but there is no neural mechanism by which we can remember or recreate our life as a Roman soldier, or a tiger in the jungle, except by charlatanry or self-delusion. Very rarely a blow to the head can result in a new 'ability' appearing, but this is usually caused by a sudden short-circuit of one brain system with another, not the rediscovery of memories and talents from a former life.

It might frustrate us that the things we want to remember quickly fade, such as phone numbers and the names of people, whereas the things we want to forget, such as bad experiences, stick around. The answer might lie in our ancestral past. Evolution has deliberately bequeathed us a forgetting machine with a selective memory, not as a flawed design, but as protection against cognitive overload, and the curse of remembering everything forever.

We can't alter the beginning, but we may
be able to write a better ending.

If we are victims of trauma, plagued by troubling images and dreams, all is not lost. What can wound us also has the power to heal us. Cognitive behaviour therapists set out to teach us how to transform malign memories into benign ones,

213

Mountains of the Mind

which at the level of the brain means changing the proteins they are coded in. We can't wipe the originals, but we can change our emotional response to them. We can't alter the beginning, but we may be able to write a better ending.

This is not the same as recalling bad memories in order to engage them in mortal combat, which can cause more harm than good. If sleeping dogs are to be woken, we need to know how to deal with their anger and pain. The 2004 film 'Eternal Sunshine of the Spotless Mind' explores the possibility of excising bad memories and replacing them with happier ones. Therapists know a different truth: the only true crossing of the Lethe, or the river of forgetfulness, is when we die. We cannot delete our past, but we can learn to accept it as part of who we have been.

When asked whether we would like to be plugged into a non-stop pleasure machine, most of us reply that we don't want to lose touch with who we really are, warts and all. Remembering that our memory is constantly playing tricks on us, we choose instead to learn how to prevent the negatives of the past from blighting the positives of the days we have yet to live.

Why do we struggle to know our own mind?

Truth telling – lying – rationalisation – self deception – ego bias – fake news – cognitive bias - handling money – calculating risk – achieving happiness - managing anxiety – resisting peer pressure

- Determining what is true is as complex as claiming to be free, making it a challenge for us to form justified true beliefs.
- It doesn't help that our brain evolved to be equally clever at telling lies.
- We are much more skilled in exposing the shortcomings of others than in judging ourselves accurately.
- Confabulation, rationalisation and self-justification make it very difficult for us to be honest and effective self-critics.
- Our cognitive biases make us vulnerable at election time to fake news and tribalism.
- We struggle with numbers, statistics and probabilities. As a result, we are not always rational or wise about how we invest in the future.
- We find it difficult to second-guess life's uncertainties, basing our happiness too often on present pleasures, not long-term goals.
- We gauge our success in life against what others possess, not what we have achieved for ourselves.
- We make bad gambles on things we can control, but worry unduly about things over which we have no control.
- We listen to all the advice on health, diet, exercise and moderation, but we do not hear it.
- Our objectivity and judgment are too often contaminated by what those around us are thinking.

215

Mountains of the Mind

Unreliable truth-tellers

Given the question marks from the previous chapter hanging over our freedom of will and the reliability of our memory, we begin to doubt whether we can ever claim to know what our brain is up to. Perhaps the flat-mind theorists are right: we hardly know our own mind. No wonder we struggle to make the right calls.

And yet to say that we never decide anything 'up top' because our brain does our thinking for us 'down below' presents us with a conundrum. Without some form of Fat Controller overseeing the tracks and the trains, our brain has no way of operating the rail network.

The trick of consciousness is to make us feel like the Fat Controller. Gazing at the control board, we sit at the end of a long chain of causes, but all we see is the big picture, and all we need to decide is which train gets priority on the main line. We don't need to know the names of all the train drivers, and what goods they are carrying. It doesn't occur to us that there are lots of other Fat Controllers overseeing branch lines all over the system. As far as we're concerned, we are the station master, the sole judge of what is true and real.

Often we lie without realising we are lying.

But are we? In a court of law, we cannot be both judge and jury. There's a very good reason for this. No other species devotes so much of its brain to deception and dissimulation, or has invented so many ways of hiding the truth. No other animal can put on a poker-face or tell a bare-faced lie. We are both counterfeiters and confabulists, if only because the successful navigation of our social life depends on high levels of artifice.

We have many motives to hide the truth, or to present reality in alternative ways. We might want to save someone's feelings, get someone into trouble, sustain belief in Father Christmas, cover our tracks, write a novel, or justify our actions after the event. Some of our lies are spontaneous, most are premeditated, and often we lie without realising we are lying.

We like to think we are truthful, but we are not always fully in control of this process, because we are excluded for the most part from our body/mind dialogue. Migraine sufferers often have no idea when the next attack is coming. Some people recovering from life-threatening illness claim to have 'true' near-death experiences such as going down a tunnel or seeing an intense light, entering a peaceful and painless out-of-body state in which their whole life flows before them, but these may be no more than altered chemical states or oxygen starvation in the brain, not foretastes of the afterlife.

Weak lie-detectors

'What is truth?' asked Pontius Pilate, knowing that no-one could answer him. He was deliberately posing an age-old moral teaser. Do you mean my truth, or your truth? Is truth a personal construct, or a fixed property of reality?

Some say the truth is intuitive, already in us at birth, others that we have to go out and make a conscious effort to find it. Some say truth is what works, or binds a group together, others that truth resides in the facts of the case, not in what we feel about them. Some search inside themselves for a truth they are prepared to live and die for: we make the truth truer by the strength of our belief. Others spend hours in the laboratory worshipping at the shrine of empirical observation: the harder we look, the more surely we can arrive at the backstop of a *justified* true belief.

In between these apparently mutually exclusive versions of the truth lies interpersonal truth, the kind of truth we can agree on without scratching each other's eyes out. It is not simple, but complex, elusive, fallible and always unfinished. We recognise it, because it rings true.

If we say we don't lie, we're lying.

Unless we are lying to each other. We all lie, and our lying starts early. We start with small acts of self-deception, such as believing we deserve more praise than we are given. Once we've learned to lie to ourselves, lying to others becomes much easier. If we say we don't lie, we're lying, or we don't know what a lie is, or we live on a desert island.

We might be telling a harmless 'little white lie' to save someone's feelings. We might be telling a dangerous lie while believing it is true, repeating as 'gospel' what someone knowingly misled us into believing. We might repeat what we believe is a lie, without realising it is in fact true.

Perhaps lie detectors (polygraphs) can throw some light on our difficulty with telling the truth. They are designed on the assumption that the body sometimes

Mountains of the Mind

tells a different truth from the mind. We can't control our autonomic nervous system, unless we invest years of yogic meditation to master its default settings. The unwilled electrical surges of our brain and our sweaty palms are likely to give us away.

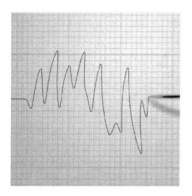

Lie detector
The machine never lies. But what if it's only picking up our stress at being wired up to it? Or is that a lie too?

Lie-detectors might not however be picking up truth or falsehood at all, only our stress at being wired up. This leads us to give a false positive, which is a problem for juries in search of the truth. Lie-detectors are now seen as psychological instruments of fear, not exposers of guilt or innocence, so they are no longer used in courtrooms

This is just as well, because human evolution over two million years has perfected two seemingly contradictory intuitive abilities: to cover up our true feelings as cleverly as we can, and to unmask each other's false seeming as skilfully as we can manage. If ever the day comes when a machine can do this on command, there will be disastrous consequences for the delicate deceptions and petty pretences that are essential to protecting our privacy and maintaining our trust in each other.

This is not yet a threat, because truth cannot be found on a brain scan, even when different colours light up. There are no neurons dedicated to truth or falsehood in our brain. Given the bewildering range of our motives, the duplicity of our intentions and the unreliability of our memories, there cannot therefore be a single neural signature or synaptic fingerprint of a 'guilty' or 'innocent' brain.

Psychopaths don't have to worry about lie detectors because they feel no guilt in the first place, so nothing shows up on the machine. Psychopaths are also very clever at masking the 'tells' that most of us give away, and that only a trained or experienced eye can pick up.

Shallow self-knowers

We kid ourselves that we are natural psychologists, good at reading other people's minds. We say things like, 'You think you're in love, but you're fooling yourself'. The irony is that we could not say such a thing about ourselves, because however good we think we are at judging others, we are poor at being honest with ourselves. We suffer from tunnel vision, boast that we could have been contenders, and are very good at believing our own publicity.

This makes us poor self-critics and shallow self-knowers. Only others see us for who we truly are, but to protect our Teflon-coated ego we routinely reject their criticisms. The blind spot of our hypocrisy is the hardest to illuminate. Even our sincerity can be an insincere deception: we justify not giving to charity on a regular basis on the grounds that we occasionally leave a little loose change in the collecting box by the till at the supermarket.

We're good at spotting other people's mistakes, but we find admitting to our own weaknesses almost impossible. The last sentence we're likely to hear ourselves say is 'You were right and I was wrong'. We are not natural self-correctors, and even after a lifetime of mistakes, few of us will ever voice King Lear's withering insight into himself as a 'very foolish fond old man'.

We learn how to block out the truths we don't want to hear. We fall into the trap of false consensus, confident that others think like us, or that they pay us any mind, when neither is true. We lapse into false transparency, thinking that others know what we want for our birthday, only to feel offended when we're not given what we wanted. We attribute false motives to others, taking the lack of a phone call as a deliberate snub, when it is nothing of the kind.

We are unconscious manipulators of other people, not deliberately deceptive but unconsciously motivated to gain a social advantage. If we want a favour, we lurk in wait for the right mood and moment. We agree with and defend people we like regardless of the argument. We favour those we know, granting them halos, ignoring their failings.

We are ten times more likely to believe something if it comes from someone we know, especially a celebrity, than from a stranger who might be much better informed. Beyond our inner circle, we are conspiracy theorists, convinced that the spooks, immigrants, terrorists or thought police are out to get us.

Our first-person perspective deceives us into laying claim to unjustified certainty. Not only do we naively boast the gift of hindsight, but we also delude ourselves that we possess foresight. We're far more likely to say 'I told you it wouldn't work' than 'I knew it wouldn't work but I went ahead anyway'. Even the little we do know is suspect, because our brain ignores what doesn't fit in with our preconceptions, and fabricates the missing parts that do. In other words, believing is seeing. This makes us bad scientists, seeing what we want to see, not what is there.

We are confabulators, making up stories to cover our tracks, not just to others but also to ourselves. We can't bear ignorance, doubt and mystery, so we fill in the gaps of a story to suit our own narrative. In experiments where objects are shown to the left eye (feeding the right brain) but not to the right eye (left brain), when asked what it has seen, the rational 'need to know' left brain makes up a story to correspond with what the wordless right brain already knows pictorially.

We peddle a narrative about how knowledgeable
or important we are.

This means we can never be fully sure we are telling the truth about anything. We don't deliberately lie, but we peddle a narrative about how knowledgeable or important we are. If we lack an explanation, we make one up, or seek out someone who can offer us a theory of everything.

Then, having invested so much emotion in our choice, we suffer confirmation bias: everything that goes slightly in our favour strengthens our self-belief. We might convince ourselves that we can sense when we are being stared at. It starts with a tingle in the back of the neck. When we look around, we notice that there *is* someone staring at us. But it's almost certainly because we happened to turn around at that moment, to find ourselves staring at them staring at us.

Mountains of the Mind

To keep our theory intact, we ignore negative results, or the hundreds of times when there was no-one showing any interest in us. We overlook the null hypothesis that the odd experience of 'knowing' we are being stared at is no more than we would expect from the law of averages. We are duped by the law of salience: we remember only what confirms our theory, like the believer who is boosted by the single prayer out of a thousand that gets answered. This is how confirmation bias works its magic: we note the hits, not the misses.

We perform a similar mental trick with negative bias: we notice the misses, not the hits. Every setback and attack on us confirms our conviction that we are right and everyone else is wrong. This makes us bullet-headed self-publicists, protecting our own interests when we are in error by justifying our own position, choosing only the 'facts' that reinforce our opinion, rejecting discordant realities, ignoring those who challenge us and sticking to the familiar.

Clever self-deceivers
We externalise blame: we didn't get the job because the interviewer wasn't fair. Or we internalise it: we didn't want the job anyway. When we fail at anything, no matter how sour the grapes, we insist they are sweet. This makes us great self-deceivers, excuse-seekers and rationalisers. We are more likely to rationalise than be rational, to defend our actions than to challenge them. In what is known as motivated reasoning, we find 'reasons' to bolster what we already believe rather than come to a consensus of what works in everyone's interest, or a balanced judgment between extremes.

The post-war generation justified corporal punishment on the grounds that it was a parental duty to keep children on the straight and narrow. As a counter-reaction, their offspring allowed their children to help themselves to what was in the fridge as a matter of entitlement. Both generations were convinced they were right, but neither could see that the middle way is best, or that the ice cream tastes better as a deserved reward.

We congratulate ourselves on doing the right thing.

After buying a new product, we rationalise our choice. We forget that we didn't know we wanted it until it was presented to us, and we were told that everyone else has one, and we were persuaded that owning one is life-transforming. But now that we've purchased one, we congratulate ourselves on doing the right thing. Similarly, after a minor car accident, we reason that it's good we pranged the car because we were going to get rid of it anyway.

Right brain knows that's not true, but left brain has to rationalise our actions, so our motives are never fully transparent, even to ourselves. We are full of cognitive distortions, telling ourselves little white lies when the truth doesn't fit or is unpalatable.

We then go out and buy a sporty replacement car with high fuel consumption, even though we know that the planet is reaching boiling point. Or we buy an old jalopy, persuading ourselves that its frequent break-downs are proof of its vintage status. Whichever we choose, we convince ourselves that it makes us happy, whining about the cost of an environmentally friendly bus fare but gladly paying the extortionate tax of keeping our gas-guzzling car on the driveway

No excuses
When we prang the car, the last person we are likely to blame is ourselves. The road was too slippery, it was the other driver's fault, we were hurrying to help a friend. Then we start to rationalise. We were thinking of changing the car anyway.

This makes us very practised at self-deception. When accused of theft, we say that we didn't realise we were stealing. If our beliefs don't match our behaviour, we change the beliefs, not the behaviour. That's why we're *right* to feel we deserve that burger after our workout at the gym, and why it doesn't matter if we under-count the calories afterwards. We cling to our pet theories and projects, even when everything around us is telling us to move on.

Mountains of the Mind

Our brain can never be certain about everything, so it compensates by creating an aura of reliability, even when it's wrong. We fail to go to the doctor, in denial that we are ill or in need of help. We react to sudden change but miss death by a thousand small cuts, like the frog that sits in the slow-warming water until it boils to death. Or we fall for popular myths: biologists point out that frogs aren't that stupid.

So are we the ones who are stupid? Not really, because there is evidence that self-deluding people are happier. After all, in many ways self-deception and delusion are our default positions, because life dumps so many lies and untruths upon us: we're urged to work hard, support the flag, vote for democracy, trust those in authority. If we doubted everything all the time, we'd go crazy.

It makes evolutionary sense to self-deceive in this way. We develop an economical set of thinking habits so that we can choose the easiest route when presented with a tough decision demanding real thought. Life is too short to rethink the big issues every day. We can't bear cognitive dissonance, because conflicts of interest make us uncomfortable. *Of course* we prefer half an explanation to no explanation at all, joy to despair, success to failure, certainty to doubt.

To assist us in this, evolution has given us not just a physical immune system but also a psychological one, to keep us on the narrow path between dangerously trusting nothing and foolishly believing everything. Our halting progress along this path depends on how successfully we negotiate appearance and reality, truth and falsity, happiness and misery.

It actually pays to be in a bad mood when we face our big decisions. When we're in a good mood, we tend to hurry our choice and be less self-critical, putting our reason on hold. A bad mood serves us better by making us more sceptical, giving us time to arrive at a wiser judgment.

Self-serving maximisers

Either way, we can't set out into the world each day with an image of ourselves as a manipulating, flawed, impressionable and self-seeking rogue, so we cling to a self-serving ego bias which 'bigs up' our own contribution and belittles the debt we owe to others. We never admit what we are really thinking, or concede an argument: *you're* the one who has to shift ground.

Mountains of the Mind

When we fill out a questionnaire, we answer every question positively. The last thing we want to do is to diminish ourselves, admit to being below average or lose face, so when asked about our own abilities, we massively over-rate ourselves. This makes us the most intelligent person in the room. Everyone is a jerk except us. In surveys, ninety per cent of us claim to be self aware, but the truth is that ninety per cent of us aren't. From this evidence, we can see that statistics are a problem for us too.

We can't bear to part with the old way of thinking.

When offered honest feedback about our behaviour or abilities, we hear only the positives, or magnify the single negative into an attack on our character. We often act irrationally to get what we want regardless, change our minds inexplicably, bear grudges, overlook the obvious, persist with actions that are self-defeating and stick to our guns, unable to reframe the problem because we have already invested too much of ourselves in our present position to lose face by reconsidering it reasonably. We believe the impossible, drawn to the counterintuitive and counterfactual because we *want* it to be true, and we can't bear to part with the old way of thinking.

We assume that our brain is a mirror that gives us a true reflection of what is there, like printing a copy from a computer screen, with no interpretation needed, but this is far from the case. Our brain can be a distorted mirror, deluded or overridden by the unconscious mind, as in hallucinations and dreams, more instinctive than rational.

We see what we *need* to: when we gaze down the street we see the people and buildings, not the litter or the power lines. We see what we *want* to: as optimists we see only the things that bolster our happy mood, and as pessimists we see only the dangers lurking in every corner. We see what we *expect* to see: all men with beards and sandals are idle dope-smoking lefty hippies. The lazy brain regards the accustomed as the inevitable, whereas the busy brain fails to see the obvious: while engrossed watching the ball in a football match we fail to spot the man in the gorilla suit run across the pitch.

Mountains of the Mind

Fickle voters

Our 'flat mind' vulnerabilities also blight our politics. If fake news is circulated for long enough, and shared enough times in the cyber-sphere, even by bots, it *becomes* true, creating a 'post-truth' reality: the truth is now what we *want* to be true, an affair of the emotions, not of reason. Our brain is a glutton for novelty, and 'fake news' is far more exciting than factual reality.

Fake news works on a simple calculus, determined by profit, not probity. A million 'hits' or 'shares' make an exciting lie more believable than a tedious truth. This is not a new phenomenon, and it has more than once pushed us into a lethal 'cry wolf' trap. In 1942, reports of a terrible Holocaust being carried out by the Nazis in central Europe began to leak out to the Allies. Memories still lingered of stories disseminated by the British in 1918 about German soldiers bayoneting babies. The propaganda turned out to be not true in 1918, so it wasn't believed in 1942.

There are others dangers with fake news. If our fears are exploited, about immigrants, terrorists or any perceived 'out group' threatening our way of life, we lose the sense of being manipulated, because pressing our limbic buttons deactivates our rational cortex, and negatives shout at us more loudly than positives. Populists thrive on appealing to nationalist sentiment, ducking responsibility for longer term solutions that involve delicate negotiations with other parties.

They know that, by and large, we vote with our hearts more than our heads. It is not unusual therefore in an election campaign for imaginary enemies to be invoked, and impossible promises made. Only after the votes are cast do we discover that political choices are more complex than was suggested by the seductive pre-election sound bites. We realise too late that, in the words of the French philosopher Michel Foucault, 'Truth is merely a mask for power'.

Democracy's appeal is that it allows us to change the status quo without violence, but only if truth is defended, justice is open, elections are fair, and the results are accepted in a peaceful handover of power. This is necessary, because political allegiance is determined not by rational calculation, but by vague notions of identity, trust, inclusion, grievance, and possibly how our parents voted. If our nation is under attack or hard up, we are more likely to vote for the status quo,

225

which usually means conservative. When times are good, we're more likely to give the other side a chance, sparing a thought for those who aren't so well off.

In cyberspace it is much harder to know
who is selling us what, and why.

Since 2016, Big Tech and social media have become major players at election time, upending the traditional 'us' and 'them' divides of class, or tough and tender mindedness. We are more influenced now by the 'digital tribe' we subscribe to. Newspapers have long pushed a particular political agenda, but we at least had a transparent view of who owned the paper, and who had an axe to grind. The difference now is that in cyberspace it is much harder to know who is selling us what, and why.

In addition, a 24/7 'breaking news' feed can make us less discriminating of what the real issues are, as well as overwhelm us emotionally. We haven't evolved to cope with chronic anxiety about disasters hundreds of miles away over which we have no control. News bulletins are presented as 'infotainment', because the editors want us to keep watching. They give us a steady feed of dramatic conflicts and gloomy disasters, not good harvests and acts of kindness, though they usually end with a story about a dog being rescued from a rabbit hole, if only to cheer us up a bit.

We like to be up to date with what is going on in the world, but we can fall foul of several cognitive biases. Impact bias means that, if all we ever hear is bad news, we are constantly cranked up emotionally. Availability bias means that our view of the world is skewed by what shouts the loudest, even though there is a quieter truth behind it. Murder rates across the world have been declining in recent years, but our perception is that we live in more violent times, because more people are reporting crimes, and the media are giving them wider coverage.

Weak calculators
We are not very good at numbers, statistics or probabilities. 'Fifty percent fat free' blinds us to all the sugar that has been added to the product to make up the deficit. We avoid the contraceptive pill after a scary story of a young woman dying of thrombosis after taking it, a one in seven thousand shot, but overlook the thirteen

thousand abortions that will be inflicted on the health system as a result of this scare.

If we have a cancer screening, we assume that an 'all clear' means we have no reason to worry, but this is not necessarily the case. No test is accurate, and something may have been overlooked. If we get a positive result, we need to remember that there a less than ten percent chance of contracting certain cancers, and that ninety percent of positive results are false positives. Our family history and lifestyle are much more likely to serve as early warning systems.

We're convinced we stand a chance of winning the lottery, which is one in a zillion, but scoff at the prospect of being served with divorce papers, which is one in three. If we remarry in haste, the odds worsen. Then again, without our willingness to take a punt, we would never fall in love in the first place. Also, doctors note that a spot of false optimism goes a long way when we are battling terminal disease.

We're not good with money. We donate £1 to help one homeless person, but when there's a famine we give nothing, on the grounds that our meagre gift is too small to make a difference. We tend to cling to what we have, because we over-focus on the present. Losing £10 today hits us harder than the promise of finding £20 tomorrow.

We respond more warmly to the gift of £100 right now than the dull logic of waiting for £105 next month. We see the point of saving £5 on a £100 purchase, but hardly think it's worth it on a £1000 outlay, even though the amount saved is the same. We're more likely to get into debt with a credit card than cash, because we can't 'see' what we're spending on plastic.

This blind spot explains why we struggle with economics too. Originally the term applied to the efficient managing of a household. Our brain can cope at this level because it evolved to oversee fair exchange and the settling of debts in a small group, 'cash on the nail' within plain sight. Modern economics is an 'invisible hand' controlling trillions of transactions in cyberspace. All we see is the price of goods on our high street, not the big forces that control supply and demand, stock market crashes, international exchange rates, local bankruptcies, global trade deals, internet scams, corporate monopolies and billionaire offshore accounts.

Mountains of the Mind

We tend to see wealth as a cake of a certain size. If the wealthy take a larger slice, or migrants undercut the market price by working for less, we think we are somehow being robbed. This 'it's not fair' glitch makes us prey to the patter of politicians who promise to protect our jobs, regulate prices, liberate the entrepreneurial spirit, boost our savings portfolios and increase the size of the cake overall, all in one go.

We don't remember that it was often these same people who deregulated the financial system leading to economic meltdown, the cost of repairs dumped on the victims through punitive austerity measures. We ignore the data that tells us that those societies work best that maintain a narrow gap between rich and poor. We forget that we are already enjoying a larger slice of the cake than previous generations could imagine, and on present models of consumption, the cake can increase in size only at the expense of the health of our planet. In other words, we can't have our cake and eat it.

Some of our difficulty with economics can be put down to basic human psychology. We're happy to earn a modest salary so long as it's slightly higher than everyone else's, because this gives us status. We're more likely to accept a salary cut if everyone else gets one too, maintaining our place in the hierarchy. If we're given a raise, the joy of having more money to spend is wiped out if we discover that others have been given more than us in the same promotion.

Being super-rich is no guarantee of nirvana.

Psychologists have established that our happiness is much increased by a lift from relative poverty to modest wealth, but after that, being a millionaire does not increase our happiness proportionately, only make us fret about the higher expectations of sustaining a more lavish lifestyle. The thought of being slightly richer cheers us up, but being super-rich is no guarantee of nirvana.

The value we place on money is relative, not absolute. How do we judge what a piece of land is worth, aside from the highest price that the market will bear? We worship gold because everyone else does, not because a nugget of gold is intrinsically valuable. It depends on who is selling, who is buying, and who else wants to buy it. Gold was so common in the Inca empire, the only metal they had, that they made toothpicks out of it. Diamonds are a girl's best friend, but only if they're pricey. Jewellers are familiar with the phenomenon that if they treble the price of their cheapest rings, they sell three times as many.

'Value for money' is therefore a fickle concept. If a museum charges a token entrance fee, we won't think it worth the entry, but if it charges ten times more, we'll tell others proudly about our visit. We persuade ourselves that blowing a hundred pounds on one memorable night out is a better investment than five forgettable nights at twenty pounds each.

Bad investors
We struggle with making money work to our advantage, partly because we don't handle 'sunk costs' very well. We have an aversion to loss. If we've paid for a ticket but don't like the show, we stick it out to the end, even though we hate it. Our emotional need to get our money's worth drives out any rational calculation we might make about the value of our time. This makes for a double loss, because we then lose our evening as well as our money, neither of which we can reclaim.

Money money money
As the saying goes, penny wise, pound foolish. It seems the larger the sum of money involved, the more we struggle to appreciate relative value.

If we have a bad start to our day, we're more likely to let that blight the rest of our morning, which is as yet full of possibility. A smarter reaction would be to start again, and write down the first hour as a straight loss. When we're already in a hole, it makes no sense to keep digging.

We struggle to think like this because we privilege quantity over quality. We hoard possessions on the grounds that losing something we definitely have will hurt far more than the mere possibility of gaining something. Divorce and bereavement hit us hard because we brood on present pain and future privation, not

229

Mountains of the Mind

the years of happiness we've banked. This makes any kind of trauma difficult, because we can't easily identify any credit that can flow from such a debit. Instead we stubbornly cling to our belongings, beliefs and bad relationships, reluctant and even unable to write them off as poor investments.

One drop in profits outweighs ten weeks of gains, because losing hurts more than winning, just as bad news 'sticks' more than good news. We panic-sell after one bad day, forgetting the twenty good ones before it, distracted by one black swan in a flock of white ones. We'd rather save pennies (a definite gain) by driving several miles to get cheaper fuel, but we hesitate to save pounds (a possible loss) by trading in our trusty old banger for a more efficient vehicle.

We want something for nothing today without
being prepared to sacrifice for tomorrow.

This blind spot in our thinking does not bode well for global heating: we're far more likely to spend money over-heating our house today than installing solar heating whose costs we won't recoup for many tomorrows. We fail to grasp that the money we spend on a daily cup of espresso coffee would buy clean water for a family for a week in the developing world.

We don't see the point when we're young of putting money aside for a pension that seems decades into the future. The global crash of 2008 occurred because too many of us, like Dr Faustus, sold our souls to the devil: we wanted something for nothing today without being prepared to sacrifice for tomorrow. Why defer pleasure when everybody else is getting what they want right now?

We are lured into a supermarket by signs promising 'big savings', 'free gifts' and 'buy one get one free', only to spend more money than we intended on goods we don't really need. Items are priced at £9.99 instead of £9.01, because our eye sees only the first figure, allowing the store to keep the difference. We spend fifty pounds to save ten pounds, which leaves us forty pounds out of pocket. We are commercial dupes, buying on impulse, drawn to the expensive product in pretty wrapping but dismissing the bulk-buy in plain packaging. We're sold a life style and cultural mindset, not a product.

Whether it's cosmetics, cars, fish fingers or washing powder being sold to us, women are persuaded they can work as hard as men, be good mothers, stay young and look beautiful, all in one go. Men are persuaded that this is no less than they should expect. To the 'persuaders', the mind is flat, and we are all trapped in a permanent adolescence, gullible, biddable and good for coughing up money.

We're far more likely to say yes to a small request if we've just declined a bigger one, partly through guilt and partly through a desire to make the other person go away. As all good salespeople know, according to the 'foot in the door' principle, once they've got us to say yes to a little thing, they've trapped us: now we are much more likely to go for the big thing they wanted to sell us all along. Then, when we've bought it, we convince ourselves that it was just what we needed, and it was always our idea to buy one.

Poor risk assessors

We are not very good at calculating the cost of good health. We might try to save a few pennies on items at the till, but when it comes to carrying out a cost benefit analysis of our physical wellbeing, which is priceless, we fail miserably. We treat ourselves to a bar of chocolate at the checkout as a 'reward' for all that hard shopping we've just done, which is why the supermarket puts it there in the first place. We gladly gorge on an expensive high-fat restaurant meal while scrimping to buy low-cholesterol products the rest of the week.

We are hopeless optimists, denying that the future can be anything but sunny. This is partly because we are poor time discounters, allowing the future, which isn't here yet, to be eclipsed by a temptation that is. We are more likely to eat the cream cake in front of us than worry about our weight next week. The temporary but immediate pleasure of a cigarette banishes any thought of future disease, so we blank out 'Smoking Kills' printed in large letters on the packet. We're even more likely to throw caution to the wind, and focus on present pleasures, if our future prospects look bleak.

For creatures like us trapped in time and chance, risk is inevitable, and for a gambler irresistible. Would we hazard a week's wages for a one-in-a-hundred chance of winning a year's salary? What about a one-in-ten shot? Money is replaceable, but our health is a finite stake. The problem is, we are not good at calculating risk as danger multiplied by exposure. We absorb more radiation from X-rays at the dentist than living next to a nuclear power station.

231

Mountains of the Mind

We stand a one in two chance of getting cancer at some stage in our life, but we're poor at calculating the odds. Which is statistically more likely to give us cancer: mobile phones or tobacco; caffeine or lack of physical activity; fluoride in our drinking water or alcohol; vaccination or being overweight; artificial sweeteners or too little fibre in our diet? The first named in each case has been demonised at some stage, but the second named is much more dangerous to our health, by an overwhelming margin.

On the African savannah, wilting flowers didn't stand much chance. Too little risk meant starving to death, too much meant being eaten by a lion. We no longer face such threats, but it remains the case that only risk-takers get the prize. Without risk there is no adventure or ambition, no way of making it to the summit of Mount Everest, or the imaginary places of the mind. Then again, if we ignore severe weather warnings, we end up perishing on the roof of the world. For every six people that reach the peak of Everest, one never returns.

We settle for risk at one remove.

Scientist have identified enzymes that catalyse different types of monoamine oxidase (MAOA) in our bloodstream. These are active in our brain, locating us somewhere on a continuum between thrill-seeking and timidity. Bull-fighters generally have low levels, explaining why they can tolerate extreme threat and deliberately seek out danger. Phobics have high levels, leaving them trapped in their fears, afraid to leave home or look down from a height.

Most of us are suspended between a craving for excitement and the lure of security. Modern life can be terribly dull, so we settle for risk at one remove, watching scary movies or bruising sporting clashes from the safety of our armchair, letting others take the hit.

Hesitant risk takers
Our MAOA-flow might change as we age, making us more sensitive to the bad news and oblivious to the good. This has consequences for the kind of leaders we choose as we grow older. We lose our youthful sense of adventure and become more protective of what we have, drifting to the right of the political spectrum. Conservatism starts to sound far less risky than socialism or liberalism.

232

Mountains of the Mind

Alongside this natural aversion to risk, our attitude to it can be influenced by social circumstances beyond our control. Sociologists note that there is a higher rate of homicide in areas of social deprivation. Where there is lower social capital, poorer economic prospects, greater pressure on mental health and higher exposure to danger on the streets, it makes sense to throw more to hazard by joining a gang or carrying a weapon.

There are also cultural influences on the level and nature of risk we are prepared to take. Travellers, Romanies and Gypsies are born into or choose a life where uncertainty is part of the appeal, appalled at the prospect of conforming, or being stuck in one place. Meanwhile, the annals of empire, the diaries of politicians, the log books of explorers, the lab notes of Nobel Prize winners and the skyscrapers of Manhattan are testimony to the rewards on offer to those prepared to speculate to accumulate, though they are balanced by equal risk of bankruptcy, failure and anonymity.

Not all risks are equally risky. When we play roulette, we throw everything on the random spin of the wheel. In a poker game however, if we are tactically skilful, good at remembering cards played, and even better at reading other players' 'tells', we can get the better of chance, at least some of the time. Most of us, unable to assure ourselves of this level of control, dare not go near the poker table, afraid of gambling away our life's savings in one evening. Instead we play our life as a game of chess, much more slowly, getting to know the pieces, pondering each move, trusting to our judgment to see us through, or at least to minimise our losses.

This makes sense, given that life itself is one big risk. Nothing is certain except death and taxes. Even classical physics is described as unswerving laws accompanied by lots of accidents. Toast dropped from the breakfast table will definitely fall to the floor, and bad luck will add the probability that it will be butter side down. When it comes to love, the future becomes positively chaotic, because logic becomes fuzzy: she loves me, she loves me not. We live in an age when undying affection and prenuptial agreements live side by side.

We are statistically much more likely to die from getting out of bed, descending the stairs or taking a bath than from sky diving, mountaineering or swimming in the ocean. Nevertheless, in our obsessive 'health and safety' culture, we do our best to minimise risk, even though this can have unforeseen consequences. We fit our cars with roll bars, air bags, crumple zones, anti-lock

233

brakes and anti-skid tyres, but all this achieves is to encourage us to drive faster on the grounds that our high performance vehicles somehow make the driver accident-proof, even immortal.

In the Ancient World, intense effort was expended on reading entrails, interpreting the flight of birds or placating the Furies. Today we read palms, tea leaves and horoscopes, but we are no closer to second-guessing the future. No-one saw Covid 19 coming down the track in 2020, and if they did, they didn't do a very good job or warning everyone else.

Even our best science and medicine struggles to establish beyond doubt what is certain, probable or unpredictable, and it is always the improbable that catches us out. The irony is that, when given a real chance to control our destiny, by watching what we eat or taking more exercise, we ignore the advice.

'Mr Right' is out there waiting for us, maybe sitting at the next table.

This is because, although economists treat us as rational maximisers, we are creatures of impulse. If we go to a speed dating bar, research shows that, after we've chatted to a third of the hopefuls, we're not likely to meet someone who offers us what the others don't. And yet we carry on, convinced that the 'Mr Right' is out there waiting for us, maybe sitting at the next table.

We're not very rational about risk. We fret at the occasional loss of every passenger on board a crashed airliner, a tragedy beyond our control. We are statistically however much more likely to die crossing the road in our local area than in a jumbo jet, a circumstance that is largely within our own control.

We are frequently prey to scaremongering. One death from an overdose of ecstasy hits the headlines, but for every ecstasy fatality, three hundred die annually from alcohol abuse. We cancel that holiday to Cape Town on account of the Ebola virus in West Africa, even though our home city London is closer to the outbreak. Two murders a hundred miles apart put us in the midst of a crime epidemic, because our brain places these shock-horrors top of the list, forgetting the millions who sleep safely in their beds.

Mountains of the Mind

Chronic worriers

Risk is an inescapable feature of life, and we are natural worriers. None of us knows what will be the eventual manner of our death, or how our children might turn out. Many of our fears were justified when we roamed the savannah: one tiny scratch could go septic and kill us. Life for our ancestors was much more unpredictable, often bordering on the tragic. Now we're much safer, but we still fret and exaggerate our fears.

Given higher living standards and longer life expectation, we might expect happiness levels to rise. The paradox is that, in the developed world, depression rates are on the up, especially among the young. There is however no cause for pessimism on a global scale. On many measures, living conditions are improving greatly for millions of people.

Worry that leads to positive and practical action is self-justifying, as legitimate concern for a crisis of our own making but within our power to address. Worry as doom-mongering, or anxiety that lacks an effective response to an identified objective, merely chips away at the mental resources we need to cope. Although our planet faces increasing ecological challenges, governments are investing in finding solutions, and scientists are developing new technologies.

We worry about dying in a plane crash, but binge drinking
is much more likely to kill us.

Some anxiety is realistic: we really do stand a higher chance of being injured if we don't wear a seat belt or cycle helmet. But misplaced anxiety is neurotic. We are statistically more likely to die of eating too many burgers or climbing a ladder than stepping on a cobra or being killed in a nuclear accident, but our limbic fears block a rational risk assessment. We over-worry about dying in a plane crash, which has a low probability, but under-worry about binge drinking, which is much more likely to kill us.

When asked, we place terrorism at the top of our list of threats, even though the government consider that pandemics and flooding pose much greater risks to public health and safety. When we look at the numbers, we learn that we are far more likely to be killed in a road traffic accident than a terrorist bomb blast, but our brain sensors are calibrated to ignore the one and exaggerate the other.

Mountains of the Mind

Terrorist attacks kill about twenty five thousand people each year around the world, but the annual toll of road fatalities tops a million.

These figures suggest that it is logical to fear cars more than terrorists, but cars were not a threat on the savannah, and marauding tribes were. Terrorists exploit this sinister logic by targeting us where we are most vulnerable. They know that bad news and fear have greater cognitive and emotional salience than 'drive safely' campaigns.

Terrorist attacks are therefore deliberately indiscriminate, their constant false alarms designed to make us permanently anxious. On the basis of one terrorist attack, we panic, shutting down the whole communications network and keeping our children indoors. We accept endless security checks at airports, surveillance cameras in the street, and loss of on-line privacy as the price of a quiet night's sleep.

Compulsive gamblers

When we feel things are beyond our control, we appeal to Lady Luck, spin the Wheel of Fortune, rely on the rub of the green, consult the almanac or dally with magic. We might say we read our horoscope in fun, but a secret part of us wants to believe it. These days science has stepped in to oust the 'God of the gaps', but we're still superstitious and gullible.

The casino always wins.

We are more rational these days, but not totally so. Part of us hangs back from trusting completely to games of chance and the roll of the dice, even if they are perfectly weighted. We are aware that the only certainty with chance is that it changes, and even if we know all the inputs, which we can't, we can never second-guess all the outcomes. But then the irrational part of us kicks in: we have a hunch, a desperate need to take a punt, or a trick that we think can beat the system. But as the betting industry knows, the casino always wins.

Some things we can't gamble with. When we take an examination, we know we can't throw ourselves on the kindness of the examiner, or a happy choice of questions: either we have prepared well, or we haven't. Playing cards is not like

236

playing chess. If we lose in cards, we can curse the fates, but if we get beaten in chess, we know it's because we're not good enough.

Cards and chess are finite games, so their losses can be contained. Life is an infinite game, so the stakes are higher. This is awkward, because we are not good rational calculators, utility theorists or clairvoyants. We put gut-feeling before fair analysis, making knee-jerk irrational gambles on the big things of life (joining a religious cult) while failing to notice the small but vital losses in our daily life (our friends begin to find us weird, and desert us).

Taking a gamble
For some, gambling becomes a life-destroying addiction. Opinions differ whether they are victims of dopamine-overdose, an underactive frontal cortex, poorly chosen friends, difficult personal circumstances or weakness of will.

We drive too fast, assume too much responsibility and borrow more money than we can repay. In what is known as the 'Monte Carlo fallacy', if black has come up ten times in a row, we place all our money on red, even though the odds are still no better than fifty-fifty. We justify the unaffordable purchase of lottery tickets with impossible odds, but are wasteful with simple certainties that could save us money.

In the hope of equalising risk and limiting our losses, we pay a hefty accident waiver on our hire car insurance, out of all proportion to the chances of a prang. Even though crime rates are at a historic low, we go out and buy more home insurance. We're normally risk-averse, but on holiday, we let our guard down and think we are indestructible: we gladly go paragliding with no safety precautions.

Mountains of the Mind

At home however, we become ultra-cautious, not letting our children play in the street for fear of abduction.

This is because we base our theories on too small a sample, and over-generalise them. Sally said her child saw a strange man in the street, so for the foreseeable future all children are at risk all over the neighbourhood, and must be kept indoors. On other issues, we choose a sample that gives us the result we want. We fit our findings to the conclusion we've already reached, believing false positives but ignoring false negatives. Mistaking a clean bill of health for low obesity-risk, we order a burger and chips to celebrate.

Tainted judges

We like to believe we are independent-minded, but we can also be insufferably self-righteous and opinionated. This can be a problem in a court of law: spouses cannot be forced to testify against each other, not just for reasons of confidentiality but for fear of clouded judgment. Apperception is when our perceptions are tainted by our beliefs and prejudices: what we see is what we want to see, or what we fear the most.

This raises issues for the legal system, because witnesses in court often 'mis-remember' key facts or faces in a trial: they remake their memories, recalling what they thought they saw, or what they heard others say. Our over-inventive imaginations have a habit of distorting our memories: white citizens shown a scene-of-crime photograph in experiments have been known on later questioning to insert black faces that were not there.

Few geniuses have thrived in committees.

Then there is peer pressure. In a different experiment, people were shown to change their mind about the length of a line, simply because everyone else in the room disagreed with them. This was a set-up: the original judgments were right all along. This leads to a disturbing phenomenon called the bystander effect: we don't intervene to help someone being attacked in the street, because no-one else seems bothered about it, which reinforces a new kind of 'normal'. On the other hand, if we are surrounded by people taking risks, panic-buying or upgrading their technology, we tend to fall in line for fear of missing out.

238

Mountains of the Mind

The fault lies neither with the individual nor the crowd, only with the suppression or application of critical reason. Some praise the wisdom of crowds and collective judgment: the average of twenty people's views is often more 'right' than the verdict of the expert. Others warn of the madness of crowds and group-think: we get swept along in sentiments that are not our own, and our guesstimates are way off-mark.

Group-think is therefore ambivalent. It can harness experience, but it can also stifle originality. Few geniuses have thrived in committees, because their forte is to challenge the consensus of their day. Though we are defined culturally by our membership of the group, our individuality resides in our ability to separate ourselves from the mass-mind. We like to say 'I know my own mind'. But do we? Can we in any meaningful sense claim ownership of it?

Can we assume ownership of our mind?

*Lazy reasoning – coloured perception - superstitious thinking –
seeing partially - choosing a worldview – changing our mind -
entertaining contradictory truths - living with uncertainty -
committing to a political cause – keeping an open mind*

- Our brain is not a flawless computer, but comes with several design faults.
- It automatically fills in gaps in our knowledge, and makes many of our decisions for us.
- These defaults started out as thinking short-cuts and uncertainty-reducers that served us well on the African savannah.
- In today's more complex world, they challenge our claim to know our own mind, as well as call into question our impartiality, rationality and completeness of understanding.
- In addition, our perception is limited. We see only parts of the whole, never the whole of reality.
- Nevertheless, in order to function in society, we must formulate a worldview, based on our hunches about how the world works.
- This involves establishing the best fit between our beliefs and reality.
- We crave certainty, but this is a luxury that no belief can guarantee.
- Convictions are useful in binding us to a cause, but they are dangerous when they blind us to other possibilities.
- Strength of belief cannot make fake news and conspiracy theories true.

- Our 'take' on things cannot be objective, only an attitude, because feelings speak louder than the intellect, and facts require interpretation.
- Our worldview can however be rational and justified, if soundly argued and based on good reasons.
- In the world of politics, democracy gives us a way of settling our disputes without bloodshed.
- To make it work, we must be able to hold conflicting ideas in mind simultaneously, be capable of living with difference, and be attentive listeners.
- If not, we fall prey to binary thinking, which traps us in destructive culture wars.
- The cause we espouse shapes who we are, so we need to choose it with care.
- The good news is that we are capable of changing our minds, something we do more often than we like to admit.
- It is a strength to admit that we don't know, it is an asset to keep an open mind, and it is a boon to know that we may be mistaken.

Cognitive misers

We like to think we know our own minds, but flat mind theorists question this assumption. They challenge the notion that there is an 'essence' called mind, and if there is, that we have as much control over it as we like to believe. The charge sheet is long: we are cognitive misers, lazy reasoners, partial seers, factual fabricators and biased believers.

When we protest that we're not racist, we may be masking the fact that unconsciously we are, but we don't know it. Stereotypes come naturally to us because on the savannah, snap judgments saved time, energy and possibly our life. We are instinctive psychological 'splitters' given to dividing the world into friend or foe, good or bad, leaders or followers, safe or dangerous. Our brain is programmed by evolution to discriminate between alternatives, sometimes violently so, more swayed by prejudice than logic, making it difficult for us to accommodate doubt, ambiguity and uncertainty.

Thousands of years down the track, we have ended up as cognitive misers, avoiding the psychological exertion and emotional discomfort of upending our settled beliefs, relying on our intuitions rather than spending time doing some hard analytical homework. We are creatures of habit, and the more we can automate our thinking, the easier our day. Faced with a tough choice, it's far simpler to choose not to choose. If two people from an ethnic group offend us, we rush to the conclusion that all such people are unfriendly and threatening, playing to an atavistic but groundless suspicion and hatred of those we don't see as members of 'our tribe'.

We're natural copy-cats.

We fall victim to the 'primacy effect': first impressions stick, true or not, regardless of what comes after. We're suckers for appearances: blue pills calm us, red pills stimulate us and white pills relieve our pain, no matter what pharmaceutical compound they contain. We're drawn to conspicuous consumption because secretly we are impressed by anyone who can afford a Rolex watch or a Tiffany diamond. We're natural copy-cats, modelling our behaviour on those we envy or admire, not realising they are no happier or cleverer than we are.

Like a good lawyer, our brain hears only the evidence that supports its case. We slip into prejudicial habits of bad-thinking that become so ingrained we can't see them for what they are, and seldom muster the courage to change. We jump to wild conclusions based on the slenderest evidence, relying on 'easy reckoning' rules of thumb rather than hard calculation, especially if the result bolsters our cause or bias.

We judge people on their looks or handwriting, and the more tired we are, the harsher our verdict. Judges have been shown to pass more lenient sentences on good-looking people, and to give out lighter punishments after lunch. So the moral is: go to court smartly dressed, and avoid morning sessions. Tall, slim and attractive people do better in interviews than short, fat and plain ones, regardless of ability. If we're short, fat and plain ourselves, we'll take it out on tall, slim and attractive colleagues.

Lazy reasoners
Such levels of misperception and self-deceit make the mind look shallow indeed, merely the effervescence of a brain determined to hold things together based on the slenderest theory of how the world works. Both neuroscience and postmodern

theory seem to have left us with at best a polycentric self, and at worst a decentred one, with no internal cohesion. We don't know our own minds well enough to lay claim to rationality or consistency, because we are lazy reasoners.

To be fair to ourselves, we can't be relentlessly rational, because we don't have time to weigh the evidence twenty times a day. Instead we rely on gut feelings and short cuts based on experience, or what we like to call intuition and common sense. We just *feel* or *believe* something is right, sensible, justified or worth pursuing.

We can never tell whether we are seeing things
as they are, or as we are.

This tacit knowledge works fine for most situations. After all, we can't prove or disprove our preferences, only live them. We therefore opt for the quiet life mentally, because self-analysis takes time and work, and is generally unsettling. But unless we occasionally put our assumptions to the test of critical thinking, we can never tell whether we are seeing things as they are, or as we are. We can never judge whether we are dancing to our own tune, or someone else's.

Our fluidity and rapidity of response may be an advantage when we're caught up in a busy and changing daily schedule dealing with the 'small stuff', but when faced with making a big call, it's a grave danger. In World War One, both sides seemed to drift into the conflict. Millions of men were sent 'over the top' to fight for what they believed was right, or what someone else persuaded them was right, only to be blown to smithereens, shredded on the barbed wire or drowned in the mud.

Even if the foot soldiers realised the futility of their sacrifice, their leaders could not break out of the stalemate of mutual destruction, or the inappropriate waging of attritional trench warfare in an age of high explosives, chlorine gas and gangrene. They were not unintelligent men, but in their heads they were fighting a previous war, sending men and horses naked against rapid-firing machine guns. They did not possess the insight, imagination or courage to press the pause button, shift their worldview, override their indoctrination, or value the lives of the men under their command. They were trapped in their predicament.

We might console ourselves with the belief that this sort of thing could never happen again. Our identities have become more fluid, we are getting to know our

Mountains of the Mind

own minds better, we are more tolerant of difference, we have 'learned our lesson', we are improving at holding contradictory ideas in mind simultaneously, even paradoxical truths. If so, this is a great advance, because our weapons are now infinitely more deadly.

> **Trench warfare**
> In 1914, lightly clad infantry were sent 'over the top' into the deadly fire of automatic machine guns. In their minds, the generals on both sides were still fighting a war of cavalry against slow-loading muskets. The result was carnage.

A cynic might observe that the only lesson we seem to have learned from two world wars is not to join combat on our own patch, but to fight proxy wars in countries far away that have no means of defending themselves. That way we can safely display to our enemies the cleverness of our drones in zapping remote villages, without risking a missile strike on our own cities, or seeing lots of 'our boys' come home in body bags.

This twisted logic, all too common on the world stage, suggests that there are deep-seated design flaws in our brain, and that we are still a long way from understanding how our mind works. We come to the negotiating table with a ready-formed worldview, defining attitude or set of core beliefs. It cannot be otherwise, because we don't just act in the world: we first have to work out what we are acting *for*.

Fabricating factfinders

First however we have to establish our facts. This sounds simple, but there is no simple nexus between fact and opinion. Facts do not speak for themselves, nor are they a smorgasbord from which we can pick and choose at will. Like a good

244

historian, we have to make a selection, having first worked out what we are looking for. Only then can we make an interpretation, by putting them to work in a theoretical framework. To do that we need robust methodologies of doubt and verification that we can all agree on, always mindful of the counterfactual that, for some of us, the fewer the facts, the stronger our conviction in our pet theory.

New facts are the lifeblood of science.

John Maynard Keynes is attributed with saying 'When the facts change, I change my mind'. Facts change in two important senses. Firstly, our enquiring mind makes new ones by observation and experiment, which are essential to the advancement of our knowledge. The psychologist Ivan Pavlov remarked that new facts are the lifeblood of science, without which it cannot progress.

Secondly, our relation to the facts changes as our understanding deepens. When we look at how differently we view the world from our parents or grandparents, we can see how capable we are of changing our minds inter-generationally. This is essential because, it we start from the wrong place with the wrong facts, our thinking will go increasingly astray as we proceed down the line.

Keynes was an economist, devoted to the 'facts' of numbers. The 'facts' of religion and politics are based on inspiration, not the latest research, on conviction, not cohorts of data, on trust, not the most recent balance of payments. Their energy derives not from objective facts, which can be reviewed in the light of new evidence, but the subjective realities of personal experience and cultural tradition, which locate us in an unfolding human narrative where the past is still felt in the present.

It has taken us four hundred years to acknowledge that these two types of facts perform distinct roles in the human mind, and form the base of different ways of knowing. In the seventeenth century, Galileo was simultaneously accused of false science and bad religion. Soon after, John Locke pleaded that the private realm of religious belief be kept separate from the public realm of empirical science. There was no longer any need to burn people at the stake for their religious beliefs, and certainly not for their scientific speculations.

These days, after bitter wars of religion and national sovereignty, we no longer imprison people for their sincerely held religious or political beliefs, nor do we lock up scientists if they discover a truth about nature that makes us think again. And yet we still find ourselves in the midst of bitter culture wars, allowing religious dogma or political ideology, sometimes a toxic cocktail of both, to dictate our moral choices. In the debate over abortion, how do we balance the rights of the unborn with the rights of women to control what happens to their bodies? How do we square the warnings given by climate change scientists with the freedoms of 'big business' to maximise profits by exploiting the earth's resources?

Biased believers

Whether facts are grounded in empirical research or personal opinion, they have to undergo some complex alchemy on their way to becoming justified true beliefs. How do we transform data into knowledge, facts into understanding, information into truth and opinions into wisdom? Unfortunately neither the best liberal education nor an apprenticeship in rational thinking automatically immunises us against bigotry, foolishness, error or evil.

> *Good reasons, no matter how persuasively put,*
> *should give way to better.*

We can use reason to put our beliefs to the test, but we can just as easily use it to find arguments for continuing to believe what we already do. In a debate, we expect to hear arguments supported by reasons, not assertions. When it comes to casting our vote, we insist that good reasons, no matter how persuasively put, must give way to better.

This is difficult, because reason, instead of bypassing the emotions, acts as their advocate. When we find a kindred spirit, or acknowledge a tribal allegiance, our brain receives a little dopamine hit, and we are drawn in emotionally, not rationally. Politicians employ impeccable logic and powerful rhetoric to reach whatever conclusion suits their campaign. They can sound very intelligent, but one definition of intelligence is being smart enough to make our not-so-smart feelings sound smarter than they really are.

We are all prey to superstitious thinking, regardless of our IQ score. Meat balls made us sick once, so we avoid them forever. In an echo of the sympathetic magic that motivated our ancestors, we believe that giving our children manly or feminine names will give them a head start in life. We carry lucky charms, or wear the clothes that we wore at our last successful interview.

Our tendency to 'think magically' increases when we are under stress. In a storm, mariners believe in protective mermaids, and dolphins that will come to ferry them to shore if their ship sinks. There might be a neurological at play here. Mountaineers often report the presence of someone walking beside them when their brains begin to suffer from oxygen depletion.

We might console ourselves with the thought that our beliefs become more informed and less opinionated with the passing years, but this is not always the case. Without the cultivation of honest scrutiny and enquiry, they may even become more extreme. Despite decades of social progress, there are still many intellectual black holes out there, populated by racists, chauvinists, homophobes, Holocaust deniers and flat-earthers. It never occurs to us that we might be stuck in our own black hole, its force field too strong to escape from.

So what makes us cling to outmoded or harmful beliefs? Much comes down to the nature of belief. What for instance is our evidence base for *believing* that global heating is a hoax or a documented fact? On what basis do we claim that we *know* this to be so? Who is 'selling' us this line of thought, and why? Have we done our best to establish whether our belief is true, or are we making it true by the strength of our belief?

Just as simply peering out of the window in the morning does not fix reality, or determine what the weather will be like today, so there is a gulf between what is true and what we want to be true. It's tempting to try to live in a world shaped by our feelings and dependent on our beliefs, and for a while, lying in bed, we can get away with it. But when we go into the kitchen, run the tap and switch on the toaster, a different kind of belief-world quickly impresses itself on us.

Forming our beliefs is never straightforward. We might assume that we arrive at our beliefs *after* we've done the looking, but belief-formation works the other way round: what we take from each moment is strongly determined by our past experience. The concept shapes the percept.

This suggests that there is no single way to map our beliefs onto the world. Instead, we manipulate the world to fit our beliefs. The nature of human perception leaves us no choice: we have to make an honest effort to arrive at a version of the facts 'as we see them', because understanding is not written across the sky.

Mountains of the Mind

Awkward anatomists

In the short term we might treat our beliefs like dishes on a buffet. Last week I had salad, but this week I'll go for the hot food. Our foundational beliefs tend to last a lifetime, which is why it makes the news when a scientist questions a theory that has dominated her thinking for decades, or an atheist declares his religious conversion after a lifetime's scepticism.

Perhaps we ask too much of the word 'believe'. The brain is a highly productive 'belief engine', so arriving at an accurate anatomy of belief is difficult. In each of the following, we are revealing more about our emotional state and cognitive processing than the objective truth of the target of our belief: I believe my friend, I believe *in* my friend, I believe it might rain tomorrow, I believe that climate change is man-made, I believe we're heading for a financial crash, I believe all gays will go to hell. Each statement answers different emotional needs, employs different neural circuits, makes different rational demands on us, lays claim to different kinds of knowledge, and calls on different kinds of proof.

Even to say 'I believe in God' cannot be shredded to a simple definition of religious belief, or the object of our devotion. Christians might say they 'believe in' Jesus as their Saviour, because to do so requires an act of faith based on a divine intervention in human history two thousand years ago. Jews are more likely to say that they trust Yahweh, Muslims that they submit to Allah, Hindus that they pay respect to the deities, Buddhists that they pursue the noble truths, and Taoists that they follow the Way.

We have never seen toast fall upwards.

Belief implies a possibility of doubt. We don't say we believe in gravity, because we don't need to. Its truth is programmed into our brain, and when we see an object fall, seeing is believing. We might miscalculate the probability of toast always falling butter-side down, but we have never seen toast fall upwards, unless we have helped it on its way.

248

Mountains of the Mind

Nor do we need proof of magnetism, because as children we spent many hours playing with magnets, watching them repel and attract each other, intrigued by the invisible force between them. In what is known as the illusion of explanatory depth, even as adults we have no idea how this magic works, but we persuade ourselves that we 'know'. In reality all we see with falling objects and interacting magnets is recurring events, but our brain turns them into foolproof belief or enduring theory. 'Pigs might fly' is our ultimate putdown of those whose beliefs we scoff at, until we see a hog soaring overhead.

Partial seers

'Pigs might fly' is an opinion, no more or less credible than 'Jesus will come again'. We are entitled to our own opinions, but not our own facts. 'Comment is free, but facts are sacred', wrote the journalist C P Scott in 1918. The difficulty is that our opinions fit so seamlessly with reality that we don't see the join: the world is as we see it, and vice versa. When we walk, we don't think consciously about where to place each foot: we just walk.

Our 'seeing' similarly feels so natural that it becomes constitutive of who we are and how we think. Common sense tells us that we see what is there, but common sense is wrong. Our seeing is not 'see through', because it is a filter that colours everything we gaze upon. From it we draw up a guide to every action, so automatic that we don't know we are applying it. It becomes our right and inevitable account of the way things really are, until proven wrong, or no longer workable.

In other words, we are partial seers, or as St Paul phrased it, 'we see through a glass darkly'. Our much vaunted independence of thought is based on the limited evidence of our senses, giving us only bounded and fragmented understanding. Whether we believe in God or quantum theory, we never see the world *as it is* objectively, only *as it appears* subjectively to us through the self-confirming loops of our perceptions.

We might think that science is our escape route from the bubble of our perceptions into objective truth, but not necessarily. The physicist Niels Bohr reminded us that physics doesn't tell us what nature is, only what we can say about it. As a proponent of quantum theory, he was not deterred by the particle/wave duality, where we don't know which is which until we observe it.

Instead he proposed a theory of complementarity, where seeming opposites do not necessarily contradict each other, because two things can share one truth. He resurrected an older teaching, that the opposite of a great truth can be an even greater truth. Given this, if we want a comprehensive view of reality, it makes sense not to put all our money on one horse, but to back several.

This is especially true in our personal and social life, where subjectivity makes it hard to break free of what we *want* to be true. Philosophers pen long screeds about what is 'true' and what is 'real', but as far as our brain is concerned, it selects perceptions that are 'cognitively fit', in the sense that they get us through another day safely, and work for us in our personal and social situation.

As the years go by, our views tend to crystallise, partly because our brain settles into fixed patterns of thought. For each one of us who remains a socialist firebrand for life, another slides into dull conservatism. Our brain is naturally conservative, and when challenged, has a habit of digging in deeper, blocking ideas that don't fit, and accepting as unquestionable truths the ones that feel familiar. In what is known as motivated reasoning, we notice only those things which support our viewpoint.

We need to be taken on mental journeys that
expose us to difference and newness.

This is why education is so vital in our early years, a time when we lay the foundations for our later thinking. When we go to school we are not only socialised, but our subjectivity is exposed to the rigours of objectivity. The referee is intersubjectivity, or encounters with other minds. Where we are out of line, cognitively or morally, our teachers and friends soon put us back on the straight and narrow. Two plus two does not equal five, and no, we can't help ourselves to what doesn't belong to us. This is the time, while we are still orienting our minds to the world, that we need to be taken on mental journeys that expose us to difference and newness.

The formation of our worldview starts early, and progresses slowly, subject to thousands of inputs that need to be made sense of. Around the age of two we learn the art of perceptual ambiguity: it could be *either* a duck *or* a rabbit, and we are capable of switching between the two. We also come to understand that others have different points of view or tastes from ours: I like ice cream, but you prefer broccoli.

Duck/rabbit illusion
We might see one or the other, but our brain doesn't allow us to see both at the same time. Are we similarly forced into binary thinking by our views and opinions?

It remains a lifelong quest to be able to balance arguments on one hand or the other. It becomes gradually harder to hold two opposing ideas in our mind at once without cognitively seizing up, so our flexibility declines. Like Tevye in 'Fiddler on the Roof', we get to the point where there *is* no other hand. Our synapses, like a flock of starlings, cease their random circling and suddenly all sweep in the same direction, leaving no stragglers to observe which way they have flown, or why.

Limited viewers

Our brain has evolved to convince us that our 'take' on the world is both freely chosen and 'right', the only one there is. We believe our eyes and the narrative of our conscious awareness. Like fish, we never see the water we swim in. All we feel is the current, and even then, only on the surface. We are never aware of the sediment of our assumptions, beliefs, opinions and prejudices underneath. If we are reading this book, we are most likely WEIRD without realising it: Western, educated, industrialised, rational and democratic. This is not a club affiliation that our ancestors on the savannah would have recognised.

The philosopher Immanuel Kant wrestled with this problem. He understood that the phenomena that come to our senses cannot by themselves give us a view or interpretation of the world. All animals receive sense data, but only humans organise them into experience and form opinions about them. Only humans have a participatory 'point of view', which also acts as a form of anticipation: we see what satisfies, comforts and makes sense for us. We can thank the later-evolved top layers of our brain for this extra processing, which gives us what Kant called a noumenal take on things (from *nous*, meaning mind), or a layer of explanation that rises above sensory perception.

Kant concluded that we live in two mind-worlds or realities, the one that appears to us 'out there', and the one we make for ourselves inside our heads. We can't choose one or the other, because we are always immersed in both. If we don't progress beyond sense data, we remain a child forever, never graduating to adult concepts. But we never reach a point where we can put sense data to one side completely. We might fast in the desert as a hermit, or smoke dope, but any sacred visions we arrive at will emanate from our brain, fashioned by what we ingest, or our early experiences.

The ability to live with difference is a good precept
for low levels of conflict.

We might find it difficult to understand what Kant is saying about the dual reality granted to us by our perceptual apparatus, but the implications are enormous. We are limited viewers, never seeing the dark side of the Moon, or the Big Picture. There is no such thing as *the* Way, only *my* way. We might find a group of people who largely agree with us, but even then we see only *our* way, not an absolute, perfect or timeless way.

Mountains of the Mind

We know this because mystics in different cultures have different visions. In other words, there are *many* ways, and they can't all be right. Even if we have no intention of becoming a mystic, we know that when we change the frame through which we look, we 'see' things differently, both literally and metaphorically. This is why polytheism appeals more to some than monotheism, and pluralism more than single vision. Socially and politically, the ability to live with difference is a good precept for low levels of conflict.

There are many factors which might influence our underlying orientation to the world. One is the prevailing zeitgeist, or mood of the time. In my own lifetime I have been aware of drifting through 1950's Cold War paranoia, 1960's optimism and rebellion, 1970's oil-crisis retrenchment, 1980's social unrest, 1990's capitalist free-for-all, 2000's terrorist threats, 2010's environmental anxiety and 2020's global pandemic. I am also aware that the view of each of these decades looks very different to a Chinese or a Russian, a teenager or an adult, a woman or a man, an optimist or a pessimist, a conservative or a liberal.

Given all these variables, we have to accept that our view of the world is at best partial, and sometimes incoherent. Aristotle was among the first to point out that we are constitutionally incapable of deconstructing all the influences that have made us who we are, and what has shaped our thinking. We can never get back to the default, so we can never give a detailed account of how we came to believe in other people, insist on fairness, object to genetic engineering, or support Arsenal football club.

On the other hand, we are under no obligation to be able to pontificate about everything under the sun, and we should be suspicious of people who do. It is a mark of maturity to admit that there are many things we simply don't know enough about to have an opinion one way or another.

Certainty cravers

And yet we crave certainty, because it is difficult to entertain several interpretations simultaneously, and to switch perspective quickly. We are system-builders who don't like admitting to being puzzled and confused. From an evolutionary perspective, this is not fickleness, but flexibility. The attitude we adopt feeds back to our brain, and if it's a fixed one, it will cramp our mental growth. If it's a bad one, it will sour the rest of the barrel. If it is ill-founded, its errors will multiply as we proceed.

Strength of conviction is no guarantee of rightness, and what we believe with all our heart is not necessarily true. We need to be able to populate our mind with ideas that challenge our default schemas, opening ourselves to change and creativity. Great minds are those that can hold several contrary ideas in mind simultaneously, and live with ambiguity. A closed mind is one that has stopped growing.

Conviction can turn out to be magnificently right or cruelly wrong. For someone like Charles Darwin, it can lead to new understanding. For Adolf Hitler, or a suicide bomber wrapped in high explosive, it can be a passion pursued to destruction, immolating others in the process.

Believing in ourselves is good for our self esteem, but not if it becomes an obsession or delusion that consumes the rights of others. Having the strength of our convictions is admirable so long as we choose wisely and well the issues we are prepared to fight for, die for or kill others for. This is never simply a question of reason, because reason is highly coloured by emotion, which is rooted in culture, which is always local.

Cultural variation means that sometimes we have little choice over our default worldview, and the assumptions that go with it. If we live in the rain forest, or on a coral atoll, our mindset will be totalised by encroaching logging companies or rising sea levels. We can think of nothing else. Our homes will be threatened, we will not be able to feed our children, and our very identity is under threat.

Elsewhere, our choices might be more negotiable. If we are born into a home with a revolver in it, in a community that has a high murder rate, in an economy driven by gun sales, in a culture devoted to hunting, in a country that was tamed at gunpoint, with a constitution that enshrines the right to self defence, we will be viscerally attached to firearms. High school shootings will not appal us, but confirm our belief in our right to carry arms, and strengthen our determination to defend ourselves, even against non-existent enemies.

Someone who has grown up around weapons will see them in a totally different way from someone who has never handled one, let alone seen one. Different parts of the brain are activated in each case, eliciting different emotional reactions when guns are seen, discussed or held. A gun is never just a gun. It is always a set of preconceptions rooted in our upbringing and experience.

Attack or defence
To some it's an object of threat, violence and death, to others it's a sporting accessory, a legal entitlement, and a guarantee of self defence.

It still remains our choice whether we want to live in a society where guns are freely on sale, teachers have to be trained how to deal with rogue shooters in the classroom, and children are taught to fire a weapon as soon as their arms are strong enough.

To 'see' is to understand the choice before us.

We can't choose *not* to have a worldview, because we cannot live without a perspective on the world, or concede that all issues are of equal weight. Our value system is the product of our yearning for meaning and significance, based on what we find intelligible. To 'see' is to understand the choice before us. Then, once we have chosen, our outlook governs every aspect of our behaviour, endowing our every thought with purpose.

Our attitude to the world is what marks us as different from everyone else, even though the world is of a piece. The world is constant, but our perception of it changes, because we are creatures of fashion. On Monday we eat meat, on Tuesday we announce that we are vegan. On Wednesday we vote for the reds, on Thursday something happens that makes us want to vote blue. On Friday we believe, on Saturday we lose our faith. On Sunday we say we are agnostic because we can't make our mind up.

Conviction seekers

Some days we fell so indecisive that we stand in awe of those who maintain strong views or convictions: how can they be so sure of themselves? But conviction is only one step away from dogmatism, which can be gloriously right or ingloriously wrong, like going flat out for God or the Devil. Both give the same neural rewards, and the illusion of certainty.

We need a worldview that keeps us cognitively on an even keel, but we should not let our craving for meaning and certainty lead us astray, or into a dead end. In his 'Republic', Plato regales us with a bewildering range of views on goodness, justice, truth and beauty. He never tells us what to think, only how to think more clearly and ethically. It's as if he is warning us against those who claim they already know, when probably all they have done is to reduce a complex matter to a simple solution. As H L Mencken observed, 'To every complex problem there is an answer that is clear, simple and wrong'.

We look through a kaleidoscope, not a monocle. Living is like peering through a stained glass window, multi-coloured and multi-perspective, never seen from a single aspect, or reducible to a single quality. Life is never all rosy, or rubbish, or easy to explain, or a conspiracy against us, so it is wise not to commit ourselves totally to One Big Idea. Doing so monopolises our attention, polarises our thinking, and results in what too easily becomes a 'clash of civilisations', in which neither can be more right or better than the other.

Life feels much easier when we reduce complex arguments to a binary choice, but simplicity achieved in this way is deceptive. Either/or thinking works well in the science laboratory, or inside our computer software, but in life, the algorithms of right and wrong take us so far and no further. Eventually we reach an important decision where we have to entertain both/and thoughts, which transcend binary logic. We have to find productive ways of engaging with the opinions of those who think differently from us, even learning to tolerate the intolerable. We have no choice but to live with the challenge of uncertainty.

We often look to science for certainty, but in fact uncertainty is essential for the progress of knowledge. Science's strength is that it is prepared to revise its opinion, or countenance a new theory. We seldom hear politicians hedge their bets or admit they don't know, but scientists do it all the time, because they must.

Mountains of the Mind

If we had heeded what scientists were telling us about global warming, which has been renamed global heating, we would have had a forty year start on solving the problem. Standing in its way are some powerful emotional drives and cognitive defences: our need to feed our family, our craving for ever higher living standards, our attachment to our private vehicles, our unwillingness to go vegan, our failure to think globally, our conviction that we can leave the solution to others.

Societal change can feel glacially slow,
and yet the glaciers are melting.

Our difficulty is that changing our thinking, or admitting we need to rethink, is cognitively expensive, and might even lose us a few friends. Distancing ourselves from the zeitgeist of our culture, which is fashioned by feelings and not rational arguments, is all but impossible, and few of us are gifted or strong enough to stand against the tide of the ideas of our time. This explains why societal change can feel glacially slow. And yet the glaciers *are* melting, at an increasing rate.

Reluctant mind-changers

Research shows that if we stay flexible in our thinking and open-minded about change, beyond the critical learning period of childhood, we are likely to enjoy a more fulfilling adulthood. This is a wise ploy given that life is part of a dynamic system in which change and disorder will always be more common than equilibrium.

Few of us however are capable of what the poet John Keats called negative capability, or the capacity to live with doubts and uncertainties. On the savannah, our brain evolved to make life or death decisions, not to contemplate its navel or debate truth. To achieve this end, it tends to impose a pattern, even though this closes out other possibilities.

We don't like living in limbo, and struggle to accept that the world is an unfinished project, but it is wise to remember that certainty is a dangerous illusion, especially in human affairs. Most of the disasters in human history have been caused by people who were utterly convinced of their rightness, unable to change course. The great Greek tragedies warn us not of the dangers of being run over by a bus, which is random, but of the perils of hubris, which is culpable failure to

Mountains of the Mind

know our limits, heed the warnings of others, and change what we believe in the light of new evidence.

There are other hopeful lessons we can learn from how we direct our attention. Occasionally we can sharpen it to a stiletto, entering a state of flow or absorption. We forget ourselves temporarily, becoming the piece of music we are listening to, or the daydream we are having.

This means two things, always working in tandem: we are what we pay attention to, and the nature of reality is shaped by the intensity of our noticing. We don't just log what is there, which is relatively easy; we also decide how to respond to it, which is much more complex.

Mercator's projection
Gerardus Mercator's projection of 1569, presenting the world to us in two dimensions, distorts the size and shape of the continents at the poles, and places Europe firmly at the centre of the action. It nevertheless continues to have a powerful hold on how we 'see' our planet's geography.

There is no 'original position' to start from, or God-centred view from nowhere, but our brain has to start from somewhere. Mediaeval maps show Jerusalem at the centre of the known world, and even Mercator's projection of 1569, still in use today, distorts the size of the poles. We have to have a frame into which everything else fits. Raw physical reality by itself is not enough: merely gathering all the facts we can about everything makes no sense at all unless we already have a scheme in which to fit the unexpected.

Our perceptions are often distorted by our emotions, previous experience and convictions. That object swirling in the wind might trigger our phobia of birds, our

258

fascination with flying, or our passion to campaign for plastic bags to be banned so that they don't end up polluting our oceans.

This means we never fully see life for what it objectively is, only as we subjectively experience it, while under the heavy influence of the 'important others' in our life. These make up our social reality, a complex construct of our family, peer group, gender, age, nationality, culture, class, education, religion, mindset and sense of history.

As we think, so the material world unfolds for us,
and as we believe, so we define our mind-world.

The world we make for ourselves is not therefore simply something given to us, nor are we entirely its creator. It is partly an attitude we passively inherit and absorb, but more importantly it is a set of convictions, principles and sensibilities that we actively form, growing out of our every thought and act, deeply moral because simultaneously emotional and intellectual. We live in two realities, the material and the mental, but they are never separate. As we think, so the material world unfolds for us, and as we believe, so we define our mind-world.

Change resisters
Cognitive neuroscientists have shown that our brain is neuroplastic: our synapses can be dissolved to form new connections. Having fallen in love, we can fall out of love, and then find a new partner. Having voted socialist all our life, we can swing over to the conservatives. We are made, but we can also self-remake, becoming more than what made us.

Habits of mind that are rooted in cultural tradition however are not so easily shifted. In the 1943 famine in Bengal, there was an acute shortage of rice. Tons of wheat were shipped in, but millions starved to death, because the starving population could not adjust to the alternative reality of eating wheat and not rice, even though their lives were at stake.

Since then, aid agencies have been more sensitive about imposing cultural change from the outside. Attitudes are embedded in traditions, beliefs, taboos, fears, superstitions and assumptions that are stronger than rational imperatives. Hearts and minds have to be won first, slowly, and from the inside.

259

Mountains of the Mind

In such instances, being open to persuasion and change can be the difference between life and death, as may be the case with taking action over climate crisis. Eventually a tipping point is reached, and a new consensus emerges. In what has become a race against time, we start to heed the warnings about death by burning, drowning or starving. We are forced into a new paradigm, or way of thinking about the world. The pieces of the puzzle remain the same, but we begin to fit them together in a new way.

In our consumerist culture, we gobble up new ideas as if they are fast food for the mind, always on the lookout for the next 'big idea'. But the march of ideas in human history has had a chequered progress, and few of us spot the one idea that is going to turn our lives upside down. The economist J M Keynes warned that the really big ideas, the levers of change that are going to drive moral advance and intellectual understanding for generations to come, are at first ignored as the random scribblings of some obscure thinker. They go on however to conquer more territory than the biggest armies. The 'background radiation' of the teachings of Jesus is still palpable, and in science, the shock waves of Darwin's theory of evolution still rumble through biology.

It is hard to stay open to new ideas, because we invest our foundational beliefs not just with self-justifying reasons, but also high emotions, making it very hard to forsake them. Political disputes, culture wars, even scientific arguments, are more frequently fought on the basis of feelings and allegiances, not facts and certainties.

We need to keep our mind open about the challenge of change, because brain scans show that instead of remaining plastic, neural circuits tend to close down once we've made our minds up about something. We have a confirmation bias that lures us into noticing only the things that bolster our beliefs: one freezing winter with more snow than we remember proves that global warming is a myth, not that weather patterns are veering towards the extreme. We also have a conservative bias to stick with what we know: rice has always been our staple diet, so why risk something new?

In small matters these biases can provide welcome relief from cognitive dissonance, but they can also blind us to bigger truths. As the poet W H Auden's wryly observed, 'We would rather be ruined than changed'. But there is no shame in changing our mind, especially when the facts change. Change of heart is one of life's great gifts, what Aristotle referred to as *metanoia*, the ability to remake ourselves in a new image. We change our mind more often than we like to think, and sometimes change is forced upon us, but when we embrace it, we give ourselves some control of our direction of travel.

Wily movers

Such fluidity doesn't make charlatans of us all, because cognitive flexibility is an asset, vital for our psychological health and emotional stability. The psychologists Carl Rogers and Albert Ellis proposed that personal growth and positive self-image are dependent on our ability to adjust our worldview to changing realities. Some took this as an invitation to relativism and self indulgence, but Rogers and Ellis were setting a tougher challenge: to think more honestly and rationally.

Leon Festinger added a further twist. Especially when we are young, we are vulnerable to the mere exposure effect, giving our heart to whatever cause presents itself to us most often. Then, once we have committed, we are so averse to cognitive dissonance or mental conflict that we make any new evidence fit our old belief, whether it does or not. In fact our faith is strengthened in direct proportion to the resistance we experience. If the prophecy fails, and the end of the world doesn't come on the fated day, it is proof that God is giving us a second chance, not that He doesn't exist. Instead of being troubled, we double down on our faith, beliefs and convictions.

Despite these glitches, most of us are quite consistent in our core beliefs, because continuity of opinion is central to our sense of self and our ability to engage with others. If we reduce our worldview to a series of randomly chosen mental snapshots that vanish as soon as they appear, consciousness ends up as an illusion founded on a fantasy, and reason becomes a whim based on a habit.

Our ability to think differently is a great strength. So long as we are not merely rearranging our prejudices, we keep open the possibility of redemption, which is just as well, given that we all hold some beliefs that, if put to the test, are slightly embarrassing if not downright indefensible.

Each of us is placed somewhere within what is known as the Overton Window. We can be persuaded to move a little to the left or right politically, to give to a new charity, or to buy a new product, but only if there is an overlap with ideas that have been in the public sphere for some time, or if our thinking is already moving in that direction. Consider how that window has shifted regarding slavery, race, immigration and multiculturalism. It is up to us how far we stick our head out of the window at election time, and how much of the view we take in.

Our hallmark as a species is that we possess the adaptive capacity to change our minds and allegiances quite quickly, not just driven by insistent emotion, but also guided by practical reason. In 1945, following the atomic explosions in Hiroshima and Nagasaki, the Japanese people did not take long to allow their passion for the imperial cause to be redirected towards the rational project of rebuilding a peace-time economy that would soon become a world-beater.

The brain is certainly capable of change, or reprogramming. If we wear inverting spectacles, seeing everything upside down, we stumble for a week or so, until our brain adjusts. This isn't so surprising, given that the image on our retina during normal vision is already inverted.

True movement is in the mind.

If the brain can change, so can the mind. There is a Zen story of three monks looking at a flag blowing in the wind. The first says the flag is moving, the second insists that the motion is in the wind, but the third remarks that the true movement is in the mind, the true agent of all change.

Changing ingrained habits of mind, cut into the grooves of deep-seated neural mechanisms, is hard, and changing habits of the heart is even harder. When was the last time we heard someone say 'I've been wrong all my life'? To change our worldview is as hard as changing our language or religion, tantamount to changing our life. We can't do it without soul-searching, and having hard conversations with those who see any kind of change as defeat or betrayal.

Sudden change such as an overnight religious conversion is often suspect, but profound change, like a tree sending down roots, requires time and sustenance. Given these challenges, we might justifiably declare a new Beatitude: blessed are those who can change their mind.

The power of self-transformation allows many young gang members, terrorists and criminals, assuming they survive the zero-sum violence of their early days, to come eventually to see the world very differently. The young brain tends to be impressionable and absolutist, seeing the world in black and white. If we do not become more mellow, forgiving and tolerant as age, we have missed one of life's great opportunities.

Whichever cause we buy into, we need our worldview as a sheet anchor while we sail through a sea of complexities. It is our lifebelt, because life is full of ambivalence and uncertainty. We need to be able to make compromises without feeling we are being hypocritical. We might have strong objections to capitalism, but we can't get by without spending money. We might hate factory farming, but we also need to put food on the table for a growing family. We might be a Christian, but we can still vote for austerity.

We have therefore evolved a capacity to entertain contradictory truths, to know and not know, to agree but disagree. Our challenge as social creatures with a large brain is that every important debate we engage in has powerful arguments on both sides, seldom mutually exclusive or incommensurate. Democratic politics would otherwise be impossible. Our opponents might turn out to be less mistaken than we are, and we need a way of seeing how right they may be. Something we have believed is wrong or false all our lives might turn out to be right or true.

It pays us therefore to keep our worldview under review, and to accept that others might not see things the way we do, because the opposite of a worldview is not a falsehood but a differently-held worldview. Hot and cold are genuine opposites, albeit on a sliding scale. If something is hot, it cannot be simultaneously cold. Political and moral views are seldom so clear cut, full of irreconcilable contradictions. We get round this by latching on to one core belief, then rationalising the inconsistencies so that they conform to it. We make them true by the strength of our belief.

Labile listeners

We can reduce our hidebound thinking be coming better listeners, as advised by the psychologist Carl Rogers, whom we met a moment ago. He used to get people on one side of an argument to listen, and then repeat in their own words *to their opponent's satisfaction* what had just been said. This courtesy was then reciprocated. Over a period, this tactic brought about a shift away from the extremes towards the centre or middle ground, the only place where democratic debate can he heard.

Mountains of the Mind

*We put most of our cognitive energy into shoring
up what we already believe.*

Such a practice takes time and patience, but it achieves several things. It stops us asking only questions that give answers that we want to hear, it helps us overcome our tribalism, and it exposes our excessive confidence in ourselves. We are all guilty of anthropic realism, or the conviction that the world works as we see it, and only as we see it. We put most of our cognitive energy into shoring up what we already believe, avoiding the challenge of new possibilities. Our emotional protectionism blinds us to the fact that our rational take on the world is much more malleable than we think, but only if we are prepared to work at it.

It might even be too malleable. Rogers staged other experiments that give us pause for thought. He asked some people to fill out questionnaires with their views on certain topics. After a lapse of time, he returned the forms and invited the recipients to summarise their views to others in the group.

But he had deliberately muddled the forms, ensuring that the participants received a set of views almost opposite to what they had written earlier. Some failed to spot this switch or remember what they originally wrote, quickly adjusting to a set of opinions they had not originally espoused. This suggested to Rogers that our views are far more fickle than we realise, determined more by passing mood than rational analysis.

If we're not vigilant, we go through life with our ears blocked and our eyes blinkered, giving us deaf spots and blind spots that we hardly notice. We get plenty of insight, but not enough outsight, because our brain, dominated by its large fear centres, nudges us towards sticking with what we know.

Compulsive world-makers

Whatever belief-complex we adopt, our brain must insist on a plan, make interpretations that fit it, and select the facts that conform to it. Only then does our mind enter the fray, as a *person* defined by core values, without which we have no foundation for passing a judgment on whether the ten million deaths in the trenches of World War One were a historical inevitability or an avoidable tragedy. Even to say we don't care is a value statement.

Mountains of the Mind

Our brain has evolved to shred the complexity of the world
down to a few simple explanations.

We are compulsive world-makers, weaving webs of meaning in which we can ensnare ourselves, and spinning yarns in which we can entangle ourselves. These 'texts' are not optional add-ons, but essential interpretations that keep us sane, at the top of our hierarchy of needs. Our brain has evolved to shred the complexity of the world down to a few simple explanations, without which we can't function cognitively and socially, or cast our vote at election time. Any anomalies that don't fit the grand scheme have to be knocked into a shape that does fit. If not, we ignore them.

We can't live without beliefs or reasons to explain why we should campaign for peace or barrack for conflict, go to work or stay at home, make friends or become a hermit, bring children into the world or stay celibate, open our doors or close our borders. In brief, we have to generate a theory of why the world is the way it is.

This world-making process begins in childhood, when we are too young to form our own narratives, theories and explanations. Our young brain starts out as a stimulus-and-response machine, convincing us that our senses take true and literal snapshots of reality. It can't absorb everything at once, so it shines a spotlight on what has grabbed our interest.

We notice this phenomenon as adults. When we are in a noisy room, we single out the one voice we want to hear, while also remaining vaguely aware of what is on the periphery of our vision, until we shift focus again. We are like a pilot in the cockpit, reducing a bewildering array of instruments to the one or two essential readings that we know will keep our plane safely aloft.

By the time we go to school, knowing how to 'narrow down' our attention becomes a key determinant of how well we are going to do. Slowly we become our own professors of perception, in control not just of what to notice, but also how to interpret what we see. Are we looking at a bird, a plane, a weather balloon, or a plastic bag blown in the wind?

Some early theorists believed that our mind is a blank slate at birth, or a hodgepodge of isolated impressions, but nature is wiser than we think. The world does not overwhelm our baby brain in a chaotic rush. Reality may look like a

Mountains of the Mind

Rorshach blob, but we are primed to see something rather than nothing. In a two way process, the world presents itself to us, and we reach out to meet it with meanings and expectations. We can merge input with output in this way because our mind secretes a kind of glue that binds our sensory inputs together.

Rorshach test
It starts out as a splurge of ink on a folded piece of paper, but it might end up as a bird, a butterfly, or a scary face. Everything depends on the experiences and expectations we bring to the image.

This means that life never strikes us as absurd. Every time we open our eyes, or view a text message, we trigger associations with previous experiences, full of symbols we recognise and significances we have learned. When we attend a concert we don't see and hear a confusion of light and sound, but musicians performing, on instruments we like, singing songs we know, to an audience that has assembled specifically to hear them. Our world is not chaotic, but soaked in symbol and drenched with meaning.

Meaning-making is partly an automatic process, but it also demands a considered response from us, starting in the nursery. At first we find that paying attention is hard work, a clash of neurons fighting for supremacy. We shift quickly from one toy to another, if only because one looks more colourful. We shout for attention so that we get noticed, which can be exhausting for our carers. In desperation they might put us in front of the television, which floods our brains with 'system one' dopamine hits, one stimulus after another.

If we are to progress in our understanding, we also need time to ponder our 'system two' responses, which happens when an adult engages us in conversation, or reads us a book. Through social exchange we learn that there are subtleties and differences in the world. Concentrating is hard work, but gradually our attention-muscle gets stronger, allowing us to start the work of creating an inner world. We can now play on our own, because we can generate our own entertainment, not at the mercy of every distraction.

By our teenage years a second 'narrowing down' of our attention is called for, not so much a settling of disputes between conflicting perceptions, but a choosing between rival world views. This is a much more cognitively and emotionally demanding task, because as well as realising we have minds of our own, we are also keen to win the approval of our peer group.

In the hormonal swirl of adolescence, our 'point of view' becomes much more complex than working out individually what we are looking at. Our thinking is socially moulded into opinions and attitudes. We want to fit in, but we also want to show that we are independent minds, not merely learning our opinions by rote. We give everything a try, partly craving certainty, but also eager to risk finding out for ourselves.

Cautious campaigners

Eventually all our choices seem to coalesce into a grandstand view of what appears before us, but we do well to remember that there are thousands of other ways of seeing, or roads we did not travel. The philosopher John Stuart Mill called each life an 'experiment in living'. He didn't mean a scientific experiment, because we cannot be sure at the outset of our hypotheses, or predict our findings. It is wise therefore not to commit to a single explanation to the exclusion of all others. This is not an invitation to relativism, but to a broad and open mindset, reserving our right to change our mind when we need to.

The hedgehog commits to a single idea, making it good at defending itself, but not so successful at making alliances. The fox, by hedging his bets, can colonise a wider range of environments, diversifying his prospects. In the political arena, we have to decide whether to be a hedgehog or a fox. This will depend on the extent to which we feel comfortable with ambiguity and uncertainty, and our readiness to take a few chances in widening our opportunities.

Democracy thrives on opposition, but it also requires consensus in a well-populated middle ground. If we live in a society where journalists are criticised by all parties for being biased, we are lucky. It means that, by offending everyone equally, we are enjoying an essential freedom to think and speak openly. We know

267

democracy is in trouble when journalists are jailed, media channels are shut down, and dissent is quashed.

Rather oddly, given the importance of this trick of the brain in giving us our personalised and persuasive picture of reality, there is no word that adequately describes it, or captures its subtlety. Apart from worldview, which is vague, other possibilities include creed, orientation, pattern of thought, mindset, private vision, personal construct, psychic map, cast of mind and explanatory framework, but none quite seems to do the job.

To a flea, the whole world is an armpit.

Other terms are too technical. Therapists refer to cathexis, or what we attach ourselves to emotionally, often obsessively so. Surfers are constantly on the lookout for the next set of breakers. Sociologists study habitus, or the habits drilled into us by our situation in life. To a carpenter, every tree is a potential set of chairs. Biologist talk of umwelt, or the ecological niche each organism finds itself in. To a flea, the whole world is a sweaty armpit.

Whatever term we choose for 'how we see the world', it has to cover not just the physical world in which we find ourselves, of things and people, but also the way we match our cognitive reality to it. The philosopher R M Hare coined the word 'blik' to describe the dense tissue of beliefs which we find so hard to unpick, or see for what it is. It is based on the German word *blick*, meaning view, but it also sounds like blink and flick, words which hint at the partiality and hurriedness of our grasp of how things really are.

Whatever name we give it, our 'take on things' is self-sustaining, overwhelming and totalising, so it lands us in a cognitive bind. Even though all we ever see is part of the whole, we are convinced that we are always right, and everyone else is always wrong. We might feel that our fundamental beliefs are self-evident or beyond proof, but this is a weakness, not a strength. To the busy mind, one belief feels as good another, so long as it gives us emotional and cognitive security.

It pays therefore is to be a cautious campaigner, while amassing a weight of evidence that supports our case. Like Fagin, we must be prepared to review our situation. The worst we can do is to declare: that's how I think, and there is

268

nothing I can do about it. There is a great deal we can do about it. It's *our* worldview, not someone else's, made true only by the strength of our believing it. Victor Frankl referred to our choice of attitude as our 'last freedom', the one thing we are left with when everything else is taken away from us.

There is no need to bind ourselves to someone else's ideology, or blind ourselves to another's truth. None of us likes being told we're wrong, but there's no shame in ditching an inadequate theory for a better one. Scientists have to do this all the time.

Democratic debaters
What then can serve as a trustworthy backstop for what we believe, about the Holocaust, climate crisis, vaccines, abortion or fracking? History and science can give us data about what *is*, which we can check out for ourselves, but they give us no sure route to *ought*. Facts answer our *what* questions, but to find out *why*, we need to weave them into a wider scheme of explanation. We have to make our own minds up, making sure we don't distort the facts to fit our opinions, or get lost in an echo chamber.

An additional complication is that we each lean towards what the psychologist Robert Sternberg calls particular 'thinking styles' or cognitive settings, which border on being personality types. Some of us are happy to be followers, others push to be leaders. Some like to operate within a clear set of rules, others are keen to make their own. Some like to keep to themselves, others crave company. Some like to focus on a single task, others comfortably multi-task. Some like to deal with specifics, others enjoy engaging in abstractions.

It is always possible that our opponents
are better informed than we are.

Given the complexity of our choices, our psychological variability, the difference in our judgments, our cultural diversity, and the fact that we can't see the bottom from the top, we are bound to disagree. We end up in different destinations because we don't all start from the same place. We have no choice therefore but to find ways of establishing common ground, and of managing our differences. In politics, as in life, we can never get everything we want, which isn't the same as getting nothing.

Politics cannot be a zero-sum or winner-takes-all game, and the solution we have found is liberal democracy, characterised by the recognition of individual rights and the rule of law. It is highly inefficient and full of flaws, but it is our best vehicle for engaging with each other's concerns without imprisoning or killing each other.

Political discussion can happen only when we allow the exchange of ideas to be also a meeting of minds, in a public forum where rational debate is open to all, and both sides treat each other honourably. There are two simple reasons for this. Firstly, it is always possible that our opponents are better informed than we are, and we hope they are respectful enough to listen to us in return. Secondly, the government that is calling all the shots this week might next week find itself in opposition.

The resurgence of populism in recent times has transformed these unwritten ground rules of democratic debate, because it pits against each other two mutually exclusive ways of arriving at the 'will' of the people: directly, through referenda, or at one remove, through elected representatives.

The problem with governing by referendum is that each one-off vote simplifies a complex debate to a single issue, and then binds all hands until the next referendum, which might not be for another generation. Millions of 'wills' end up as a simplified argument, which compromises the capacity of representatives elected every five years to debate complex issues as they arise. Representatives are not delegates who do as they are told, but individual minds and consciences, responsible to their voters, free to revise their opinion and adapt policy quickly in the light of changed political, social and moral circumstances.

When these two 'wills' conflict, of the people and their representatives, there is confusion about where the will of the people resides. Capital punishment by hanging was abolished for all offences except treason by UK parliamentarians in 1969, and completely abolished in 1998, but 'popular' polls suggest that a majority of the population 'will' it to be reintroduced for certain offences, overruling the 'will' of the politicians they freely elected to represent them.

There cannot therefore, despite the claims of populist leaders, be a clearly defined 'general will of the people' on any particular issue. Immediately after each

270

referendum, some voters die, some become eligible to vote for the first time, and some change their minds either way. A referendum is a snapshot of a moment in time, coloured by the events that lead up to it, and unable to revise its thinking in the light of new developments. After the 'people' have spoken, it is both illogical and dangerous to label those who have been outvoted as 'enemies of the people', as this makes them enemies of themselves.

Even in Ancient Athens, the birthplace of democracy, which means 'rule of the people', the ideal was intrinsically flawed at the outset. Only a small percentage of free males were allowed to vote, and women and slaves were excluded. On the plus side, the small number of voters allowed them to hear their candidates directly, and certain key posts were decided by the drawing of lots, giving everyone a potential shot at running the city state. Given the dominance of today's 'political class', being ruled by a butcher, baker and candlestick maker taking it in turns might be a kind of 'populism' worth having.

Liberal losers

It was partly the glib optimism of the liberal intelligentsia that created the conditions for populism to thrive in the first place. It has been too rational and psychologically naive, overlooking the emotional grievances of those who feel left behind, angry at being taken for granted, threatened by change, and uneasy about globalism. Internationalism is a noble cause, but it butters no parsnips for those who feel they are losing their jobs, identity and control over their lives.

Populism is not new, nor is antipathy to privilege and elitism. Julius Caesar knew that the populace were more interested in bread and circuses than policies and principles. His reward, so long as he continued to lavish them with the spoils of war, was to be deified.

Caesar achieved dictatorship by force of arms, but modern demagogues have more subtle means at their disposal. In today's hyper-reality, governance is presented as a game show, popularity is determined by poll ratings, and facts are on sale to the highest bidder. Vital issues are decided not by rational argument, but by corporate money, the loudest voices, and control of the air waves.

Take for instance the issue of global heating. Temperatures may be rising, and climate events becoming more severe, but in the American Senate, some senators deny climate change, despite having been taught the same science lessons at school as those who take on trust decades of data amassed by researchers. For these climate change deniers, their political allegiance is stronger than empirical evidence or rational argument. Their thinking is not dispassionate but motivated, overshadowed by tribal loyalty and corporate interest.

The existentialist philosopher Martin Heidegger had a theory to explain how science and feeling can end up working against each other. We have two ways of mental processing, the theoretical and the experiential. One tells us how the world works, the other how to live in it. In the science laboratory, it is fairly easy to be calmly analytical about the options facing us, but when our livelihoods and identity are at stake, we have to do more than process the world. We have to find a way of living in it, and of carrying people along with us.

The most dangerous worldview is the one held by
someone who has not viewed the world.

This brings our emotions into play, which Heidegger believed always get the whip hand over facts and reasons. The irony for Heidegger is that in the 1930's he dallied with Nazi ideology, so even he was guilty of privileging feelings over facts. His hypocrisy reminds us that, after we've crunched our way through all our school lessons aimed at getting us to think rationally, we still need to make a commitment to a cause, so we might as well make a wise one, bearing in mind Alexander von Humboldt's opinion that the most dangerous worldview is the one held by someone who has not viewed the world.

Political partygoers

We might be tempted to pin political affiliation onto genes, neurochemistry or character: we are born to be liberal, socialist or conservative, just as we can be labelled introvert or extrovert. But nothing in the mind/brain is as simple as this. The flag we rally round has nothing to do with the dominance of our left or right brain, or whether it is our fear-dominated amygdala or rational cortex calling the shots.

There is some evidence that first-born children tend to be more radical in their views than later siblings, but there is no fixed 'hard right' or 'soft left' personality type, or combination of genes which turns us into authoritarians or anarchists.

Mountains of the Mind

Facial recognition technology claims it is possible to tell our political affiliation merely from the look on our face, but there is no calculus by which our class, gender, education, race, place of birth or upbringing determines how we cast our vote on election day.

Our squabbles over freedom, justice and equality depend on our default view of human nature. Are we intrinsically good at heart, or do we need to be kept firmly in our place? These are gut feelings and approaches to the world, played out in the busy social arena, not capable of being proved right or wrong by rational argument.

Debates about human nature and what makes for the ideal society are as old as human language, enshrined in long-running religious and philosophical disputes. We might agree with Thomas Hobbes: people are essentially flawed and not easily changed. Life is potentially brutish, so we need a strong state to keep order.

Or we might be disciples of Jean-Jacques Rousseau: we are born naturally good, but are corrupted by the vices of society. We are perfectible, capable of transcending ourselves, so good government is that which enables us to flourish, by revolution of the status quo if necessary.

The following table comes with many health warnings. The surge of populist sentiment in 2016 in Britain and America showed that traditional left-right divisions based on class have been superseded by 'culture wars' fought over much more complex issues.

Also, voting 'right' does not automatically mean we are prolife, or fiercely protective of our borders. Voting left does not commit us to being prochoice, or globalist in our outlook. Loyalties are so tribal and open to media spin that pollsters find modern elections too close to call.

Liberalism is a confusing term, signifying left in Canada and right in Australia. Then there is neoliberalism, which takes the usually centrist instincts of liberalism much further to the right.

7

	Left	Right
Parties go by different names, but they always signify a left/right divide.	**Labour** **Liberal** **Democrat** **Socialist**	**Conservative** **National** **Republican** **Neoliberal**
Vision	Entitlement, social justice, mutual aid, help for the left behind, tough on the causes of crime.	Desert, choice, responsibility, law and order, help for those who help themselves, tough on criminals.
Aspiration	Collective obligations. Equality of opportunity to ensure that everyone has the same life chances. Social mobility for all.	Individual freedoms. Prizes for those who make it, creating a natural hierarchy based on talent and initiative. Reward merit, not birth.
The State	'Hands on' government. State ownership of 'goods' that no single person can afford, such as schools, hospitals, transport, utilities.	Minimal state. Private enterprise to encourage efficiency, competition and profit for those prepared to invest in the public good.
Tax	Progressive tax to boost public services. Take from higher earners to spread to those whose income is capped, or who are jobless, or who are in need.	Low tax to encourage business innovation, and to leave us free to buy private health and schooling. Austerity for low earners to encourage them to strive harder, and to discourage scroungers.

Whether or not we've heard of Hobbes or Rousseau, we do readily divide ourselves into rival camps, based on the slenderest differences. The political debate is often reduced to economics, the touchstone for our views on social justice, even though earning enough to pay our bills takes up at most a third of our lives. Our Faustian struggle with conflicting siren voices is neatly summed up in the opposing views of two American political philosophers. They both died in the same year, 2002, but that is about all they have in common.

274

Mountains of the Mind

Robert Nozick insisted that what we earn belongs to us, and if the state is to lay claim to any of it, it can only be a minimal amount, which we grant under duress. Possession is nine tenths of the law. Those who have less cannot look for handouts from those who have plenty: they need to get themselves sorted.

John Rawls started from a very different premise. Society will always have its needy, and much wealth is inherited, not earned. He advocated an 'original position' argument: what if the prince had been born a pauper, and vice versa? Entitlements need to be distributed in society in a way that levels the playing field for all.

Egalitarian-minded socialists warm to Rawls's theory of social justice, but conservatives favour Nozick's birthright arguments. Nozick has the edge, because the status quo is hard to budge: every piece of land and property is already owned by someone, and no one has the right to take it away or give to anyone else. The thought experiment is therefore pointless.

In the real world, things are never so simple. In logic, the middle ground is excluded: black cannot be white. But in life, most of us bob up and down in a sea of grey, floating around on most issues. If we're lucky enough to live in a liberal democracy, we are seldom forced to swim in a particular direction, nor are we ever left to drown.

None of us fits neatly into any particular political paradigm. Nor do we ever find out which party colour we 'naturally' are, because we are born into a society where many of these choices have already been made for us. The world comes to us as a package.

Democracy's virtue is that it allows us to respond as a moral agent, to choose the kind of world we want our children to grow up in. No matter how rational our political allegiances appear on the surface, they start in our gut. Left, right or centre of the political spectrum, we have differing ambitions and passions motivated by reactionary fear or cautious hope, strong self sufficiency or risky mutuality.

What marks us out is where we place ourselves along an ideological continuity. This will flow from our core beliefs about what makes for the common good. Whatever our political persuasion, we each have our own notion of utopia, a 'no place' in our mind that we want to turn into *our* place. Who doesn't want a world where people are treated fairly, effort is rewarded, suffering is minimised and poverty is 'made history'? What we find difficult to agree on is how best to bring this about, or who to trust with controlling the levers of the future.

We might drift into our political persuasion, but usually we are looking for answers to difficult questions that first occur to us as teenagers. Do we accept things as they are, or are we duty bound to change them to what we believe they ought to be? Should the bonds of society be tightened or loosened? Do we see equality as a birthright or something we have to earn? Do we see others as essentially untrustworthy, or do we sense an intrinsic goodness in each other?

Are we driven by traditional 'family values', or do we have no objection to abortion on demand, gay marriage and euthanasia? Do we want to see money spent on youth clubs, or more young criminals brought to justice? Are we convinced that the market will sort things out, or are we obliged to intervene to ensure the 'left behind' can flourish?

The time to worry is when the verbal sparring stops.

Most political parties occupy the middle ground on these issues, which is why they sometimes sound alike in their bandying about of 'feelgood' words like fairness, choice, progress, justice, opportunity, change, sovereignty, prosperity and national destiny at election time, meaning everything and nothing.

'Freedom' is the slipperiest word of all. The right sees the left as freedom's enemy, and themselves as the true defenders of liberty. Equality is a threat to freedom. The left replies that, without basic rights and protections, freedom is dead in the water. There is no liberty without equality.

Some of us switch off at this point, while others are driven by a quasi-religious belief in the state, the party, the free market, human rights, social activism or utopian anarchy. Win or lose, such verbal sparring is an important part of being politically engaged. The time to worry is when it stops, because that suggests that democracy is being slowly strangled, or is dying through apathy.

Volatile voters

Neither side has a monopoly on truth, empathy, intelligence or rightness. Some socialists can be ruthless and intolerant in their pursuit of social justice, some

276

conservatives can be compassionate and forbearing in their championing of self-determination.

Conservatives start from the premise that life is intrinsically tough. They hate the idea of welfare, because they believe it goes against the grain of human nature, weakens individual responsibility, rewards shirkers and is unfair to workers. In one sense, evolutionary neuroscience backs up their argument. Our brains have shrunk in size since our ancestors left the savannah, possibly as a result of less challenging life styles. Life's prizes go to those who strive to ascendancy.

Conservatives believe that the best government is the least government. Competition is good for us, hand-outs weaken us, and social capital is made by those who, in the first place at least, look out for themselves. Society works best as a collective of self-reliant individuals, whose spontaneous aspiration for personal betterment ends up benefiting the whole.

Conservatives don't like sudden change, which is where the idea of 'conserving' the hard-won lessons of the past comes in. Gradual reform reduces the risk of throwing out the baby with the bathwater. To this end, society needs a natural ruling class dedicated to guiding the 'little platoons' in taking care of the nation's delicate social fabric and proud history.

They are deeply suspicious of socialist 'blank slate' thinking, or the idea that we are somehow perfectible. Our mind is written on at birth, with some simple strictures: look after ourselves, protect our own, defend what we have, be wary of strangers.

Look what happens when these defaults are forgotten: sudden and violent revolution. In the French, Russian and Maoist Revolutions, millions died on the anvil of ideological zeal, with little gain in equality or happiness. Conservatives don't like meddling do-gooders and 'bleeding heart' reformers, who end up undermining traditional values, interfering with society's normal checks and balances, and sacrificing the general good on the altar of their naive agendas.

Human nature is geared towards self-interest, social hierarchies are formed naturally, and the future is uncertain, so policies must reflect these realities, starting with the protection of private property. Our instinct, indeed our first duty, is to take responsibility for ourselves. The only help we need from government is a few strong institutions of state, especially police, law courts and the military.

Mountains of the Mind

'Freedom' means choice, low tax, sovereignty, a minimalist state, thriving business, strong trade, and being left alone to get on with our lives.

Socialists, at the opposite end of the political spectrum, are accused by the right of being woolly in their thinking, but they can be as precise as conservatives in their pursuit of what makes for a better society. They accuse conservatives of being hard and rigid in their convictions, perpetuating the injustices of the world. We are collectively responsible for each other's welfare, and it is the duty of government to be interventionist, taking an active role in challenging injustice, spreading wealth, raising happiness levels for all, protecting the vulnerable and, where necessary, transforming the institutions of the state.

They ask not for revolution, but for organic change based on progressive policies that keep pace with the opportunities and shifting values of a changing world. They accept that we are all born with individual differences and natural endowments. What hold us back are the structural inequalities of society. The legal profession is forever closed to us if we're not given a good basic education, a chance to go to law school, and a job as a lawyer if we're good enough.

Our individual differences and abilities are more likely to flourish if society's structural inequalities are minimised. This allows a meritocracy of talent to emerge in each generation. Social mobility is increased, social envy is reduced because the best people are seen as taking the best jobs, and social inequality is kept to a minimum, avoiding a yawning gap between the super-rich and those on zero hour contracts.

If only things were that simple. We can work towards equality of opportunity as an ideal, and we can accept equality of outcome as a variable, but there is a problem. If we eliminate all structural inequalities in society, we clear the way for our genetic differences to flourish unhindered, so there will always be a pecking order. We have evolved as strivers, and one way or another, our biology will out. In a race, there can't be prizes for everyone.

Also, those who are given a leg up in the first generation to climb the ladder of opportunity by dint of effort and talent, claiming their meritocratic rewards, will want the best for their children, thereby perpetuating new structural inequalities for the next generation. This means that, to maintain equality as a living ideal, the playing field must be kept level for every child in every generation, not as a one-off social reform.

278

Mountains of the Mind

Capital is not exploitation but liberation.

Government intervention, taxation of the wealthy and redistribution of wealth are therefore, say the left, constant necessities, otherwise social justice is unachievable. A good government must curtail the freedoms of a few to ensure equal distribution of rights for everyone. In reply, conservatives insist that welfare and egalitarianism are pipe dreams without wealth-creation, and rights are hollow unless they are earned. Capital is not exploitation but liberation. It is the ingenuity and hard work of entrepreneurs that pays the wages of teachers and nurses.

Socialists point out that it is the labour of the workers that adds value to the economy, and it is their taxes that pay the salaries of judges, ministers and generals. Rather than leaving social justice to 'winner takes all' market forces, they favour worker cooperatives, progressive taxes and managed redistribution of the national exchequer.

Children struggling in socioeconomically deprived areas are more likely to be given a brighter future by proactive policies, not leaving their chances of going to university to the vagaries of trickle-down wealth. Fairness does not arise automatically from a richer economy or technological innovation, though these might be necessary preconditions for it. If we today enjoy better schooling, health care, employment rights and pension entitlements, even the right to vote, it is because these 'capabilities' have been won by hard political struggle, not because our 'betters' were feeling generous.

Somewhere in the middle sit the liberals, persuaded that society is a pact of free individuals who come together in a voluntary rational agreement, underpinned by law. In other words, we're all in it together, so there is no need to drift towards the extreme ends of the political spectrum. For this reason, liberals are often drafted in to help form a coalition government, which encourages more listening and forces policies onto moderate middle ground. The downside of this is that they are often accused of sitting on the fence on important issues, or being wishy-washy. Centrists and moderates often have the best answers, but unless elected to power, their arguments are seldom heard.

Neoliberal disrupters

Political labels can be confusing, but liberals are not to be confused with neoliberals, who introduced an extreme form of conservatism in the 1980's based on the writings of a handful of earlier hard line 'market first' economists. Neoliberals have such an evangelical passion for individual freedom that the idea of mutuality is completely redrawn. The only equality that matters is that anyone can make it to the top, because in doing so, they create wealth for everyone else.

Neoliberals are sometimes called communitarians, which sounds cosy, but not when their policies are looked at closely. Their ideas appeal to Big Business, fossil fuel companies, conspiracy theorists, the Alt Right and the Evangelical Right, because profit, power, personal interest and private conviction are privileged over all else.

Inflated boardroom salaries, billionaire bonuses and lavish superyachts are justified on the grounds that, if the rich are allowed to get richer, by a process of 'trickle-down economics', the poor will be less poor than they otherwise would have been. Everybody gets more, because a rising tide lifts all ships. The reality is otherwise. The gap between the rich and the poor widens even further, so although the poor are relatively less poor in real terms, they *feel* poorer and less equal within society as a whole.

Neoliberalism was responsible in the 1980's for encouraging a 'fat cat' corporate culture of 'casino' investing and trading, without any penalty for the perpetrators when the market inevitably crashed in 2008, wiping out the life savings of many ordinary people. The result in the public realm has been weakened labour organisations, watered down workers' rights, a zero hour 'gig' economy, impoverished public services, austerity for those who were not to blame, grievances which populist demagogues exploited freely, and a cavalier regard for the delicate fabric that holds society and earth's ecosystems together.

We get the leaders we deserve.

Neoliberalism's greatest achievement, if such it is, is to break down the old class divides that used to dominate our politics, and force us to rethink what politics is for. It is no longer a question of ideals or rational arguments. It is whether we can get to the top, bend the truth to our own agenda, make our country great again, take back control and vent our spleen against imagined enemies. Perhaps its worst legacy is that it has changed the type of person who is drawn to going into politics. As the saying goes, we get the leaders we deserve, and if bullies, blusterers, braggarts and bigots are what we're looking for, we can have no complaints.

In a predominantly binary system of faith-based politics, fomented by the Wild West of social media, arguments become more polarised, then pushed to the extremes. It's worth noting that, whether we find ourselves living under an extreme-right fascist autocrat or an extreme-left totalitarian 'beloved leader', usually surrounded by a Praetorian Guard, the result is the same: rational debate, respect for the truth, freedom of thought and individual liberty disappear. There are many hybrid systems throughout the world, but it's sobering to realise that at best only half the population of the globe lives under systems that can reasonably be described as liberal-democratic.

Careful choosers
Which causes are worth living and dying for? In Jonathan Swift's satire 'Gulliver's Travels', the Big Endians and the Little Endians spend their whole lives bitterly disputing which is the 'correct' end to crack open a boiled egg. We might refer to this as a storm in an eggcup.

Storm in an egg cup
Are we a Big Endian or a Little Endian? Hard or soft boiled? One or two eggs? Battery or free range? With toast, or fresh bread cut into soldiers? Wars have been fought over less, and it's time to take sides.

Mountains of the Mind

Choosing what motivates us to get out of bed in the morning is a little more consequential than this. There are plenty of causes to choose from that are life-affirming, but there are just as many that can slowly deaden the heart. The world needs people driven by passion, but we must be careful what we wish for. 'Your soul takes the colour of your thoughts', advised the Stoic emperor Marcus Aurelius. On the other hand, we need the anchor of a few firm beliefs, without drifting into what John Stuart Mill described as 'the deep slumber of a decided opinion'.

If we under-commit, we are liable to drift, but if we over-commit, we gradually become shaped by what we oppose. We lose our ability to turn back, to empathise with those who oppose us, and to understand their argument. If we are not careful, we lose respect for those who do not see the world as we do.

Experiments in visual perception show that once we have learned to see something a certain way, we can't *not* see it that way. So is it just a case of keeping our eyes open? Not quite. John Locke pointed out in the seventeenth century that our senses present to our brain the primary qualities of things: we can all agree on the weight of an apple, or the length of a piece of wood. Secondary qualities are added by our mind: the apple might taste different to each of us, and we can disagree over who owns the forest from which the timber is taken. This is apperception, or the interpretation we make of our sensory inputs. Mine is bound to differ from yours, because it relates to our personal experience.

This means that emotion has a key role in the formation of our philosophy of life. We might think that the way we tip our hat to the world is entirely a rational affair, but emotion is as much part of our biological hardware as reason. From the get-go, experience determines what we *feel* about what happens to us. Our reaction to a strange dog in the street will depend almost entirely on our previous encounters with canines. It's not a case of our feelings being right or wrong. It's whether they refer accurately to the world. Just as we can mistake a bush for a bear, so we can mistake a friend for a foe.

Problems begin when our feelings become stronger than the facts.

Our understanding is never therefore the product of a simple assembling of facts. Our attitude derives from how we *interpret* the facts. Normally facts and

282

feelings work in harmony: if we're unsure about our feelings, we go in search of more facts, and if we're unsure about the facts, we consult our feelings. Problems begin when feelings become stronger than the facts. In what is known as motivated perception, we see what we want to see. Before we know it, we are putting our feelings before the facts.

The dangers of this were clearly on display during the presidency of Donald Trump. He and his supporters were so desperate to see the world their way that the truth became a function of the strength of their belief. If the facts didn't fit, 'alternative' facts had to be found.

His opponents responded by insisting on the 'true' facts, but this led to the back-fire effect, which is a serious problem for those combating conspiracy theories: the more counter-evidence is presented, the more strongly the conspiracy is believed. Forget the notion of truth as correspondence to reality, or as cohesion in a wider frame of reference. Truth is a matter of opinion, and my truth is truer than yours, because I believe it more strongly.

Strength of belief in the cause we espouse reminds us, if we need reminding, that we do not live by logic alone. Nor do we inhabit some super-rational realm of scientific omniscience. Paradigm shifts have been common in the history of science: as knowledge advances, new facts come to light, which is an invitation to change our mind. The flat-earth theory was abandoned by scientists, not because all the old astrologers died, but because it no longer stood the scrutiny of the new knowledge as revealed by astronomers through their telescopes.

Even so, as cosmologists and astrophysicists are the first to admit, we ain't seen nothin' yet. There will be more new knowledge, new facts, new theories, new insights, new controversies and new choices. We will always find ourselves having to make our minds up on one thing or another, whether in the private or public realm. Before we do, we need to remind ourselves of the words of Bertrand Russell: 'All human knowledge is uncertain, inexact and partial'. Or we can heed the advice of the Quaker Book of Faith and Practice: 'Think it possible that you may be mistaken'.

Can we learn to think more clearly?

*Establishing cause and effect – seeking a theory of everything -
justifying our belief – types of theory – maps and nets – scientific
literacy – evidence checking – unconscious gremlins*

- Theory-making is an extraordinary cognitive and imaginative feat.
- Without it, we cannot see what lies beyond our senses, or advance our understanding.
- Theories act as nets and maps, but what they catch, and where they guide us, depends on our knowing where and how to look.
- Scientists may or may not discover a Theory of Everything.
- It matters more that we understand how theories about people and theories about things engage our intellect and emotions differently, giving us different types of knowledge, and requiring different types of proof.
- All of our theory-making benefits from careful evidence gathering and rigorous testing.
- Science has to have an unequivocal relationship with the facts. When the facts change, scientists must be able to change their minds.
- Religious beliefs and facts work to a different logic, made true by our faith in an end greater than ourselves.
- Evolutionary theory challenges our notion of who we are, and quantum theory stretches our comprehension of how things work, but both theories hold up experimentally.
- To become better theoreticians, we need to be sufficiently scientifically literate to recognise a good theory when we see one.
- To become better thinkers, we need to make conscious as many of our unconscious assumptions as possible.

Mountains of the Mind

Tentative explainers

Given all the glitches and gremlins in our brain, and the deceptions of our mind, can we learn to think more clearly, especially if we keep our distracting emotions under wraps? Scientists like to think so, relying on scientific method and evidence-based theory-making.

Scientific theory-making does not however come naturally to the human brain. Intellectual acrobatics are required to get beyond superstition and divine intervention. It is not the crow of the cock that triggers the rising of the sun every morning, and thunder is not the roar of an angry god. But even when the right questions are asked, and appropriate models created, causes remain elusive, and explanations are as rare as hen's teeth.

At school we are taught a straightforward algorithm for being a good scientist, involving hypothetico-deductive reasoning: formulate a hypothesis, work out how it can be tested, test it, then revise the hypothesis. This was the approach of Gregor Mendel between1857 and 1863, when he cross-bred thirty thousand pea plants to test his theory about the heritability of traits such as height and pod size.

This was a labour of love and persistence, with no recognition in his own time, but it would have been useless without a specific hypothesis to guide it, which is the real stroke of genius. There's no point conducting an experiment for the sake of it, or gathering data willy-nilly. Scientists have to be prepared to revise their thinking in the light of new evidence, which is in stark contrast to political conviction and religious belief.

We are all mini-scientists to a degree. After two or three tumbles of our tower of wooden blocks in the nursery, we formulate a hypothesis about heavy objects always falling to earth. Through the art of induction, we learn that where there is fire, there is smoke. Deduction allows us to reverse our assumption: where there is smoke, there will be fire.

But it's never quite as simple as this. Induction can deceive us, because there is such a thing as smokeless fuel. Also, deduction doesn't work every time: a pile of damp leaves can smoulder for days without flickering into flame. These troubling anomalies warn us that working out cause and effect, or arriving at an explanation, needs a more subtle approach. Television detectives know all about this. After gathering all the clues, there will be many red herrings to be eliminated before they can deduce, on the balance of probability, 'whodunnit'.

Mountains of the Mind

Connecting smoke with fire is fairly easy, because the first quickly follows the second. The time lag of sexual reproduction posed our ancestors a much bigger challenge. It is reckoned that the links between copulation and birth, nine months apart in our species, and longer in bigger animals, were not fully understood until about twelve thousand years ago, coinciding with the domestication of dogs, which have shorter breeding cycles.

New knowledge is liberating, but it can also have far-reaching societal consequences. Once the male biological contribution was understood, there began a slow but radical shift in human culture and gender relations. Women went from being venerated as mysterious fertility goddesses to brood mares in a male-dominated world.

The biology of sexual reproduction seems obvious now, but hindsight is a wonderful thing. It's common knowledge now that dirty hands spread germs, contaminated water carries cholera, thalidomide taken during pregnancy leads to foetal deformity, earthquakes are followed by tsunamis, lack of citrus fruit results in scurvy, and aspirin relieves a headache. But establishing cause and effect in each case took years of patient research, often accompanied by determined opposition.

In case we think such disputes are easily settled, debate still rages over whether cannabis 'causes' psychosis, phone masts 'cause' cancer, fossil fuels 'cause' global heating, and vaccines 'cause' brain damage. The challenge for scientists is to fight ignorance with information, but first they must establish the difference between cause and correlation.

For decades the tobacco industry fought the charge that smoking causes lung cancer on the grounds that non-smokers die of lung cancer too. The fact that rates of lung cancer are higher among smokers is mere correlation, not evidence of causation. Smokers tend to be extroverts, so maybe there are other factors at work, such as personality type and lifestyle.

When the data started to show that non-smokers also contract lung cancer through passive smoking, Big Tobacco started looking for other aggravating causes, such as genes or psychological factors, anything but the carcinogenic effect of nicotine on the lungs.

Scientists don't win such arguments easily, or straight away, because they have to factor so many variables into their thinking. Nature does not give up her secrets willingly, and causation, explanation and proof are challenging concepts. It is not a safe hypothesis that, just because something has happened over and over again, it will definitely happen again tomorrow. Repetition is not the same as causation. The turkey had a theory that food was delivered on time twice a day. It discovered on Christmas Eve that its theory no longer held up.

Another problem for theory-making scientists is that, however hard they try, they can't act as dispassionate observers of nature. They start with prior beliefs, which are human, the work of a human mind, not of a number-crunching zombie. As science advances, scientists have to become ever more daring and subtle in their theorising, no easy task when simplicity and fixity disappear before them, leaving only the grin of the Cheshire Cat. Some feel that at best they only achieve an illusion of understanding.

Physicists are the first to admit that there is much yet to be explained. At the level of the universe, which is as large as we can think, dark energy accounts for ninety-five percent of what we see out there, but at the moment they have no idea where it comes from. In the quantum world, which is as small as we can think, 'entanglement' or 'spooky action at a distance' takes place between particles millions of miles apart, but created in the same cosmic moment. Even Einstein struggled to account for the how and why of this one.

Smoking kills
The warning on the packet is plain enough, but it took decades to establish a direct link between nicotine and lung cancer beyond coincidence and correlation. The 'theory' has been proven, but even so, many choose to ignore it.

Such phenomena are well beyond the power of common sense to comprehend. They force constant revision of existing theories, or the creation of new ones, such as multiverses, many-worlds hypotheses and parallel realities, as if we are all in

Mountains of the Mind

The Matrix, but don't know it. There is no definitive proof for such speculations, and yet quantum theory, despite its wackiness and challenges to classical physics, remains our most successful theory of material reality.

> *The more models we have, the more we can*
> *challenge our present limited understanding.*

Alchemists once searched for the Philosopher's Stone, or the mysterious key that could open all chemical locks, allowing lead to be transmuted into gold. We smile at their naivety now, but at the time they were pushing the boundaries of what could be known, with the techniques available to them. The dead ends they backed out of were necessary to point us towards today's through roads.

The modern quest is for the fabled Theory of Everything (TOE), and perhaps future generations will look back and be amazed that it took us so long to find it. Or maybe it doesn't exist. Some say science is achieving ever closer convergence of understanding, but it has also broken into many sub-specialisms speaking mutually unintelligible languages.

All rely on theory-making, theory-testing and theory-revision, but not necessarily following the same agenda. This is the only way that human knowledge can advance, even if there are some wrong turnings along the way. The more inventive models we generate for exploring how things work, the more we can challenge our present limited understanding.

The key strength of a theory is not its rightness, but its ability to be proved wrong. Along comes one black swan, and bang goes the theory that all swans are white. Many times in the history of science a theory has been corrected, amended or possibly abandoned. With powerful arguments on all sides, great minds continue to wrestle over whether the universe is random or designed, life on earth is a fluke or an inevitability, the future is determined or open-ended, evolution happens at the level of the gene or the group.

All theories start as speculations, perhaps wild or counterintuitive. If they are to become more than this, they must survive ruthless interrogation, and the answers must be subjected to unforgiving peer review, otherwise they become self-fulfilling prophecies, 'true' by default.

Mountains of the Mind

If physics presents its share of conundrums without looking for them, the human sciences spark controversies of their own making. In the 1960's, following a few anthropological findings of smashed or scarred human bones on stony ground in East Africa, the theory that Homo sapiens is a 'killer ape' began to take hold, fuelled by media exaggeration. Were our ancestors noble savages and peaceful cohabiters, or ignoble warmongers and violent aggressors?

The story in the bones could be read either way. The Cold War paranoia of the time edged the debate towards an ancestral legacy of bloody slaughter. Then, as more finds emerged over the following decades, a different back-story gradually emerged, of altruism, caring and cooperation. How else could our ancestors manage to drag huge stones over a hundred miles to construct megalithic monuments like Stonehenge, other than by the collaboration of many clans?

Faithful lovers
What makes a belief different from a theory is that we might cling to a belief regardless. This is especially true of religious belief. Faith is described as believing without seeing. If we can see it, like stones falling or magnets attracting, we don't need faith or explanation. It makes no sense to say we *believe in* things we have no cause to doubt. The challenge for the religious believer is to cleave to the faith when there is every reason *not* to do so, and to accept suffering as a paradoxical mystery.

These are the times when faith is sorely tested and the soul is encircled by doubt in the face of life's ultimate concerns. The writer C S Lewis, despite losing his wife to cancer, and struggling to reconcile the idea of a God of love presiding over a world of suffering, clung to his faith that there was a deeper purpose beyond the pain of this life.

His faith was not mere assertion, but warranted by experience and study, making him both intellectually convinced and emotionally committed. It was not provable by scientific standards or analysable by logic, because it was grounded in trust, which is intuitive and interpersonal. He had reasons to believe, but they were fed from a spring which reason itself could not replenish. He felt that his life was held together, not by isolated articles of faith, but by a unity of practice and belief. For him, love was sustained by more than a passing rush of oxytocin to the head.

Mountains of the Mind

Such a conviction might sound like a forlorn hope that the soul somehow survives the death of the body, but that does not make it irrational. In many ways faith is tough-minded, critical and reasonable. Some claim they believe that love survives the grave, and that God is present in the very midst of despair, *because* these things are absurd, even scandalous. Others say they believe in them in order that they may gradually come to a deeper understanding, which denial and scepticism make impossible.

Blaise Pascal believed, but he criticised God for not making himself more obvious. The hiddenness of God makes faith infinitely harder, especially during times of tribulation. If 'proof' comes at all, it comes after the leap of faith, or the commitment to the cause, not as a precondition of it.

Human love is a brief taste of a much greater divine love.

It is interesting to compare Lewis's faith in the redemptive power of love in this life with Sir Arthur Conan Doyle's occult fascination with departed spirits in the next. Each lost his partner through illness, but emotionally trusted and rationally assented to a very different spiritual reality. Lewis opted for a living faith that, though taxing his considerable intellect to the limit, was grounded in the core teaching of Christianity, that human love is a brief taste of a much greater divine love.

Like so many of his generation, Doyle was appalled at the number of deaths in the Great War, including close family and friends. The creator of Sherlock Holmes, the master of logical deduction, fell for some fake photographs made by two schoolgirls, of fairies at the bottom of their garden. He was swept along by the legacy of a Victorian cult of refusing to let go of the dead, and attended séances designed to summon up the spirits of the departed, especially that of his first wife, who died in 1906.

We might admire Doyle and Lewis for their fidelity and devotion to what they believed, or we might dismiss them both as deluded. Their desperation for an explanation left them in the grip of a conviction, believing in something with no evidence that would satisfy a sceptic, and clinging to it regardless, a mind-state that some regard as bordering on a thought disorder.

Mountains of the Mind

This charge is both naive and unjustified, as it fails to plumb the deep well of human longing, as well as tacit understanding. Doyle and Lewis did no harm, because they were merely seeking solace, and they had no designs on other people's freedom to believe. Beliefs only become dangerous when they become emblems of tribalism, denying others the right to hold their own beliefs, or are used as justification for doing injury to others, seen in their most deadly form in the fanaticism of a suicide bomber. The poet W B Yeats warned how extreme belief in a cause can reach a 'passionate intensity', creating a 'terrible beauty' for the believer, but pain and suffering for those left outside the charmed circle.

Religious beliefs make special demands of us, but our every day belief-making system runs on fairly simple algorithms. We remain right in our beliefs until they are proven wrong, but only if they are falsifiable in the first place. If not, the algorithms get twisted to our personal agenda, with no foundation in fact.

We might for instance know someone who was beaten in a job interview by a candidate of equal ability from an ethnic minority. If we perceive this as the consequence of a policy of positive discrimination, leading to 'immigrants' taking jobs unfairly from hard-working white folk, no rational argument will persuade us otherwise. Our belief has now become a superstition, a one-off event that we have turned into a universal theory, regardless of how statistically inadequate the sample is.

'Immigrants are stealing our jobs', like all beliefs and theories, may be right or wrong. It fires the same neural areas as the proposition 'Immigration is the lifeblood of our country's economy and culture', so how do we choose between them?

The easiest response is to go for the theory that everyone else believes in, because that involves the least cognitive effort to interrogate or defend. We naturally prefer being liked to being right, and don't want to lose friends by sticking our neck out. It's easier and safer to stick with COWDUNG, or the Conventional Wisdom of the Dominant Group, but as Mark Twain advised, 'Whenever you find yourself on the side of the majority, it is time to pause and reflect'.

We tend to go with the flow because scepticism does not come easily to us. It can also lead us down a blind alley. 'Hard' scepticism borders on nihilism: our senses are so unreliable that we can't know anything for sure, and our opinions are valueless, because they are based on beliefs that cannot be proved.

What we need is a healthy scepticism based on what we can *reasonably* claim to know, but this is tough too, because it is potentially socially isolating. Sticking to received opinion and tagging along with everyone else allows us to tick over comfortably, but doubt taxes the grey matter and stresses the nerves because we have not evolved to live with uncertainty and ambiguity. We are tempted to go for pat answers, because deep down we are lazy thinkers. Clearly defined answers and choices make for an easy life, but few days pass without the need to commit ourselves one way or another, or decide whose side we are on.

Fallible theorists
Not all theories are formed in the same way, because each is a particular way of seeing, or intellectual toolkit for understanding the world, calling on different mental processes and kinds of knowledge to support it. The physicist poring over millions of data-sets generated by a particle accelerator faces a very different challenge from a sociologist looking for trends in suicide patterns, not to mention a potential suicide looking for reasons to carry on living.

Whatever our discipline or purpose, and whatever we are looking for, we need a theory to tell us where and how to look, and a method suited to our quest, otherwise we are just data-collecting for the sake of it. This does not mean we can opt for any crackpot theory. There are plenty of bad ones about, such as Social Darwinism, a twisting of Darwin's original evolutionary theory into a struggle dubbed 'the survival of the fittest'. This phrase was neither coined nor approved of by Darwin, but used to justify late nineteenth century views on slavery, imperialism, eugenics, and the superiority of the Great White Race.

Social Darwinism fails as a theory because it is a creation of ideologues, not backed up by experiment or data. Seeing competition or cooperation in nature depends on where and how we look. Peter Kropotkin published 'Mutual Aid' in 1902, showing that altruism comes as easily to our species as aggression. We need only observe a busy shopping centre for a few minutes to see that we gain far more as a species from regulated mutuality than from chaotic self-seeking.

'God created the world' is more an assertion than a theory. The danger of relying on it as a theory is that everything and nothing serves to demonstrate its

292

truth, or to put it another way, it can be neither verified nor falsified by empirical observation. 'Intelligent Design' posits the existence of a supernatural creator, but it provides no mechanism by which fossils that look like dinosaurs could evolve into modern birds and reptiles, except to say that it pleased God to arrange things like this.

Darwinism has survived as a strong theory because it has been tested to destruction. It has weathered major revisions and syntheses with other disciplines, but emerged stronger as a result. As physics and biology have grown ever closer, it has been able to expand even further. Genetics and natural selection, though 'true' at the fundamental level of the theory, are now seen to be inadequate to explain life's diversity, or the complexity of 'superorganisms' such as a beehive, the human brain and consciousness. Scientists now use a new language, of quantum effects, emergence, mathematical attractors and self organisation, not because Darwin asked the wrong questions, but because he laid the foundation for a thousand new ones.

Creationism and Intelligent Design are not theories, but faith claims, incapable of being subjected to scientific method. Darwinism starts from the way things are, stripping away assumptions and prejudices. Creationism and Intelligent Design oblige us to work back to front, arranging the facts to fit the theory.

It may be comforting to believe that we have been specially placed on this planet, and as a narrative it is a lot easier to understand than quantum theory. But as science advances, and belief in magic and miracles fades, scientific explanations demand less of our credulity than an invisible supernatural being within our imagination but outside of time and space.

All theories are in a constant struggle for survival.

A good theory is a triumph of intellect and imagination, each holding the other in check, and combining to make a powerful tool of analysis that never strays too far from what it sets out to explain. Karl Popper called science a dialectic of conjecture and refutation. A theory is a conjecture, or guess about how something in the world works, and it remains a good theory as long as it survives repeated attempts to refute it.

Darwin's theory of evolution by natural selection is still going strong after nearly two centuries for two reasons: no better explanation has been proposed, and each new discovery fits neatly into a growing picture of understanding. Interestingly, it also accounts for its own 'fitness' and success. All theories are in a constant struggle for survival, because they give only probabilities, never certainties, as Darwin would be the first to admit. The weak ones are relentlessly squeezed out by the stronger.

Double agents

We have evolved to live as double agents, in a world of people and a world of things, echoing an ancient religious teaching that the kingdom of heaven is both inside us and outside us. Our theories therefore have to be flexible enough to embrace both, approach data differently, and apply different reality tests. There is a big difference between having a theory that our friend no longer likes us, and a theory about what keeps aeroplanes up in the air.

Our brain has not evolved to worry about aerodynamics, but we worry very much about what the other people in our life are getting up to, or thinking about us. Our 'theory of life' is in the last resort much more important to us than any theory of how the world works. When we are on our deathbed, we reach out to the people around us, not the certificates we have been awarded, the fortunes we have amassed, or our copy of the periodic table. But when we are at thirty five thousand feet, we need a science of what keeps things aloft. Aerodynamics is largely about numbers, so as well as the language of the heart, we also need the language of mathematics.

In the social sphere, human actions and beliefs are measured by words, marinaded in metaphor and symbol, without which we can't 'prove', as in confirm, the flavour of our life, or the feeling of what we are trying to understand. It requires proof of a very different kind to understand why aeroplanes stay up in the sky.

Private conviction gets us through each day, but when we board an aeroplane, we do so in the knowledge that *everybody* believes it will fly, not just the pilot. We can safely fly on *any* day of the week, regardless of whether it is Friday the thirteenth. A hundred years of successful aviation history feed into this confidence, and even when there is a crash, accident investigators do not rest until they have found the reason.

What keeps planes in the air is what the philosopher Daniel Dennett calls cranes, not skyhooks. A crane is a physical process such as aerodynamic lift that can be explained by the laws of nature, whereas a skyhook is an appeal to a magic force beyond our comprehension.

This distinction does not stop some people from believing that witches fly on broomsticks, or taking their favourite fluffy bunny with them when they fly, just in case, or kissing the ground on landing to bank some good fortune for the return flight. Science has largely replaced superstition, but not completely.

Isaac Newton traded largely in the world of things. He is often described as the last magician, because he 'outed' the physical forces that keep the Moon suspended in the night sky, and carry aeroplanes through the air, theoretical 'laws' that up to then had been mysterious and invisible. Albert Einstein built on Newton's genius, 'seeing' far beyond our solar system into deep space, tweaking Newton's laws to show what happens to time and space across the vast universe.

Albert Einstein
1879-1955
Einstein didn't exactly stick his tongue out at scientific orthodoxy, but he realised that looking and experimenting were not alone sufficient to break through to new understanding. What he really needed was a new theory, but before he set out in search of a solution, he first needed to invent the problem.

Mountains of the Mind

Einstein did not prove Newton wrong. What makes a theory great is its ability to provide a stepping stone to the next breakthrough in understanding. If it is a bad theory, it must make way for a better one. This is a wise counsel, given that in our own lifetime we can list many occasions when the things we believed today turned out to be not true tomorrow.

Einstein saw theory as a 'striving toward unification and simplicity'. This suits the scientist, who relies on the laws of physics, which brook no negotiation at all, and are confirmed every time a plane lands safely. NASA scientists have no reason to question a theory that can predict exactly when and where their space probe will arrive on Mars.

All we have to go on is fallible hunch.

This guarantee does not work well as a prediction of what people will do, because they are neither unified nor simple. When Newton lost money on an investment, he remarked that he could predict the movement of stars, but not the madness of men. Our relationships with each other depend not on natural laws but on what evolutionary psychologists call theory of mind. All we have to go on is fallible hunch, and our only 'proof' is looks and comments, open to interpretation and dependent on intuition.

The good thing is that our people-oriented theory of mind comes easily to us, because our species has had tens of thousands of years of practice in second-guessing each other's intentions. We tend to believe that what we see is what there is, and most of the time this is enough to get us by socially.

Scientific theory, barely a few hundred years old, challenges this common sense view of the world, on the basis that the mind sees more than the eye. Cognitive scientists have given us reason to interrogate the 'reality' given to us by our visual processing system. From the millions of photons entering our eyes, our brain selects the bare minimum to make sense of a situation, privileging some data and ignoring the rest, giving us only what is good enough to get by without leading us into danger. As a result, seeing is not necessarily believing, because our brain gives us only its own theory of what is there.

If we don't see things as they are, but only as our brain gives them to us, we are double agents indeed. That doesn't mean that we are living on the film set of

Mountains of the Mind

'The Matrix', because evolution has ensured that our brain is not all there is to our perceptual apparatus. We are embodied creatures, so when we see an apple on the lawn, we can physically pick it up, touch, smell and bite into it, instead of mistaking it for a tennis ball.

Even with this assurance, there are still blind spots. We think we see everything, but we don't: we see only what is in the centre of our vision. If we gaze at a focal point we realise that our brain is 'guessing' everything that surrounds it, unless of course we shift our gaze to a new point. In other words, instead of giving us a precise photograph, our brain composes the picture, compressing huge amounts of data into a single visual 'experience', filling in gaps, but not necessarily seeing exactly what is there. It sees only what is adequate for the situation.

X-ray seers

At the microlevel for instance, what we see as a solid object is mostly made of empty space. This kind of extra-sensory 'seeing' that a scientific view of the world demands is much more taxing on our grey matter, asking us to *conceive* beyond what we can *perceive*. No wonder the physicist Richard Feynman called scientific method 'a mighty test of human reasoning ability'.

We assume that reality fits the human mind, or vice versa, but the universe has no obligation to make sense to us, nor is science obliged to give us meaning. It is a method of enquiry, and its explanations are not intended to justify our being here. Many of nature's operations are still a mystery to us. To understand them at all, we must make theoretical models of reality. These cannot reveal to us ultimate reality, but they can take us as close as we can get to it, given the limits of our intellect. We are also dependent upon the acuity of the questions we ask, the sensitivity of our latest equipment, and the replicability of our measurements.

Considering these limitations to our knowledge, it is remarkable that we presume that the universe is comprehensible in the first place. To temper this arrogance, we have gradually become more aware of our ignorance than our knowledge. Scientists have realised that theories don't explain the world, because we never see it as it really is. All we get are the phenomena that show themselves to our limited senses.

Mountains of the Mind

Each discovery therefore teeters on the edge of uncertainty, because there will always be new elements, planets, microbes and laws out there yet to be brought into view, made real by our investigations. Dark matter, dark energy, parallel universes and virtual dimensions may be hiding in plain sight.

The challenge then becomes, if we are denied the confirmation of direct observation, how can we claim to 'see' the invisible? Having reached the limit of what can be known, are we merely inventing theory-castles in the air, based on what we already know? How do we get to the very bottom of the rabbit hole?

For many decades, mathematics was seen as an intellectual abstraction, very clever but outside time and space, not particularly informative about the nitty gritty of the world. Beyond what Stephen Hawking called the event horizon, classical physics breaks down, and we enter a world of intangible mathematical speculation and pontification.

That has all changed. Armed with the mathematical compass held by William Blake's 'Ancient of Days', modern physicists sound more like theologians than scientists, speculating about quantum entanglements, superstrings, wormholes, spacetime manifolds, no-boundaries, singularities and black holes.

These are more than conjectures. In 2019, the first grainy image of a black hole emerged from deep space. Theories arrived at by mathematical calculation give us 'X-ray specs' to see further and further. Einstein was quite confident about this. Theory means 'way of seeing', from the same root as the word theatre. He believed that a good theory brings into view what has not yet been seen, such as his own revolutionary theory of relativity. As a result of his mathematical 'seeing', we are all now familiar with time that is relative and space that is curved.

The closer we get to what we think matter is 'really' made of,
the further it recedes from us.

A good theory therefore, no matter how ethereal, is one that brings into focus what has always been there, but not yet observed or understood. More importantly, it reveals what is *not* there, or what cannot be seen, preventing us from following false trails, or making mistaken claims about what we know. It keeps us humble by suggesting that, the closer we get to what we think matter is 'really' made of, the further it recedes from us.

298

Mountains of the Mind

Nature presents these baffling challenges to us because so much of it resides in the realm of the very large or the very small, well beyond the middle range of our perceptions. The question then arises, how can we 'prove' a theory about what we cannot see?

The answer is that a good theory allows us to make predictions, not as an act of faith with random success, like a soothsayer, but by dint of our intellect, with a high degree of accuracy, like a scientist. If we can't achieve this, the theory is either wrong, or needs to be radically tweaked.

A theory remains valid only as long as it survives thousands of repeated attempts by independent minds to prove it wrong, known as 'peer review'. The great breakthrough for medicine was the invention of randomised controlled trials, banishing forever the mountebanks and quacks who sold their snake oils and wonder cures to anyone gullible enough to buy them. Penicillin turned out to be a better antibiotic than all of them for the simple reason that it could be seen to work, over and over again.

Frequent fliers

Theories need therefore to be kept under constant review and revised accordingly, no matter how counterintuitive the conclusions may be. Aviation is now a universal technology, but in the nineteenth century, some doubted that heavier-than-air machines could get off the ground, and if they did, the passengers inside would fall to bits. Today, aviation wins our confidence because international law demands that the circumstances of each crash or fault are fed into the system, and the judge of success is the high safety record of the industry, not whether we *feel* that planes can't possibly get off the ground.

Friends are not so predictable or unchanging. The only reason we keep them is because we *feel* they still like us, and we like them. In other words, we rely heavily on intuition, emotion and experience, forming our theories of human behaviour after the event. Once we have settled on our theory of what makes people tick, we modify it as we go along, which is just as well, given the inconstancy of our feelings and the mutability of other people's behaviour.

This is what makes economics an awkward 'science'. It was once called the 'dismal' science, because all its theories are true some of the time. How do we forecast which or when? By what means do we choose meaningfully between rival

299

theories (speculate to accumulate v save for a rainy day), or judge what makes for a sound investment?

Unlike physicists, economists are unable to make accurate predictions, as all investors know. Their theories do not describe an objective reality. As consumers we are often described as 'rational maximisers', but we are just as likely to change our purchasing behaviour in the light of the latest fashion. Conspicuous consumption sees some of us purchase a particular product not because it saves us money, but because it sends a signal that we have money to burn.

And yet this in itself verges on becoming a 'law', or kind of scientific truth, because we all behave like this. Our spending habits are not as mysterious and volatile as we think, because we are rational maximisers only up to a point, after which our rationality becomes 'bounded'. We are not naturally 'big spenders', but tend to hedge our bets, too loss averse to take a risk with our hard-earned cash.

When our fickle behavioural responses are ramped up across the whole population, they become predictable enough for bankers, insurers, retailers, accountants and hedge fund managers to make reliable forecasts about next quarter's profits, though as we know from crashes, recessions, bankruptcies and bailouts, nothing is certain. There will always be 'acts of God'. In that sense, natural scientists have an easier job than economists, because physical matter does not change its character according to the latest boom or bust.

Or does it? Quantum theory has challenged our understanding of what is 'real', as well as proving devilishly difficult to understand. In a quote attributed to Richard Feynman, one of the subject's co-inventors and a brilliant teacher of it, 'If you think you understand quantum mechanics, you don't understand quantum mechanics'.

God does not 'play dice' with the universe.

If we envisage reality as a snooker table, Newton gave us the classical physics of balls colliding. Armed with the right mathematical formulae, we can calculate after the shot whether the black will fall into the pocket. Einstein's theory of relativity introduced bumps and curves into the game, but it's still playable.

Not so with quantum theory, which blurs the distinction between the game and the player, as well as making it impossible to predict the winner. Einstein was so

300

unsettled by this that he declared that God does not 'play dice' with the universe in this way.

The fact remains however that at the level of the very small, the rules of classical physics become paradoxical. In the world of large bodies such as ours, we can only be in one place at a time, but in the quantum world, particles can be in two places at once.

Implicated players

The more we take matter to pieces, the less solid it becomes, more like music than matter. It is not a 'thing' at all, but a fluctuating field that alternates between being a particle and a wave. It is not possible to see both at the same time, and we don't know which it is until we open the lid of the box to look inside. Then our act of looking fixes the wave/particle duality in something called 'a collapse of the wave function'. *We* have decided the outcome, or created a fraction of quantum reality. *Our* looking has made the difference.

Physicists are understandably puzzled by all of this, because it challenges their very ability to be objective about reality. How can they predict an outcome if they don't have a way of measuring that doesn't change with the thing it is measuring, or with the person doing the looking? They are like the dreamer who changes the nature of the dream by waking up and thinking about it.

One solution is to conclude that reality is made inside our brain, or we create the world by participating in it. If photons of light don't collapse into their wave or particle function unless and until we look at them, this suggests that reality is made inside our brain. We might as well say that the sun and the moon disappear if we close our eyes, because their existence depends on our perceiving them. Matter is just so many 'bits' of information, not made into the 'its' of awareness until we gaze up into the night sky, bringing the universe into being by our act of looking.

All it takes to endow the whole cosmos with consciousness is one human mind. This does not open the door to solipsism. All it takes is for two solipsists to agree on the same observation, and we have the beginning of objective knowledge.

Some say quantum theorists multiply entities beyond what is necessary to make their theory work, making reality more exotic and mystifying than it really is. According to the principle of Occam's Razor, the fewer assumptions a theory has to rely on, the better. Nevertheless, in addition to up, down, strange, charm, bottom and top quarks, they have given us pentaquarks, heptaquarks and octaquarks, ad infinitum.

The key point about quantum effects is that they work.

We don't need to invoke poltergeists or second comings as explanations of quantum strangeness, because physics is weird enough already. Experiments show that events in one region of space time can be instantaneously affected by events many light years away. To date no theory offers an explanatory mechanism for this, but that doesn't matter. The key point about quantum effects is that they work, in both the physical and biological worlds. Without them, our phones could not carry messages, our computers would grind to a halt, plants could not photosynthesise, and tadpoles could not turn into frogs.

Scientists are similarly baffled by their inability to predict the rate at which uranium decays. They hate randomness and unpredictability in the physical world, but there is no known way of predicting when a radioactive uranium atom will emit an alpha particle. This conundrum lies at the heart of the famous 'Schrödinger's Cat' paradox. If we leave a cat in a box with some uranium, we have no way until we open the box of knowing whether the cat is alive, or dead from radiation poisoning.

Peter Higgs
b 1929
Fifty years before it was experimentally found, Higgs used theory, hypothesis, mathematics and a lot of imagination to predict that the particle that bears his name, the Higgs boson, was 'really there', just waiting to be spotted.

This puzzle convinces some scientists that there are truths we haven't yet seen. The Higgs boson 'appeared' fifty years after it was theoretically predicted. By the same reckoning, calculations point to there being WIMPs out there, or weakly interacting massive particles. They *have* to be there, because they 'theoretically' hold the universe together. It's just that we haven't yet worked out a way of 'seeing' them.

In situations like this, the theory has to come first as a rational deduction, even if empirical proof is a long time coming. Democritus theorised over two thousand years ago that matter was made up of small particles that could not be divided any further, which he called atoms. This seemed a wild claim at the time, but in 1919 Ernest Rutherford not only 'found' an atom; he also showed experimentally that he could split one. In other words, Democritus was not only on the right track, but could have ventured even further along it.

Hypothetical deducers

This powerful combination of inspired guesswork and exacting investigation explains why scientific method is described as hypothetico-deductive, making a speculation that is then tested beyond a reasonable doubt. In practice scientists use every means available to them to crack open the mystery of matter. Many apply Bayesian statistics, relying on models that make sense of reality in the light of previous beliefs based on tacit knowledge. The longer the models work without need for adjustment, the 'truer' they become.

Theory still matters however, because without an ability to predict phenomena we haven't yet seen, we're stuck forever with the tiny part of reality we have observed. The theory guides us to what we are looking for. Gazing up at the night sky or relying on traditional pictures of the firmament as a spangled ceiling is not enough, as Galileo realised as he peered through his newfangled telescope. What he needed was a new way of seeing.

A billion facts or experiments cannot generate a new theory, nor can streams of data. Darwin had all the descriptive data he needed. His true goal was one grand explanatory theory or organising principle to make universal sense of it all. Some believe that his theory of evolution by natural selection is the greatest idea anyone has ever had, potentially uniting matter and meaning in a single theory.

Mountains of the Mind

Even so, Darwin was not so rash as to believe that his theory could explain *everything*, including the origin of life. Instead, his goal was to propose a mechanism, once life had been kick-started in some 'warm little pond', to transform it from a few chemicals into the mind of a Leonardo. He knew that a good theory gains its strength from having a defined focus. It also depends on praxis, or its ability to unite theory and practice. No-one has ever seen a species evolve in real time, but evolution can be observed in action in our own lifetime, and fossils of intermediate forms keep being unearthed.

As children, we are natural biologists in our understanding of living things in our environment, and natural physicists in our exploration of matter. As we grow, all we need on an everyday basis is a theory of what works based on what comes to our senses, even though our perceptual system gives us only a partial glimpse of what is 'really' happening. Physicists dig deeper than this, but that does not mean they are the only people who see things as they really are. They make a much humbler claim: their theories take them inch by inch closer to understanding, but not necessarily all the way.

For all their sophisticated methods and equipment, they are still like mediaeval knights seeking a vision of the Holy Grail, looking for a particle that will make all their sums work, binding together the four forces that seem currently to operate independently of each other. Perhaps this will shed light on dark matter and dark energy which make up most of the universe, uniting all the other particles they have found in their giant colliders. Perhaps each particle is an aspect of a super multi-tasking particle that is right under their noses, so obvious that they can't see it for what it is.

There are too many threads to weave into one
grand design or finished tapestry.

Others think they are chasing a will o' the wisp. Reality is not one, but a conglomeration of lots of smaller theories that are individually designed for their purpose. Just as no single mind can hold all the information, so no single theory can explain all the phenomena. There are too many threads to weave into one grand design or finished tapestry.

Mountains of the Mind

Aristotle's intellect was broad enough to range over the whole of what was known in his day, and Aquinas endeavoured to reconcile the realms of faith and reason, but we now sense that the universe may be too complex or full of surprises for us to dream of a final theory. Currently 'Big Bang' theory is in pole position for explaining how the universe began fourteen billion years ago, but this might be the first chapter in a story which, like the universe itself, just keeps expanding into a cosmos with no edges.

There are still many lacunae in our knowledge. Most astrophysicists agree that the universe is bursting into infinity, but can't agree whether it is expanding at an even rate, or will eventually start to shrink, folding back in on itself. Time might be cyclical, not linear. There might have been a Big Bounce before the Big Bang, meaning that we're heading for a Catastrophic Crunch, after which the whole shebang will start up all over again.

Meanwhile, back on our own planet, there may not be a theory of or for everything, but there is a kind of convergence of many disciplines, pointing tentatively towards what the physicist Steven Weinberg called 'the deepest idea in the universe'.

In what are known as Big History and Big Geography, academics pool many resources and methods of enquiry to work out how life began and diversified on our cooling ball of rock, how and where our species evolved, which migrations took place and when, and what part climate, landscape and weather patterns played in the development of culture and civilisation. Clues as varied as fossils, meteor strikes, genetic markers, languages, tree rings, lie of the land, ocean currents, extreme weather events and archaeological remains combine to retell the myth of Genesis, as written by a scientist-God.

In case anyone thinks that the story is nearly complete, and that science is nearing its end, it is only just beginning. Also, in the true spirit of the humility of science, most of the narrators of this expanding saga sense that not only is there much yet to learn, but that there may be whole ways of looking at and understanding ourselves that we have yet to discover.

Speculative scientists

The philosophy of science sounds like a contradiction in terms, but it provides valuable insight into how scientists go about their work, and on what foundations they build their knowledge. We might look to science as our guarantee of ultimate truth, but ironically what makes science right is its readiness to be wrong.

Science doesn't claim to be flawlessly true, only to take us as close to the truth as rational enquiry can get, based on probabilities, not certainties. That which survives repeated attempts to falsify itself stands a better chance of being true than something that hides from scrutiny, claims to be infallible, insists it is always right, or is unable to revise its understanding. Unlike in the personal and social realm, scientists do not adjust the world to fit their theories: they adjust their theories to fit the world. They draw up a map that consistently leads the traveller home. When this ceases to be the case, they know the map must be redrawn.

Theory-making and theory-testing play vital roles in showing us truer maps and diagrams of how things work, as opposed to how we *think* they work, but how? Empiricists insist that things can only present themselves to our minds through our senses, but rationalists point out that our senses often mislead us, and by themselves are not proof of anything.

Merely watching our ice cream fall out of its cone to splat on the floor gives no explanation of gravity, or proof that it will happen again tomorrow. We need a way of going beyond our senses, without straying into wild speculation. This is where theory comes in, a combination of sense and reason that seems unique to human cognition.

A metaphor might help us to understand how this can be so. We start out wanting to catalogue all the fish in the oceans, so we go 'deep fishing', feeding all the data about every fish we find into a super-computer. But without some sense of what is classed as a fish, what constitutes a species, and how fish reproduce, we have no idea how to proceed.

Our theory-net determines which fish we catch,
and what conclusions we can draw.

What we need is a theory to act as a net, the right size net, cast in the right place. If we cast it too wide, we just get fished-out. If we cast it too narrowly, and the holes are too small, we catch too much to look at closely. If the holes in the net are too big, we miss the small fry. Our theory-net determines which fish we catch, and what conclusions we can draw.

306

Mountains of the Mind

Einstein went fishing, but he neither collected facts nor conducted experiments. His forte was the thought experiment, playing with ideas established by his predecessors, moving them around in his head, measuring them against his own calculations and speculations. This allowed him to generate a new theory of time and space, which he could test against available data.

He is regarded by some as the last lone genius who was capable of picking the low-hanging fruit of scientific discovery by the power of thought alone, largely as a hobby in his spare time. Theory-making and theory-testing have now become a powerful combination of highly specialised teams and international funding, using equipment and computing power that Einstein could only dream of. Some boldly predict that science will have completed its grand scheme by 2100, drawing the last bits of knowledge into one comprehensive frame.

In the humanities, new truths often demolish old ones, but science is more like adding new bricks to a wall. Einstein did not swing a wrecking ball at Newton's edifice: he added another course of bricks. He showed that light and gravity are not absolute values, but relative, changing with the position and speed of the observer. The faster we go, the slower time passes. It gets even stranger: we can never catch up with a ray of light, because it recedes from us at the same speed, regardless of how fast we chase it.

Ironically, his discoveries made him a victim of his own iconoclasm. Having set physics in a new direction, he was uncomfortable with the implications of quantum theory which grew out of his work on relativity, stating that he did not believe God would meddle with the laws of the universe in this way. He struggled to dispense with his prior beliefs, even though quantum theory's counterintuitive discoveries hold up experimentally. Einstein demonstrates how theory can on the one hand usher in new knowledge, but also be an impediment to the next step forward.

Trusted experts

Science's claims to disinterested knowledge can occasionally be compromised, allowing theory to be put before fact. Research can be tainted by commercial pressure to be the first to the finish line, and scientists can find themselves giving 'expert opinion' that they are paid to deliver. For several decades, Big Tobacco provided scientific 'evidence' that smoking has no link to lung cancer, even that smoking is good for us. In case we think that argument has been won, the same obfuscation might be happening today with the dangers of vaping.

Big Pharma knows that there is Big Money to be made.

America's opioid crisis, trapping a million and a half people in addiction, is not the result of a philanthropic desire of pharmaceutical companies to relieve the nation's pain, or of their investors to increase everyone's happiness levels. Big Pharma and its shareholders know that there is Big Money to be made. They have also worked out that they can cash in by developing detox pills for the addictions they themselves helped to create.

Scientists are generally cautious about over-trumpeting the benefits of new drugs, gene therapies, environmental solutions and dietary advice, though the media are not so scrupulous. 'Miracle cure for obesity found' grabs our attention, but when we look behind the headline, we find a host of nuanced caveats, careful provisos and guarded reservations.

We need to be trained in statistics, nutrition and ethics to work out the medical risks of adopting low carb, paleo, vegan or red meat diets, not to mention the impact of our craving for burgers on the health of the rain forest. Meanwhile, the unelected entrepreneurs of Silicon Valley are busy designing a utopian high-tech robo-future for us that we haven't been consulted about.

There is an old saying that science is a good servant but a bad master. Science itself is neutral: it is knowledge that can be put to good or bad use, as Eve discovered after biting into the apple. The true masters of science, as in the funders and directors of it, are entrepreneurs and politicians. Scientists seldom become either, as their research does not allow time to run a business, and they find the outcomes of politics too unpredictable.

And yet what scientists do, or what they declare to be possible, is deeply political, because it affects us all. The greatest mathematical and engineering minds were brought together in the 1940's in the USA to develop the atom bomb, and later the much more destructive thermonuclear bomb. Out of this extraordinary technical achievement grew guided missiles, space flight, the nuclear industry and computer technology. But it also took us one step away from Armageddon.

Mountains of the Mind

The motivation of these boffins and wizards was to beat Nazi tyranny, and then to counter Soviet threat, but many were also driven by the belief that if something is theoretically possible, it must be done. Some later regretted their involvement in making weapons of mass destruction, but by no means all. Perhaps they foresaw that, without their genius, there would be no international air travel, modern medicine, artificial intelligence, internet or iphone.

Despite this fashioning of how we live, we have an ambivalent relationship with science. We don't always 'trust the experts', or pay heed to what the science says. We are largely science-illiterate, and some are anti-science, protesting outside research laboratories, trampling down fields of genetically modified wheat or refusing life-saving vaccines, caught in an ethical storm of misinformation, disinformation and conspiracy theory. Meanwhile we are silent about the development of ever more sophisticated killing machines, the stockpiling of biological pathogens, mass surveillance systems and joy-rides in space for the super-rich.

The problem for 'proper' scientists is that their work is hard and unglamorous. We are more likely to learn the names of doctors who harm their patients and researchers who breach ethical guidelines, than those who strive to find solutions to global heating, make our roads safer, tackle pollution, eliminate plastic, develop new antibiotics, pioneer new medical techniques, reduce the burden of pain or develop cures for dementia.

There are rare exceptions. Marie Curie and Rosalind Franklin are remembered for dying early from radioactive poisoning in the pursuit of their research, and Jonas Salk is honoured for giving the life-saving polio vaccine to the world with no expectation of financial reward. Franklin and Salk were not awarded the Nobel prize, but Curie received two, both the first woman to be lauded in this way, and still the only woman to receive a prize in two different fields.

Finding better theories
Given all the unknowns that we do not know about, we need a steady flow of new theories, some of which may be wacky, but one of which is going to be transformative. In 1912 Alfred Wegener was laughed out of court for suggesting that once upon a time, the continents were all part of one huge land mass. Now his theory of continental drift is universally accepted.

Mountains of the Mind

Instead of believing what we see, iconoclasts like Wegener teach us to see what we believe, not as part of a weird cult, but for carefully presented reasons. Starting with Copernicus and culminating in quantum theory, science has constantly forced us to live with paradox and uncertainty: universes multiply, randomness rules, time bends, space warps, matter is not solid, reality lies beyond our senses, particles defy prediction.

Andreas Vesalius
1514-1564
If it wasn't for Vesalius challenging hide-bound medical practices, we would still be subjected to the casting out of demons, leeches sucking our blood, and vile herbal remedies poured down our throats.

Innovators have to take risks if they are to see what others have not yet seen. In the seventeenth century, Thomas Willis had no equipment to detect electrical activity in the brain, but he laid the foundations for neuroscience, just as Darwin did for genetics, Maxwell for radio waves, and Freud for the science of sleep.

When a new theory is proposed, it must show it is capable of being proved wrong, and surviving constant rigorous scrutiny. If it makes claims that are not founded on empirical or historical data, it will suffer the fate of homeopathy, telepathy, Marxism and psychoanalysis, failing to qualify as scientific. It must be able to account for the negative results as well as the positive.

We might suppose that weak theories, like struggling species, are deselected from the meme-pool. If something about it isn't right, it has to adapt to new realities, or become extinct. The evolution of human thought however is not quite so straightforward. Old theories die hard, and new ones may take centuries to be accepted.

The physician Vesalius found this out when he tried to overturn Galen's outmoded theory of humours that had dominated medical practice since the second century. Galen proposed that the health of the body is controlled by the balance of four fluids or humours. We still talk of being in a good humour, or out of humour.

In one sense Galen was working from empirical evidence: our body does exude certain fluids when it is ill. It was the theory that was wrong. For centuries doctors believed they were saving their patients by 'bleeding' them. Imagine their cognitive dissonance when they were told they were slowly killing them.

Scientific theories are not infallible, and their agenda is seldom free of society's ambitions and emergencies. Research is driven by socio-political imperatives, reflecting the priorities of the society that funds and practises it: yesterday it was space travel or drone warfare, today it is carbon capture or alternative antibiotics, tomorrow it is artificial intelligence or genetic modification.

New scientific theories remain our best hope for the future.

Whatever challenges present themselves to us, new scientific theories remain our best hope for the future, especially when they are also the best explanations we have so far, given our present state of knowledge, the tools at our disposal and the limits of the human intellect.

This does not mean that science can easily put to bed all of its disputes and uncertainties. Anthropologists argue whether our species migrated out of Africa or Asia. Biologists cannot decide whether the first life forms emerged in a warm pond, in thermal vents at the bottom of the ocean, in an impact crater, under an ice sheet, in a desert, or hitching a ride on a meteorite. Cosmologists sway between many-worlds hypotheses and parallel universes. Evolutionists are divided over whether single genes are the prime agents of selection, or kin, group and cultural factors play important parts. Particle physicists cannot agree on a unified theory of space, time and matter. Neuroscientists tackling the 'hard problem' of consciousness line up under 'global workspace', 'integrated information' and 're-entry processing' banners.

311

Mountains of the Mind

What keeps researchers of all complexions in pursuit of ideas without becoming ideologues is their search for answers in data and analysis, not in opinion and dogma. When new information comes to light, which it does all the time, they are the first to incorporate it into their thinking and theorising. But they have to be realists too: they need results which guarantee the renewal of their research grant.

Vulnerable ideologues

Science has its share of controversies, but our theories about people and society make even the hottest scientific disputes look tame. Applying natural science to lived experience and political sentiment does not take us far. For most of our evolution, biology directed our progress as sophisticated primates, but our cultural evolution in the last hundred thousand years has added immense psychological complexity to what makes us tick.

Science is presenting us with moral challenges which our present social theories are ill prepared to handle.

Science is our best tool for answering our what and how questions: which forces help aeroplanes to stay aloft? It is not intended to tell us why we should be bothered to find out in the first place, to provide us with laws for living, or reason with us why we should reduce our carbon footprint by flying less. It cannot referee our culture wars and police our info wars. And yet it is science that is presenting us with moral challenges in genetic engineering, artificial intelligence and information technology, which our current social theories, political systems and moral codes are ill prepared to handle.

It's impossible to live a social existence without being part of an ideology of one sort or another, serving as a theory of how society is meant to work, or works best. The twentieth century saw fascism and communism come and go, only to be revived in different guises in different places.

In the West we consider liberal democracy to be superior to all other 'isms', but it has been sorely tested by populism. It is difficult to come up with a theory of or about populism, because it sets out to cause deliberate disruption and defy rational analysis. It distrusts experts, is intrinsically anti-theory, and prefers actions to words.

The resulting seesawing between order and chaos is reflected in the political arena, where theories are treated not as self-evident truths but as weapons in culture wars. Politicians thrive by picking up public concerns. They don't need to invent these, because they are already being stirred up by rival theories coming from the social sciences. No sooner has one child psychologist insisted that parents have a vital role in shaping their children's future, another gatecrashes the party by declaring that the genes and the peer group do all the talking.

We can't escape these culture wars, because we can't duck having a view on emotive issues such as the sanctity of the family, child rearing, abortion, euthanasia, capital punishment, knife crime, life after death, taxing the wealthy, legalising drugs, or keeping children safe online. We might classify our feelings on such matters as convictions, not theories, because they are visceral, impacting our emotions and our relations with others.

Such beliefs are only partly rationally arrived at, but that doesn't mean they are irrational. Religions and philosophies are not sciences, but they were the first systematic attempts of our species to create a unifying theory of the puzzles of being alive, how to live together and what makes the world go round. They are based on the premise that the universe is comprehensible, there is a coherent scheme of things, and there are laws that create a cosmos, not a chaos.

Science is not a departure from these vital early foundations, but an extension of them. Its method is very different, relying on reason to arrive at justified true belief, not revelation, conviction or revered custom. This does not mean that we cannot apply scientific rigour to our personal and social thinking. Despite our strength of feeling, we can hold our convictions to the same standards, constantly trying to falsify or verify them.

If for instance we belong to a religious sect that regards vaccination as a violation of God's right to determine life, we can consult the findings of science, avoiding the siren voices which either distort the data or try to undermine it by spreading doubt in our minds. If, having weighed the evidence, we are still of the opinion that we should not allow our children to be vaccinated, we must accept not only that we are putting their lives at risk, but also potentially sacrificing the lives of other people's children not yet born, because we are allowing a pathogen to

313

flourish and mutate unopposed. We must be made aware that a conviction based on dogma is not a substitute for a choice guided by reason.

If we have a prejudice loosely disguised as a theory that immigrants are creating a shortage of school places, affordable homes and hospital beds in our area, or driving down wages and pushing up crime figures, we can either believe the stories circulating on social media, or ask ourselves: how would a scientist put these claims to the test?

Rigorous testers

Darwin's theory of evolution held up when he first formulated it, and it still makes sense of most of the facts and processes of the natural world as understood so far. It has been accommodating new findings as they emerge for a hundred and fifty years. Some say it is only a theory, but it has been constantly tested, and so far not found wanting. Another criticism is that it bears no relation to how we live our lives, but when we start looking, we realise that no part of our life is left untouched by it.

Unless we believe in alien invasion, the only rival to evolutionary theory is creationism. This appeals strongly to our anthropic pride by placing us firmly at the centre, and comforts us by implying Providence at work, even in the fall of a sparrow. Creation came from the sky.

Evolutionary theory's version of how we came to be here is much more mundane, though no less fascinating: creation came from the mud. Although there *appears* to be design in the three and a half billion year journey of DNA, any meaning we attribute to it is ours. Evolution is not providential, because it does not assume the role of a supervisory planner.

Creationism falls at the first hurdle of scientific method. It can be neither confirmed nor falsified, which puts it in the same category as telekinesis and astrology. It is based on intuition and revelation, positing the 'skyhook' of a supernatural creator, not the 'crane' of a biological process which can be empirically observed and grasped by logic unaided by faith. Evolutionary theory operates in cosmic time and space, but creationism leaves us with eternal regress. If we believe that the world sits on the back of a giant turtle, we are left wondering who made the turtle. Or perhaps, as the lady insisted, it's 'turtles all the way down'.

Global heating qualifies as a scientific theory, because year-on-year data confirms it. It will take many years of global cooling before scientists are tempted to revise their thinking, posit a different theory, or put the whole thing down to sunspot activity.

Given the triumphs of science and technology, it seems odd that so much superstition and belief in magic remains, even today. Magic is an attempt to control nature, belonging to an age when its workings were poorly understood. Many were drawn to the Faust myth, of selling one's mortal soul to the Devil for the prize of immortal knowledge. As late as the seventeenth century, the Magus John Dee, adviser to Elizabeth 1, was more interested in divination and astrology than in science and astronomy. Even Isaac Newton, who came soon after, wrote as many books on the occult as on light and gravity.

Surveys show that as many people still believe in angels and demons as in evolution and vaccination, so the legacy of magic lingers. Genetic research is treated with suspicion, while large numbers are drawn to 'strange goings on' in the paranormal realm, such as poltergeists, UFO's, out-of-body experiences, clairvoyance, astrology and reincarnation.

When we make a rational enquiry, we find that there is no mechanism capable of standing up to critical scrutiny to explain how we can hear the voices of the dead, be abducted by aliens, walk through walls, see something that hasn't happened yet, or have our future influenced by stellar pulses billions of miles away. But we should always keep an open mind. If Capricorns consistently commit suicide more often than Libras across all cultures, or go on to found their own businesses, there might be some astrological phenomenon we haven't yet identified.

There cannot be any laws of friendship which parallel
Newton's laws of gravity.

As if things 'out there' aren't controversial enough, our 'in here' interpersonal relations take our fallibility to another level. We might feel abandoned by a friend, only to find out that we are mistaken: she doesn't dislike us at all, but has simply had an off day, and now wants to spend some time with us. We simply misread the

315

signals. There cannot therefore be any laws or theory of friendship which parallel Newton's laws and theory of gravity.

We might say we 'believe in' our friend, as loyal and trustworthy. Even if there is the odd fall from grace, we just believe this is true, and we will probably take the belief to our grave. The belief has no backstop, because it needs none: trust is its own justification. It doesn't make sense however to say we 'believe in' a theory such as evolution or creationism unless we first ask ourselves whether we've fully understood it, and this calls for a lifetime's curiosity, as well as considerable intellectual effort.

Committed minders

Only a personal commitment to finding out for ourselves can ensure that we remain ideologically sound. Not all ideologies are bad, and even to decide not to hold to an ideology is to take up an ideological position. Some ideologies however skew the data towards their own end, lure us with certainty where there is only probability, put theory before the fact, and substitute dangerous myth for exacting truth. Even our most developed system of knowledge is riddled with gaps, inconsistencies and mutabilities.

Our brain alone won't make us ideologically strong or wise, because it doesn't particularly care whether we are predominantly liberal or conservative, religious or atheist, anarchist or fascist, technophilic or technophobic, creationist or evolutionist. It simply insists that we adopt a theory about the world into which everything can fit, or be dismissed if it doesn't. Everything else is an act of mind, or an expression of our personal values.

Our brain is doing its best for us.

Despite all these subtle controls exercised by our biological brain, it is nevertheless doing its best for us, on our side, spotting dangers, looking out for our interests, connecting thought and action, building a picture of the world and protecting us from making fools of ourselves.

It has had thousands of generations to perfect some strategies that, though operating below our conscious radar, save us from a lot of grief and embarrassment: knowing who to trust, when to delay, how to listen, why not to rush to judgment. Our ability to hold conflicting points of view in awkward tension is a valuable asset in a world where certainty is ambiguous, truth is elusive and change is inevitable.

The trick is to make conscious as many as possible of our unconscious processes, so that we can place these automatic programs under our mindful control, especially in times of confusion, contradiction and contrariety. We have to confront our cognitive gremlins.

Unconscious operators

Sigmund Freud alerted us over a hundred years ago to what he called the 'psychopathology of everyday life', the many ruses and deceptions we employ to carry off our public persona. We're gullible, vulnerable to stale habit, insecure, constantly seeking distraction and self-justification. Our dislikes are embedded in our amygdala, where they are ruled by subliminal reactions of fear and disgust, not conscious responses of openness and curiosity.

Research by cognitive scientists in the decades since has confirmed Freud's suspicion that, like the iceberg, the bulk of our thinking goes on below the waterline. When we drive on autopilot, arriving at our destination with no memory of turning left or stopping at a traffic light, we are reminded that much of our mental activity is hidden from us.

Evolutionary psychologists put a slightly different spin on the human condition: we are brainy but flawed and frightened primates. Freud did not however believe that we are slaves to our unconscious urges, default assumptions or ancestral cravings. On the contrary, he thought we could give ourselves a degree of control over our mind by plumbing its depths. We have to 'out' our bad thinking habits, which are normally ensnared with our hang-ups. To this end he proposed the 'talking cure' of psychoanalysis to help us convert the 'id' (it) of unconscious action into the 'ego' ('I') of conscious choice. 'Where *it* was, there shall *I* be'.

Despite the claim of flat mind theory that our reasons are never pure but always motivated, they are nevertheless *reasons*. Our behaviour might occasionally be bizarre, but we never deliberately set out to act illogically, embrace false beliefs, enslave ourselves to a cult, behave unreasonably or do crazy things. Our intention is usually to make sense of our confusion, defend our fragile sense of self, and present a positive face to the world.

Sigmund Freud
1856-1939
Freud maintained that most of our thinking goes on out of sight, in our unconscious. From the mountain top of consciousness, we never get to see what's going on down in the valley. Flat mind theory shows us how, by 'outing' how our mind works, we can make a better job of integrating climbing the lower slopes with the view we get from the summit.

Social psychologists generally follow Freud in teaching us to 'game' our own minds: knowing our foibles gives us a shot at behaving more rationally. Avoid impulse buying on the assumption that it will cheer us up, steer clear of the bakery section in the supermarket while we are buying food for dinner, give ourselves an hour to calm down before we rattle off that angry email. On a broader level, avoid splitting the world into 'goodies' and 'baddies', and deliberately seek the company of those who disagree with us. Remember that lies travel six times faster than truths, and evil shouts more loudly than good.

It's not of course as simple as that. Freud realised there is a third level of the psyche, above the ego, the 'superego', which is the weight of restraint and convention placed upon us by our parents and moral guardians. There are also the 'folkways' of our culture, which may be laced with hidden prejudices and blind spots. This makes it doubly difficult to know why we do what we do, or believe what we believe. We feel a passion, perform an act or utter an opinion without the slightest idea why. On the rare occasions that we feel guilt or regret, we have no idea that it is our brain doing this to us.

Freudian psychoanalysis ruled the roost for the first part of the twentieth century, providing a valuable service for those who could afford it, and felt the need to talk. In the 1960's, Aaron Beck pioneered a different approach to debugging the mind. He agreed that we never see ourselves for who we truly are, but he didn't believe in Freudian depths. Instead he saw the mind as a rapid succession of distracting images which we can learn to control.

It pays to acquaint ourselves with those processes in our brain
that remain tantalisingly beyond our conscious control.

In his view, our subterfuges, tendencies to blame others, bad thinking routines, repetitive behaviour and self-defeating attitudes are not personality failures, but errors of thinking, or unproductive cognitive habits that can be retrained through a process he called cognitive behaviour therapy (CBT). We can learn by our own resources to exercise some influence over our default networks. Having to give reasons for our attitudes helps us to reconfigure them, not just temporarily, but next time, and the time after.

This is a smart response that has the potential to confront 'system one' reflexes that shortcut 'system two' reflections. It calls on us to take ownership of our mind, as something more than a biological machine. It pays to acquaint ourselves with those processes in our brain that, despite our best efforts, remain tantalisingly beyond our conscious control. But how can we upgrade our thinking, while staying true to our feelings?

Upgraded thinkers
Earlier in the book, we met Francis Bacon and his warning against 'idols of the mind', by which he meant relying on what has always been thought, what those around us think, what our gut tells us to think, and what it is currently fashionable to think. With so many influences and distractions, how can we possibly claim to think for ourselves, or manage to upgrade our thinking?

Mountains of the Mind

In previous chapters we have discussed how difficult it is to be rational about our feelings, disabuse ourselves of our prejudices, and see the world for what it is. We can't subtract our mind from how we see and feel, leaving our brain to operate as a flawless thinking machine. We don't just churn out propositions, we have to decide what we value, learn to judge wisely and practise being reasonable.

The laws of logic can help us to a degree, showing us how to disinfect ourselves from bad thinking habits. We can enrol ourselves on a 'critical thinking' course, learning to avoid the fallacies of the slippery slope, the straw man, circular reasoning, emotive language, false dilemma, appeal to authority and biases of a dozen kinds. We can go on a statistics course to learn the difference between cause and correlation, and how not to over-generalise from too small a sample. Bacon would be impressed.

Cognitive research confirms that dispassionate, critical thinking is an uphill task. Our mind does not stand alone, detached from its body. Its metabolism is modulated by enzymes and hormones. We are played upon by fickle feelings, seduced by sexual desire, enchanted into love, abandoned in sleep and lost in dreams. We face existential challenges of freedom, responsibility, loneliness and finding a meaning in our life.

In addition, we are bounced between two types of thinking, a fast and intuitive circuit grounded in our emotions, and a slower analytical one governed by reason. 'System one' instinct and gut feeling were reliable guides for settling disputes quickly on the savannah, but as language evolved and society became more complex, more subtle 'system two' thinking was needed to resolve conflicts and settle disputes fairly.

We see system two system two thinking in all its glory in our law courts. Judges need time to reflect on their judgments, and plaintiffs need to see reasons for not taking the law into their own hands. The fact that our law courts have a backlog of cases shows how we still struggle to restrain our system one disputes, and how hard our system two thinking has to work to resolve them.

We have seen how, at election time, when policies are laid out clearly, we vote with our gut, not with our logic. When we fall in love, we yield to the spell of the person we see the most of, who is also an idealised version of ourselves. When we feel enmity towards the out-group, it's because we don't see enough of them, or see too much of ourselves in them.

Mountains of the Mind

This does not mean that system one thinking is inferior, only that we need to understand what it evolved for, and how to integrate it into our post-savannah existence. We still need to decide quickly whether we can trust someone, to listen to our body when it is telling us to slow down, to work out automatically whether an object is too heavy to lift, or whether it will fit through a doorway. We don't need to weigh or measure it. System two thinking might consider itself more 'cool', but it occasionally complicates things. We over-think a problem, or ignore a hunch that we should have trusted.

The trick is to know which type of thinking suits a given situation. It's simply not the case that system one is irrational, while system two is a paragon of reason. In most situations we make the best judgment and arrive at our best decision by integrating them, because our brain is expert at both.

We can become 'smart' thinkers through slow reflection
and engagement with other minds.

'Smart' thinking is therefore an alliance of our brain's default system and our mind's intervention. Neuroscientists have shown how the gift of neuroplasticity enables us to use our mind to change our brain. We can master our bad thinking habits. We can integrate our fast and slow thought processes. We can become smart thinkers, given not just to speed and intelligence, but to slow reflection and engagement with other minds.

New neuroscientific techniques are lifting the lid off our skulls. Voxel based morphology (VBM) can trace not just where in our brain we are doing our thinking or formulating our theories, but the volume of its activity. The deeper reaches of the flat mind can now be seen on a scanner.

The supposition is that, the 'noisier' the signals, the tighter the connections, the more intense the intellectual activity, the denser the reasoning, the subtler the beliefs, the richer the emotions, and the more intricate the personality of the brain's owner. This means that the mountains of the mind are real, and not all of our mental landscape is predictably flat. If shallowness of thought has its own neural signature, so does depth of mind. Perhaps VBM is doing little more than giving us visible evidence of what for centuries we have intuitively recognised as wisdom, but without the aid of a scanner.

Mountains of the Mind

Conclusion

What you look hard at seems to look hard at you.
G M Hopkins

Our mind is flat, if by that we mean that we often catch ourselves thinking on autopilot, or uncritically. Our dependence on our brain is brought home to us when we drive it to breakdown by starving it, denying it sleep, stressing it out or plying it with narcotics.

But our mind also has mountains to climb. Brains are born singly, but our mind faces challenging journeys of self discovery and social integration. As well as mastering the periodic table, we also have to find meaning, become accepted, and live the life of reason.

We rarely step back to think of our mind in an objective way, but flat mind theory suggests that we should. This is difficult, because it is always *our* mind, the only lens through which can look. We might occasionally say 'my legs are too old to climb that hill', but we don't objectivise our mind like this, or nag at it for being faint-hearted. It is not an alter ego we single out for blame or praise. Someone else might accuse us of being flat-minded, but from inside the dugout, we hear only *our* reasons for thinking and behaving as we do.

When we read a psychology text book, we get a glimpse of ourselves from the outside, but when we respond, we do so from the inside, because we have no view from anywhere else. We don't see our mind as the 'global workspace' of our consciousness, but as part of the continuum of how we explain ourselves to ourselves.

We are not strangers to ourselves, but self-interpreting subjects, enigmas with depths to fathom. We assign meaning to our actions, we create alternative worlds, we surprise ourselves, we see ourselves as part of a human narrative, with guess who in the starring role.

Mountains of the Mind

We live our life top-down, as a self-directing person with an open future. Unless we have a clinical neurological condition that hijacks our sense of agency, we knowingly choose from a range of options, without which freedom, responsibility, commitment and sacrifice make no sense to us.

We cannot come up with a theory of everything that includes our own theorising, because unlike the hands in M C Escher's drawing, we cannot emerge from the picture to sketch ourselves. We are caught in a strange loop, implicated in our own enquiry, our impartiality compromised. Without our mind, there is no point to the universe, and without our awareness, there is no science.

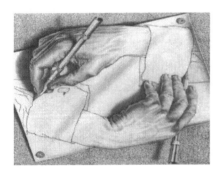

Caught in the frame
M C Escher's 1948 sketch of two hands drawing each other encapsulates the conundrum of the mind trying to deconstruct itself.

But we can learn to integrate the above with the below, and the inside with the outside. Although we are born as single brains, we have evolved as social minds. It is our mind that turns biology into being, and converts flatness to depth. To plumb the depths of human rationality, and scale the heights of human minding, we must embrace all of our ways of knowing, understand all of our stories, and sample the view from all perspectives. The effort repays itself because, as Hopkins wrote in his journal, 'What you look hard at seems to look hard at you'.

Bibliography

'Mountains of the Mind' is a crossover book, or attempted synthesis of what are often seen as mutually exclusive ways of looking at how we got here, and who we are now.

It covers a wide range of topics, few of which get to be mentioned between the covers of a single book, but I have listed those titles that helped me develop my thinking in bringing the inside and the outside, above and below, the peaks and the troughs together.

Not all the books address the mind's flat or mountainous terrain specifically, and those that do tend to promote one aspect at the expense of the other.

Abbott, Edwin – *Flatland* 1884 A satirical novella billed as a romance of many dimensions.

Aslan, Reza – God: *A Human History* 2017 A dispassionate account of how the idea of God originated and evolved.

Begley, Sharon – *The Plastic Mind* 2009 How our brain can adapt, renew and transform itself.

Blackmore, Susan – *The Meme Machine* 1999 An analysis of how the science of memetics can assist in understanding the spread of ideas.

Brown, Andrew – *The Darwin Wars* 2002 An account of why, despite disputes among evolutionary theorists, Darwin's brilliant idea still rules the roost.

Burnett, Dean – *The Idiot Brain* 2016 What our head is really up to.

Bowker, John – *The Sacred Neuron* 2005 How reason and emotion combine to give us our beliefs.

Caputo, John D – *Truth* 2013 Why the truth is so hard to define, difficult to establish, and easy to fake.

Chater, Nick – *The Mind is Flat* 2018 Depth of mind is an illusion, and our brain makes things up as it goes along.

Cialdini, Robert B – *Influence* 2007   The psychology of what makes us say 'yes' to persuasion.

Critchlow, Hannah – *The Science of Fate* 2019   A study of the ways in which our future is already determined by our biology and brain activity.

Damasio, Antonio – *Descartes' Error* 1994   A reminder of the important role of emotion in rationality, and vice versa.

Dasgupta, Partha – *Economics* 2007   A short introduction to the subject's theoretical strengths and weaknesses in forecasting the future.

Dawkins, Richard – *The Selfish Gene* 1975   A key text in promoting the 'modern Darwinian synthesis', but it underplays the role of culture.

Dennett, Daniel – *Freedom Evolves* 2003   An account of how the feeling of freedom can evolve from natural qualities of the brain.

Doidge, Norman – *The Brain that Changes Itself* 2007   Case studies of the power of the brain to self-renew.

Dweck, Carol – *Mindset* 2006   Our power to change the way we think.

Eagleman, David – *Livewired* 2020   The brain seen from a dynamic neuroscientific perspective, though it barely mentions the existential dimension.

Fine, Cordelia – *A Mind of Its Own* 2007 How our brain distorts and deceives.

Gilbert, Daniel – *Stumbling on Happiness* 2006   Not so much about happiness, more our mistaken search for it.

Gladwell, Malcom – *Blink* 2005   How we often think without thinking.

Goodwin, Matthew, and Eatwell, Roger – *National Populism* 2018   How populism presents a threat to liberal democracy.

Haidt, Jonathan – *The Righteous Mind* 2013   Why we are so divided on politics and religion.

Holloway, Richard – *A Little History of Religion* 2016   Religion's strengths and weaknesses laid bare by a sceptical cleric.

Johnson, Steven – *Mind Wide Open* 2004 Why we are what we think.

Kahneman, Daniel - *Thinking Fast and Slow* 2012   The unconscious influences on our decision making.

Henly, Carolyn and Sprague, John – *Theory of Knowledge* 2020   How theory operates to give us reliable knowledge across different domains.

Hoffman, Donald D – *The Case Against Reality* 2019   How our brain evolved to give us a 'good enough' picture of reality, not an accurate one.

King, Jamie – *Conspiracy Theories* 2009 What are they, how they arise, and why we fall for them.

LeDoux, Joseph – *The Deep History of Ourselves* 2019 The four-billion-year story of how we progressed from a blob in the mud to a conscious brain.

Levitin, David – *The Organised Mind* 2014 How to think straight in an age of information overload.

Linden, David – *The Accidental Mind* 2008 How love, memory, dreams and God are 'accidents' of evolution.

Lynch, Aaron – *Thought Contagion* 1998 How memes act like viruses and spread through society.

Marcus, Gary – *Kluge* 2008 How our mind is not 'designed' but the product of haphazard evolution.

McGilchrist, Iain – *The Master and his Emissary* 2010 How the evolution of the brain has shaped the way we think.

Mlodinow, Leonard – *Subliminal* 2013 How our unconscious mind rules our behaviour.

Montagu, Ashley – *The Nature of Human Aggression* 1976 Is violence innate, or the result of genetic and environmental interaction?

Newman, Robert – *Neuropolis* 2017 The inadequacy of explaining everything in the mind through the filter of the brain.

Ornstein, Robert – *Multimind* 1986 How our mind is not single but modular.

Pang, Camilla – *Explaining Humans* 2020 Human behaviour seen through the eyes of an autistic scientist.

Pearl, Judea – *The Book of Why* 2018 A careful analysis of how scientists formulate their hypotheses and arrive at their conclusions.

Pinker, Stephen – *Enlightenment Now* 2018 A plea that rationalism is our only hope against cognitive gremlins and default thinking.

Rosling, Hans - *Factfulness* 2018 How a closer look at the facts can show us ways in which we are wrong in our assumptions about the world.

Shermer, Michael – *The Believing Brain* 2011 How our brain is a belief engine that puts beliefs before explanations.

Sigman, Mariano – *The Secret Life of the Mind* 2017 The hidden forces that drive our thinking.

Sloman, Steven – *The Knowledge Illusion* 2017   Why we claim to know more than we do.

Strauch, Barbara – *The Secret Life of the Grown-up Brain* 2010   How the brain gets wiser as it gets older.

Tavris, Carol and Aronson, Elliot – *Mistakes Were Made* 2007   How we justify our foolish beliefs, bad decisions and hurtful acts.

Thaler, Richard – *Nudge* 2008   How we can be nudged to better decisions about our health and happiness without infringing our civil liberties.

Tomlin, Sarah – *What would Freud Do?* 2017   An entertaining survey of what different psychologists and psychotherapists have to say about the flat mind.

Watson, Peter – *Convergence* 2016   A narrative account of how the sciences are gradually 'converging' towards a unified theory.

Wrangham, Richard – *The Goodness Paradox* 2019   The evolution of the strange tension between virtue and violence in the human story.

Wilson, Edward O – *The Meaning of Human Existence* 2014   Not as metaphysical as it sounds, but an attempt to integrate the science and humanities.

Wright, Ronald – *A Short History of Progress* 2004   A sceptical look at our claims that things just get better and better.

Yalom, Irvin D – *Existential Therapy* 1980   A therapist reflects on the 'ultimate concerns' of meaning, purpose and free will that are considered in this book.

Index

Printed in Great Britain
by Amazon